EQUILIBRIUM AND ECONOMIC THEORY

The division of the economics profession into separate groups – using different 'family languages' and eyeing each other with suspicion and often with intolerance – is reflected in the deep disagreements concerning the meaning and the usefulness of the notion of economic equilibrium.

The book provides an up-to-date picture of the main conflicting positions on this crucial issue, with a view to analysing the nature of the different evaluations and their methodological implications. The treatment of equilibrium is examined from the viewpoint of the most important contemporary schools:

- neoclassical economics
- neo-Ricardian economics
- post-Keynesian economics – in the two streams of those who follow Joan Robinson in denying any interpretative role to equilibrium in economic theorising and those who maintain, instead, the need for a notion of equilibrium re-defined in a classical and Keynesian spirit

The critical comparison of these positions highlights both the main sources of conflict between the various stands and their different underlying pre-analytical visions.

Giovanni Caravale, Professor of Political Economy at the University of Rome 'La Sapienza', studied at the University of Rome and at Trinity College, Cambridge. He has written several publications on the theories of growth, value and distribution as well as in the fields of macroeconomics, methodology and the history of economic analysis.

ROUTLEDGE STUDIES IN THE HISTORY OF ECONOMICS

EQUILIBRIUM AND ECONOMIC THEORY

Edited by Giovanni Caravale

Econ)
7/22/98 6t

London and New York

339.5
E642

First published 1997
by Routledge
11 New Fetter Lane, London EC4P 4EE

Simultaneously published in the USA and Canada
by Routledge
29 West 35th Street, New York, NY 10001

© 1997 Giovanni Caravale

Typeset in Times by J&L Composition Ltd, Filey, North Yorkshire

Printed and bound in Great Britain by
Hartnolls Ltd, Bodmin, Cornwall

British Library Cataloguing in Publication Data
A catalogue record for this book is available from the British Library

Library of Congress Cataloging in Publication Data
Equilibrium and Economic theory / edited by Giovanni Caravale.
    p.   cm.
Includes bibliographical references and index.
1. Equilibrium (Economics) 2. Comparative economics.
I. Caravale, Giovanni.
HB145.E676   1996
339.5–dc20
96–33541
CIP

ISBN 0–415–14299–7

PUBLISHER'S NOTE

Professor Caravale sadly died soon after the corrected proofs of this book, *Equilibrium and Economic Theory*, had reached the printer. The publisher would like to express its condolences to his family, and is proud to contribute to the diffusion of Professor Caravale's approach to the study, development and teaching of Political Economy.

CONTENTS

CONTENTS

CONTRIBUTORS

Giovanni Caravale is Professor of Political Economy at the Faculty of Political Sciences, University of Rome 'La Sapienza'.

Pierangelo Garegnani is Professor of Political Economy at the Faculty of Economics, University of Rome III.

Bruno Jossa is Professor of Political Economy at the Faculty of Law, University of Naples.

Giorgio Lunghini is Professor of Political Economy at the Faculty of Economics and Trade, University of Pavia.

Luca Meldolesi is Professor of Economic Policy at the Faculty of Economics and Trade, University of Naples.

Pier Carlo Nicola is Professor of Mathematical Economics at the Faculty of Mathematical, Physical and Natural Sciences, University of Milan.

Paola Potestio is Professor of Monetary Economics at the Faculty of Economics and Trade, University of Pescara.

Domenico Tosato is Professor of Political Economy at the Faculty of Economics and Trade, University of Rome 'La Sapienza'.

Alessandro Vercelli is Professor of Economic Policy at the Faculty of Economic Sciences, University of Siena.

Gerd Weinrich is Associate Professor of Financial Mathematics at the Faculty of Economics and Trade, Catholic University of Milan.

ACKNOWLEDGEMENTS

I wish to thank Sally Carter, desk editor at Routledge, Sergio Nisticò, Fabio D'Orlando, Eleonora Sanfilippo and Federica Piperno of the University of Rome 'La Sapienza' for their intelligent and patient co-operation in the preparation of this volume.

INTRODUCTION

Giovanni Caravale

The notion of equilibrium – an essential point of reference in the field of economic studies – is employed with such diverse meanings that confusion and misunderstanding inevitably arise in the literature. At its thirty-second Annual Scientific Conference (Rome, October 1991), the Società Italiana degli Economisti organized a specific session on this theme in order to supply a picture, as complete and up to date as possible, of the conflicting positions held on the matter by some important schools of thought. The aim was to analyse the nature of these different evaluations, and to discuss the methodological implications of the various stands.

The present volume – which collects the proceedings of the above-mentioned session (in spite of revision and completion which the contributions have undergone, there has been no alteration of substance) – obviously does not offer unanimous conclusions or definite results. However, in so far as it will be able to accomplish the results indicated above, it will represent the occasion to reflect on the sense and relevance of theoretical research in the field of economics.

Owing to its character, the subject implies the continuous overlaying of methodological questions on analytical problems, as well as on themes in the history of economic thought – making every attempt to classify the various contributions extremely arduous. In spite of the inevitably arbitrary nature of such an endeavour, I have deemed it useful to group together the essays in four sections on the basis of the 'external' criterion of each essay's main subject matter: (1) the idea of equilibrium in economic theorizing (Caravale, Lunghini, Vercelli); (2) equilibrium in the neoclassical conception (Nicola, Tosato, Weinrich); (3) equilibrium in the classical conception (Garegnani); (4) equilibrium in the Keynesian conception: theoretical analysis and hints for economic policy (Jossa, Potestio, Meldolesi).

Transversely, within the contributions grouped in the above mentioned sections, there exist profoundly different viewpoints concerning the vision of the world, the explanation of value and distribution, and the

1

relationship between the requisites of formal coherence and of relevance to the interpretation of reality.

In order to do justice to such differences (also witnessed by Lunghini's comment on Caravale, Tosato's comment on Garegnani and the subsequent rejoinders of the authors) a highly detailed discussion would be required, well beyond the limits of this intentionally brief introduction. These differences, however, will not escape a careful reading. In fact, apart from the categorizing by 'external' criterion, the volume can be read from different viewpoints. One of these consists in the effort to point out the existence (perhaps not always explicit but certainly operating in depth) of three different approaches.

The first closely ties the legitimate use of the concept of equilibrium to the requirement of logical and analytical coherence, and ends up by giving such a requirement greater importance (also of a normative nature) than that of being the kernel of a theory able to grasp the essential features of the real world. The second also accepts the idea of a close association between the concept of equilibrium and the aspects of formal coherence, but views such an association (in a Robinson-like perspective) as a reason for rejecting the notion of equilibrium as an instrument incapable of contributing to the explanation of the complexities and the contradictions of actual economic systems. The third approach emphasizes instead the essential role of the notion of equilibrium in economic theorizing and assigns equal weight to the requirements of logical coherence and of adherence to the essential features of reality.

The identification of such 'hidden threads' is not sufficient, of course, for the 'erection of a building', that is, for the construction of a theory. Perhaps, however, it can make it easier to attain a goal which is at least equally important in the presence of a proliferation of analyses which, though elegant, are often insensitive to the question of the meaning and relevance of economic theorizing – the goal, in the words of Ludwig Wittgenstein, of 'having a perspicuous view of the foundations of possible buildings'.*

REFERENCE

* Wittgenstein, L. *Culture and Value*, ed. G.H. Von Wright, translated by P. Winch, Blackwell, Oxford, 1980, p. 7e.

SUMMARIES

1 THE NOTION OF EQUILIBRIUM IN ECONOMIC THEORY

Giovanni Caravale

The chapter suggests a classification of the main approaches followed in the literature what concerns the crucial notion of economic equilibrium, and offers a critical evaluation of these. For the approach termed 'neutral' (implicit in optimal growth models) the chapter identifies a reason of weakness in its agnosticism towards the questions of realism and of convergence. For the 'apologetic' approach (implicit in neoclassical economics) the chapter emphasizes the difficulty to consider, after the debates of recent years, the equilibrium position there defined as a logically coherent expression of the real forces at work in economic systems. The chapter then criticizes a third approach, recently proposed in the literature, which he terms 'heretical', basically for two reasons: (1) because it incorrectly lumps together early classical and neoclassical economics from the viewpoint of equilibrium as an optimal position; and (2) because, for what concerns Marx and Keynes (the only ones, together with Schumpeter, who reject, according to this approach, the notion of equilibrium), it ends by preventing full comprehension of certain fundamental aspects of their theoretical research which appear instead firmly grounded on the notion of equilibrium.

As an alternative the chapter suggests a different notion of equilibrium, of a classical and Keynesian flavour, *per se* free from both apologetic and critical implications. This notion should express a simplified representation of the dominant forces at work and thus should constitute a potential centre of gravity for the economic system – a *long-period position in the logical sense* with respect to which the age-old and unsolvable question of the *actual* convergence loses much of its relevance.

3

2 EQUILIBRIUM, REPRODUCTION AND CRISIS

Giorgio Lunghini

The aim of this chapter is to reconstruct the concept of 'equilibrium' in the history of political economy. According to the current view, the relevant distinction is between classical and neoclassical schools of thought. The chapter maintains that the relevant distinction is instead between the orthodox view of capitalist equilibrium and the heretical analysis of the conditions of reproduction of the capitalist mode of production. According to the classics (as defined by J.M. Keynes) the economic system is governed by a natural order, which guarantees – in a régime of *laissez-faire* – a perfect equilibrium: an equilibrium which exists, which is unique, stable and, in some sense, an optimum one. It is as if the capitalistic economy were a cooperative economy. The heretics' view is the opposite. *This* mode of production, as any other one, is not a *natural system*, it is a *historical system*. It may attain an equilibrium, but only *by accident or design*. Crisis, and not a perfect equilibrium, is our normal lot.

3 EQUILIBRIUM, DISEQUILIBRIUM AND MACROECONOMIC THEORY

Alessandro Vercelli

In recent decades macroeconomics has focused on equilibrium positions and paths, neglecting the analysis of the dynamics of the economic system in disequilibrium. This depends in part on the diffusion of methods which tend to concentrate the analysis on equilibrium states (like game theory and stochastic processes theory), and in part on the growing success of theoretical approaches (like new classical economics and atheoretical econometrics) which justify an exclusive attention to equilibrium positions. In the meantime concepts of equilibrium and disequilibrium have multiplied without sufficient effort being made to clarify their logical connections or to specify the scope of different kinds of equilibrium analysis. In this chapter a taxonomy of different concepts of equilibrium utilized in macroeconomics is suggested in order to clarify the foundations and limits of different kinds of equilibrium analysis. There are good reasons for emphasizing the importance of equilibrium analysis, but it requires solid dynamic foundations referring also to disequilibrium behaviour. These conclusions are not weakened by the new methods and approaches which have recently blossomed in macroeconomics.

4 'CATHOLICITY' OF GENERAL EQUILIBRIUM

Pier Carlo Nicola

The chapter argues that some equilibrium notion is central to economic theory and asserts that, ideally, every model must possess at least one equilibrium solution, possibly only one. Outside an equilibrium state every sequence of current states ought to converge in time to some equilibrium. The chapter critically discusses some definitions of equilibrium, in particular with respect to general equilibrium theory. The aim is to show that, by enlarging step by step the notion of one-period general equilibrium, this notion has been notably enriched, so that today all economists, more or less aware of this, have Walras as their main ancestor.

5 EQUALITY OF RATES OF RETURN IN MODELS OF GENERAL ECONOMIC EQUILIBRIUM WITH CAPITAL ACCUMULATION

Domenico Tosato

The chapter analyses the problems raised by the condition of equality of the rates of return on capital goods in general equilibrium models. Walras's formulation of a one-period (i.e. temporary equilibrium) theory of capital accumulation is considered and compared with the Arrow–Debreu formulation based on an intertemporal equilibrium model.

The chapter shows first that the inequality of rates of return in Walras's theory is not the consequence of a composition of the capital stock 'inappropriate' – with the given technology – to the production of the outputs required by the preferences of consumers, but of a systematic forecasting error of future prices of capital goods and of future rental values of their services, attributed to savers by a simplifying assumption of the theory. The chapter further shows that uniformity of rates of return is restored when, as assumed in intertemporal equilibrium models, agents are in a position to make maximizing choices on the basis of equilibrium prices for every future date.

The chapter draws from these results elements for a critique of the thesis that the concept of appropriate physical composition of capital and the notion of 'long-run position' may be useful methodological tools for the study of structural change.

6 THE THEORY OF EQUILIBRIUM WITH STOCHASTIC RATIONING

Gerd Weinrich

The chapter represents the theory of equilibrium with stochastic quantity rationing as an extreme attempt to overcome certain deficiencies of the theory of equilibrium with rationing and fixed prices. It argues specifically that the version of the model with stochastic rationing not only corresponds to a legitimate desire for greater realism and generality but that stochastic rationing is a necessary ingredient in any satisfactory theory of trading in the presence of sticky prices and quantity rationing.

7 ON SOME SUPPOSED OBSTACLES TO THE TENDENCY OF MARKET PRICES TOWARDS NATURAL PRICES

Pierangelo Garegnani

In the literature connected with the present revival of the classical approach to relative prices and distribution, the idea has been advanced (Steedman) that the divergence of the 'market' prices of the means of production from the 'natural' levels may prevent the tendency towards the 'natural' prices of the products. If sufficiently wide, that divergence could in fact result in the association of a profit rate below its 'natural' level, and a market price above the 'natural' level, with a consequent (initial) fall in output and further rise of the market price and vice versa.

The purpose of the chapter is instead to claim that the above possibility does not prevent the ultimate tendency of market prices towards their natural levels. The chapter argues that this can be seen as soon as attention is shifted away from the divergence between market and natural prices, and is focused instead directly on the more basic divergence among the market rates of profits. With reference to an economy with n single-product industries the chapter demonstrates that the fall in the output of the commodities showing the minimum level of the profit rate in the economy – and hence, under conditions which are shown to be sufficiently general, the increase in that profit rate – is sufficient to ensure that simultaneous convergence of the prices of all products to their natural levels. This will be so whatever the initial deviations of the market prices of the means of production from their natural levels, and the possible initial 'perverse' association of high market prices and low profit rates, and vice versa.

The chapter argues then that the same argument focusing on profit rates, besides ruling out the difficulty regarding the means of production, allows more general positive conclusions. This is confirmed also by pointing out that some negative conclusions on the subject reached in the literature (Nikaido) have in reality been based on hypotheses which, on closer economic examination, turn out to be unacceptable because in contrast with the competitive postulate of a high relative market price in the presence of a supply of the product below its 'effectual demand', and vice versa.

8 THE CONCEPT OF EQUILIBRIUM AND THE REALITY OF UNEMPLOYMENT

Bruno Jossa

The chapter emphasizes the existence of a lasting tradition of thought, beginning with Keynes and still alive today, according to which the labour market may be in equilibrium also when there is an excess supply of labour. In this tradition of thought are to be placed, first of all, those who believe that the NAIRU (the non-accelerating inflation rate of unemployment) is different from the NRU (the natural rate of unemployment). Central in this tradition of thought today are also the theory of efficiency wages and the explanations of rigid money wages in terms of rational behaviour.

The importance of the demonstration that there is no underbidding is due to the 'degree of liberty' which it gives to the economic system. Also the so-called theory of hysteresis belongs to the same tradition of thought when it argues that the supply curve of labour coincides with the demand curve.

9 LONG-PERIOD POSITIONS AND KEYNESIAN SHORT-PERIOD EQUILIBRIUM

Paola Potestio

The chapter compares the concept of equilibrium in the classical tradition (and of the modern theory that draws inspiration from that tradition) with . the concept of equilibrium emerging from the main body of the *General Theory*. The aim of the comparison is to analyse the basis of an idea which is very common among critics of neoclassical theory, namely that an analytical approach which is alternative to the neoclassical one can be developed, bringing together essential features of both the classical and the Keynesian analyses. The chapter maintains that this kind of project has actually a very indirect relationship with the *General Theory*. In fact the radically different role that expectations play within classical and Keynesian analyses gives rise to two alternative concepts of equilibrium. This conclusion holds also for the long-run positions, the definition of which directly derives from classical analysis.

10 THE NOTION OF OPTIMUM DISEQUILIBRIUM

Luca Meldolesi

For policy as well as for methodological reasons the debate about equilibrium may be developed along a path which is different from, though complementary to, the one usually followed; a path that runs between theoretical and applied economics (and between the discipline and other social sciences). The chapter draws from the well known controversy on balanced *vs.* unbalanced growth and emphasizes the relevance of Hirschman's notion of optimum disequilibrium: the unbalance that calls in, and enlists for development, the additional, previously dormant, resources that generate the highest average rate of growth. The chapter explores some theoretical points entailed by this notion and concludes that equilibrium is a ghost, though a beneficent one.

Part I

THE IDEA OF
EQUILIBRIUM IN
ECONOMIC THEORIZING

B41,   11-35

1   EØ, DOO, EOO

THE NOTION OF EQUILIBRIUM IN ECONOMIC THEORY

Giovanni Caravale

The theme of our Society's annual conference this year is not, I believe, the outcome of a casual choice. When a discipline is permeated by a widespread sense of unease – underscored by communication difficulties among its 'practitioners' and by the frequent superimposition of semantic problems on theoretical divergences – debates on the fundamentals of the discipline and questions of method, in themselves always critical, tend, by force of circumstance, to assume primary importance.

It is natural that this should occur in our discipline, faced as it is with a series of common concerns:

1 the questioning of fundamental concepts in both the traditional and heterodox analytical frameworks, which have long functioned as pillars for basically opposing views on the working of economic systems (think of the notion of marginal productivity of capital in the former and of exploitation of labour in the latter);
2 the collapse of theoretical consensus in the field of macroeconomic theory, marked by the fall of post-war Keynesian orthodoxy and the attempt to substitute for it theories (implausible to many) of the formation of expectations and the working of markets;
3 the profound doubts that are emerging about the possibility of utilizing econometric results as a criterion for choosing from among competing theories;
4 the deep disagreements on the 'nature and scope' of economic theory, which have led the profession to splinter (to an extent not encountered in other disciplines) into separate groups that use different 'family languages' and eye each other at a distance with suspicion and intolerance.

All this has led our Society to consider it not only useful, but also necessary, for us to turn our attention to the concept of equilibrium, the pivotal notion for reflection in the field of economic theory; a notion which, however, is employed (when taken beyond the neutral 'minimal' sense[1] as a mathematical solution to a model) with such different values and

11

implications that the attempt to restore some order in this intricate and delicate matter seems to be fully justified.

Fully aware of the arbitrary nature of the exercise, in what follows I shall present – mainly, though not exclusively, in order to open the debate – a classification of the major positions on economic equilibrium. This is a classification – to borrow Vercelli's terminology (1987, 1991) – of the 'specific semantic' notions of economic equilibrium, i.e. the indication of the 'dynamic endogenous forces' singled out from the differing theoretical approaches used to define equilibrium. The evaluation (also critical) of some of these 'approaches' will constitute the basis of what I hope will be a more constructive set of considerations.

It seems important to emphasize from the outset that the term 'approach' refers here both to the pre-analytical vision in the sense of Schumpeter and to the analytical notion of equilibrium. The two concepts are abstractly distinguishable, but clearly interconnected – the connection being realized through the model (perhaps Vercelli's 'heuristic model'), which simultaneously expresses the 'vision' and generates the equilibrium solution. On the one hand, the vision influences the specific way in which the notion of equilibrium is conceived (the characteristics attributed to it, or for the existence of which proof is sought); on the other, this latter notion can – by virtue of its characteristics – contribute to supporting the vision of the working of the economic system.

THE 'NEUTRAL' APPROACH

A first approach that can be usefully identified is the one I suggest to term 'neutral'. Here, the definition of economic equilibrium, predominant over the pre-analytical vision, consists of the abstract definition of a possible state of affairs in which conditions occur that guarantee the 'smooth' working of the system, either at a single point in time, or through time. This definition does not necessarily imply either the belief in a spontaneous tendency to realize these conditions (which would attribute to it an apologetic character) or the opposite view that the world would never be able to mirror them (thus making it assume the character of a critical tool). It is obvious, however, that were it possible to show that conditions for optimal working tend to occur spontaneously, or, in contradistinction, that they can never occur, the approach would lose its neutrality and take on apologetic connotations in the first case and critical ones in the second.

A great deal of the theoretical literature on growth appears to be characterized by a neutral approach to the notion of equilibrium: from the identification of the Harrod–Domar conditions for steady state balanced growth (the stress on the aspect of knife-edge instability is here accompanied, as is known, by studies of varied inspiration on potentially stabilizing 'counter-tendencies') to Pasinetti's definition of the conditions of balanced growth in a multi-sectoral model (1981).[2]

An approach of this type is certainly useful for specific purposes. For example, it provides the means to indicate the macroeconomic conditions under which the flow of income, generated by new investment, is able to ensure the full utilization of the newly formed production capacity and the employment of the increasingly available labour on the markets. This approach can constitute, on the other hand, a point of reference for the identification of some general guidelines for economic policy (this is certainly true of the relationship between the Harrod–Domar analytical framework and the so-called incomes policy in its original meaning[3]). It can also contribute to explaining the intricate relationships that characterize the growth process in a multisectoral economy where each sector has, for example, different rates of growth of productivity and of the demand for goods.

Yet – in spite of this – the 'neutral' approach seems inadequate: on closer inspection, it does not seem to be able to represent the central reference point of economic theorizing. To play this role, the notion of equilibrium should in fact express the quintessence of the fundamental forces that are actually at work, i.e. it should summarize those elements which, by virtue of their 'dominant' character, act as a centre of attraction, or gravity, for the economic system (in the sense that will be discussed further on).

THE 'APOLOGETIC' APPROACH

The second approach to the question of equilibrium – which can be called 'apologetic' – is closely connected with the view of the economic system as an harmonious whole, undisturbed by class antagonisms or conflicts of interest between opposing social groups, i.e. as a mechanism capable of spontaneously bringing about a situation, an *equilibrium*, characterized by:

1 the best possible allocation of available resources with respect to the needs the community expresses through the market (hence a situation of social optimum);
2 the full utilization of factors of production (primarily, the labour force); and
3 a fundamental distributive equity realized through the application of the same criterion in determining the prices of the services of all factors of production.

Neoclassical economists insistently stress that their theoretical construction deals with a hypothetical situation that does *not* describe the reality of the world in which we live[4] (which is why, with reference to our classification here, the theoretically defined equilibrium position would take on not an apologetic character but a neutral one). Yet, in spite of this, it seems clear that neoclassical theory does not simply represent the outcome of a refined intellectual game, completely removed from reality, but has been constructed – through the talented contributions of many scholars who devoted a life-long effort to this aim – to represent a 'mirror' of reality, or at least some relevant aspect of it. Thus the considerations relating to the apologetic approach can be attributed to the fundamental inspirations of neoclassical theory, if not to the single theorems that have been defined within its context.

Here the structure of the system and the behaviour of economic agents guarantee that possible deviations from the equilibrium position will be promptly corrected and will therefore be only temporary. In spite of the many specifications and distinctions put forward (for example, by Hahn 1973), equilibrium thus presents itself as simultaneously efficient, optimal, equitable and stable.[5] The basic hypotheses for defining equilibrium are the absence of uncertainty and abstraction from historical time, which enables the analysis to nurture the idea of its universality and its unlimited applicability in time and space. This very idea is also ascribed a logical value, to indicate the absolutely general nature of the theory (its 'catholicity', to use Nicola's expression – see Chapter 4) compared with which many other theories – or all other theories – represent only particular cases (see also Hahn 1982).

In so far as the equilibrium position identified by this theory is meant to express forces operating in real economic systems (through the definition of a position of rest that exerts attraction on actual variables), it responds to the above-mentioned requirement of acting as a centre of gravity; i.e. of representing a position that the system spontaneously tends to reach.

The problem is that – for a series of reasons that cannot be ignored – it is increasingly difficult to believe that the equilibrium position defined by neoclassical theory can represent a logically coherent expression of the fundamental forces at work in real economic systems. These reasons relate both to the realism of the theory and to its logical coherence. These reasons can be expressed in term of:

1 the limitations deriving from basic assumptions (see e.g. Dore 1984–5; Arrow and Hahn 1971; Hahn 1973, 1981, 1982);
2 the devastating outcome – at least at the level of logical coherence, if not at the (less fundamental) level of practical relevance – of the 'Cambridge debate' on the theory of value and distribution;[6]
3 last, but obviously not least, the consistent and systematic gap between the spirit of the conclusions that are drawn from theory and the actual reality of contemporary economic systems.[7]

It is interesting, and in a sense paradoxical, that all these reasons for weakness are closely – and negatively – linked with the methodological credo of one of the greatest and most significant figures of the neoclassical

14

school, Alfred Marshall. It is well known, but nevertheless worth recalling, that in a letter to A.L. Bowley of 3 March 1901, Marshall – after having written that in his view 'a good mathematical theorem dealing with economic hypotheses will not [*per se*] be good economic theory' – advised Bowley to follow a procedure which he summarized in six points:

1 use mathematics as a shorthand language rather than as an engine of inquiry;
2 keep to them till you have done;
3 translate into English;
4 then illustrate with examples that are important in real life;
5 burn the mathematics;
6 if you can't succeed in (4) burn (3). 'This last,' he added, 'I did often.'

THE 'HERETICAL' APPROACH

In a recent essay Lunghini (1989) suggests a different approach to the question of equilibrium that I propose to label as 'heretical'. The approach is presented in fact as an alternative to the traditional apologetic approach, because of its 'critical' use of the apologetic notion of equilibrium, and forms the basis of Lunghini's proposal for a re-interpretation of the whole history of economic thought. This proposal can be summed up in two propositions:

1 the thesis concerning the existence of only one possible notion of equilibrium, as a necessary, optimal and desirable position which represents the result of the operation of spontaneous and natural forces. This notion of equilibrium is closely linked with an optimistic vision of the working of capitalist economic systems in which considerable trust is placed in the 'presence and efficiency . . . of laws . . . that guarantee the reproducibility of capitalist production and distribution of material products'. In terms of the present classification, this latter notion of equilibrium represents the essential element of the apologetic approach;
2 the thesis that this approach is contrasted only by the isolated positions of Marx, Schumpeter and Keynes, who, although in different contexts, made fundamental contributions 'to the critique of economic theory as an ideology of equilibrium'. These contributions tend – according to Lunghini – to show that, in the working of the capitalist system, the norm is represented not by equilibrium but by crisis, so that, substantially, the capitalist process represents the negation of the notion of equilibrium.

Lunghini's interpretation – barely smoothed out by some observations on the nature of Keynes's, contribution (ibid., e.g. 73) – revolves around the

15

idea that equilibrium is indissolubly associated with the characteristics of necessity, normality, uniqueness, stability and optimality:

> The real opposition is between the two extreme views of the capitalist system. The orthodox and hegemonic view, first of the classical economists then of the neoclassical economists, envisages the economic system as supported by a natural order, or by moral principles, so that it gravitates, by force of circumstances, towards a configuration of unique, stable and optimal general equilibrium. The structure of the system and the way its elements act guarantee that eventual departures from the configuration of equilibrium . . . are surely temporary . . .
>
> The heretics' viewpoint turns around the perspective: the capitalist system – like every other system – is not natural, but artificial, historically determined . . . . The capitalist system too is capable of some sort of equilibrium and, in fact, it exists. This equilibrium, however, can occur only by accident or as the outcome of a plan; crisis, not equilibrium, is the capitalist norm.
>
> (Ibid., 17)

Lunghini's interpretation encompasses the entire history of economic thought, identifying two opposing lines of thought. On one side is the apologetic group of classical and neoclassical economists which, according to Lunghini, finds its common basis in the idea of the 'naturalness' of the economic order. On the other side are the heretical economists whose common aim is to evaluate critically the established orthodoxy in the face of which they happened to be working and to dethrone equilibrium analysis, thus placing themselves outside and against the perspective of equilibrium.

This is clearly an extensive task, which Lunghini undertakes with his usual competence and elegance. The interpretative suggestion raises, however, the following doubts:

1 it lumps together the classical and the neoclassical schools under the viewpoint of the orthodox notion of optimal equilibrium;
2 it limits the interpretation of equilibrium in Marx to the analysis of reproduction schemes (to the exclusion of the transformation problem); and lastly;
3 it runs the risk of precluding the possible interpretation of unemployment in Keynes as a true equilibrium rather than as a transitory phenomenon.

With regard to the first point, it should be stressed that Lunghini's thesis – that '[t]he orthodox and hegemonic view, adopted first by classical and then by neoclassical economists, envisages the economic system ruled by a natural order [that leads it to gravitate] by force of circumstances towards a configuration of general equilibrium [which is] unique, stable and optimal' (Lunghini 1989: 17) – has two dangerous implications. On the one hand, it substantially negates the specific character of the classical approach, which, as Lunghini well knows, is the basis of the fundamental 'reconstructive' contributions of our discipline after the 'crisis' of the traditional approach; on the other hand, it excludes the modern classical-type prices of production theory from the fundamental logical anchorage of equilibrium (Lunghini writes, for example, that '*Production of commodities*, with regard to the concept of equilibrium, . . . says nothing,' ibid.: 87).

With respect to the second point it must be emphasized that Lunghini's treatment of Marx is centred on the theme of reproduction schemes (both simple and enlarged), with respect to which Marx's heretical approach is correctly pointed out. ([He] – writes Lunghini – 'demonstrates only the *possibility*, not the necessity of equilibrium,' and stresses that '[t]he true face of equilibrium is crisis, which the dominant theories, on the contrary, have always seen . . . as an exception', ibid.: 49).

However, the fact that Lunghini limits his conception of equilibrium to the orthodox notion as an optimal and desirable situation leads him (incorrectly, in my view) to eradicate, from the context of equilibrium, the 'fundamental' (the adjective is Marx's) problem of the 'transformation' of values into production prices. This problem, not even mentioned by Lunghini in the work referred to, can in fact be understood only within the logical context of equilibrium,[8] correctly viewed as a centre of gravity not implying value judgements.

With regard to the third point, Lunghini's position on the concept of equilibrium in Keynes – in spite of a certain amount of contradiction[9] – remains anchored to that 'real opposition' between the orthodox and the heretical vision, which is based on the idea of the uniqueness of the concept of equilibrium as an optimal and desirable situation. In fact, Lunghini notes that Keynes 'directly reformed' the notion of equilibrium (ibid.: 61) and that '[f]or Keynes capitalist equilibrium is not only possible, but it is also normal, in the sense that some equilibrium always occurs [even though] it is iniquitous' (ibid.: 73).

These observations should have led Lunghini to radically restructure the logic of his interpretation through the explicit admission of the existence and the importance of a notion of equilibrium *different* from the apologetic one and, in any case, through the recognition that Keynes's contribution cannot be represented in terms of the 'critique of economic theory as an ideology of equilibrium' (ibid.: 16).

Since all this is lacking, Lunghini's interpretation, as it now stands, comes into conflict with the interpretation of Keynesian unemployment as a non-transitory phenomenon.

In conclusion, it can be said that the basic logic of Lunghini's proposal, in spite of the qualifications introduced, remains anchored to a conception of equilibrium as a conceptual tool that can be used either as an apology for the capitalist system or for a critique of it, but not as a tool that can and must be used in order to understand how this system works.

To facilitate this very understanding, a different approach to the problem of equilibrium should instead be identified that sides neither with the apologetic approach nor with the heretical one. The following considerations indicate the general features of such a line of research.

A DIFFERENT APPROACH TO THE EQUILIBRIUM PROBLEM

Equilibrium and economic theory

The point of departure of these considerations is the close link between the notion of equilibrium and the general conception of economic theorizing.

Political economy can be defined as a social science whose principal aim is the identification of the 'laws', or uniformities, that regulate the phenomena of value, production and distribution in given social and institutional contexts, with a view to providing – although not in an immediate or direct way – useful points of reference for those who are responsible for the choices of economic policy. That is to say, it represents a systematic attempt to comprehend how real economic systems work in order to aid the identification of tools and solutions for the problems of the time (to 'comprehend in order to take action' as Luigi Einaudi said).

The central focus of the theorizing process, as defined above, is the identification of the 'model', i.e. a simplified representation of the world (or that portion of it which constitutes the object of the analysis) that should be able, however, to capture the essential features and the fundamental traits of the reality under examination – something akin to what happens when an artist draws a landscape or a portrait and makes no attempt to reproduce faithfully every single aspect of the reality he is observing, but simply tries to fix on paper the most important elements.

The approach suggested here as an alternative to the apologetic or heretical approaches and which could be labelled the 'natural equilibrium' approach (the term deliberately refers back to the classical tradition) is strictly connected with the idea of economic model specified above. It refers in fact to a 'stylized' representation of economic reality that should have a series of essential, strictly interconnected, methodological properties. In order to constitute the focal reference point of the attempt to interpret this reality, equilibrium should simultaneously represent:

1 a 'significant' position;
2 a position that expresses the 'rational' choices and behaviour of 'active' economic agents also in the presence of uncertainty;
3 a 'long-period position in the logical sense'.

Let us consider the three points in turn.

The significance of the equilibrium position

The first feature of equilibrium stresses the need for the representation to be meaningful, i.e. able to capture the essential traits of the reality which is the object under inquiry. In this regard it is worth emphasizing that in the construction of a model through an inductive process (Vicarelli 1984) observation of the reality plays a fundamental role. However, for the theoretical construction to make sense, the representation must obviously make it possible to analyse such reality better, more systematically, in greater depth than could be done on the basis of the mere description of observable elements. In other words, in order for the model to be meaningful and consistent with the fundamental function of economic theorizing, it must not refer to a state of things removed from reality. The representation of the theory may very well be, and in a certain sense *must* be, 'abstract'. It cannot constitute a faithful reproduction (on a scale of 1:1) of all the aspects of reality (that would be, at one and the same time, impossible and – even if it were possible – useless); but it certainly must try to express the essence, the fundamental features, of the reality under examination.

The significance concerns, on one hand, the realism of the reference framework and, on the other, the importance assigned – in this context – to the 'dominant' forces.

1. From the first point of view, the requirement of significance refers mainly to the *institutional context* that is hypothesized for the economic system. This concerns both its historical-juridical profile (type of economy, juridical treatment of ownership and relations between single parties, relations between these parties and the State, the overall degree of development, the structure of financial institutions, etc.) and the behavioural profile of its economic subjects (presence or lack of rationality in choices, presence or lack of uncertainty, mechanisms regarding the formation of expectations, etc.).

The satisfaction of this condition – although obviously not implying that the theoretical model be totally faithful to the observable reality – appears essential in order to avoid the construction of theories which, explicitly or implicitly, presuppose institutional frameworks or hypotheses of behaviour of economic agents so far removed from reality as to render the theoretical model a difficult tool to use for the interpretation of the working of actual economic systems.[10]

2. Once a significant institutional context has been outlined, the definition of the equilibrium requires the identification of the forces which play a central role; that is, of those forces which – to adopt the expression used by the classical economists – have the characteristic of being 'dominant' or 'systematic', and which are, therefore, held to be different from those other

forces which, although belonging to reality, have a transitory, and not systematic, character. This implies, in other words, the ability to distinguish between dominant and systematic forces on one hand, and temporary and non-systematic forces on the other: the definition of equilibrium must be based *only* on the former. To obtain this result, a twofold difficulty must be overcome. In fact, on the one hand the temporary, non-systematic forces also belong to the sphere of the real; and, on the other, the dominant, systematic forces have a more 'hidden' character in respect of the former.

The classical economists' distinction between natural prices and market prices illustrates the point well. Market prices certainly belong to the reality of the economic system, yet the analysis does not take them as an essential reference point for the construction of the model. It reserves that role for natural prices, defined as the prices which guarantee a uniform profit rate in all sectors and hence the equilibrium position of the system. On the other hand, natural prices – that play the role of the system's centres of gravity – are more concealed, less 'observable' than market prices. By their very nature, they can be conceived as the result of a theoretical calculation, or as expected by economic agents (on these aspects see Caravale 1994a). In neither case do they 'emerge' clearly to the surface to be *directly* perceived. Classical theory, however, is constructed around the idea that reality can be perceived only by hinging on this concept – natural prices – taken to be the expression of the 'dominant' and 'systematic' forces of the economic system, from production conditions to demand conditions.

Equilibrium as an expression of rationality

The second property equilibrium should have is that of constituting a position that expresses the rational choices and behaviour of 'active' economic agents also in the presence of uncertainty. The salient aspects here are:

1 the postulate of rationality;
2 the relation between this and the presence of uncertainty;
3 the distinction between 'active' and other economic agents who do not share this characteristic.

The equilibrium position assumes importance as a central reference point in economic theorizing only if it is conceivable as a consequence of rational choices and behaviour. The idea of rational behaviour in economic agents has always been present in the theoretical analysis of economists, from the classical school down to the present day, and is, therefore, a central element in the construction of the various explanations of the working of economic systems developed during the course of the history of economic thought.[11] What varies is obviously the meaning attributed to this characteristic and the context in which it is placed.

In the neoclassical conception, in both its traditional and its contemporary version, the idea of rationality is strictly associated with the hypothesis of the adequacy of the information available for the identification of an optimizing behaviour. This hypothesis implies either precise knowledge of the consequences of the possible alternatives from which the choice is made in order to maximize utility, or the possibility of assigning a precise distribution of probability to the various possible alternatives with a view to reaching the same objective – the maximization of utility.

The rationality referred to in the present context is directly linked with the notion introduced by Keynes (1921), which marks a radical change from the neoclassical one, since it focuses on the need to analyse human behaviour under conditions of uncertainty, i.e. of limited knowledge.

The essential point is that the presence of uncertainty – i.e. of conditions under which each alternative is specified by an 'unknown' probability distribution which is not objectively definable, nor accessible to economic agents – leads *neither* to a paralysis of action in economic agents *nor* to irrational behaviour on their part. It implies only that the way each economic agent imagines the consequence of each possible behaviour – although characterized neither by full knowledge of the results nor by a known distribution of probabilities (objectively definable and accessible)[12] – constitutes a reasonable basis for economic agents' rational choices.

The hypothesis of rational behaviour (also under conditions of uncertainty) which assumes importance for the purposes of defining equilibrium does not, however, regard to the same extent all economic agents whose presence is hypothesized in the economic system. It refers only to the agents who, through their decisions, are able to modify the outcome of the economic system they operate in: 'active' economic agents. The distinction, of clearly Keynesian inspiration,[13] between the latter and other agents who, although present, have no opportunity of playing an 'active' role, assigns a central function to the decisions made by entrepreneur-capitalists on the basis of their expectations for the future.[14]

From the viewpoint of the rationality of active economic agents, a necessary condition for the achievement of equilibrium must be fulfilled: the equality of the profit rates expected by economic agents in the various sectors.[15]

This condition may represent the focal point for the tendency of actual variables to move towards equilibrium under the influence of rational choices made by agents also under conditions of uncertainty. This aspect can well be brought to light with reference to the Keynesian investments function, where decisions concerning the increase in production capacity, for various capital goods or various sectors, proceed until they reach the point where the expected profit rate equals the interest rate.[16] These decisions, which are rational, but which can yield wrong results if the expectations are not realized, express the system's *tendency* to move towards the equilibrium position corresponding to the given initial set of conditions relating to the relevant variables (Marshallian short-period conditions plus long-period expectations).

Lastly, it must be observed that this way of conceiving the rational choices made by 'active' economic agents under conditions of uncertainty may supply a link between microeconomics and macroeconomics capable of overcoming the limitations of neoclassical analysis of the 'microfoundations', which is based on the idea of the maximizing representative agent, and is strictly connected, in the case of competitive markets, with the notion of equilibrium as an optimal position.[17]

Equilibrium as a long-period position in the logical sense

1. The third requirement for a position of equilibrium to be meaningful is represented by its capacity to exert a relevant force of *attraction* over actual economic variables. This is the question of so-called convergence. Particularly important from this point of view is the way in which the adjustment process and its characteristics are conceived – in other words, the meaning that must be attributed to the idea of *attraction*.

With a purely *chronological* conception of the adjustment process, the analysis must inevitably tackle the unsolvable problem of reconciling the emphasis placed (correctly) on the position of rest (in which all impulses towards change disappear under the given conditions) with the awareness that the conditions that characterize the equilibrium position necessarily change over time.

In effect, when the initial position is taken randomly, it cannot be generally thought of as an equilibrium position. However, if the economic system has a sufficiently 'attractive' centre of gravity, the variables will tend to adjust towards the equilibrium position with a movement that will necessarily last a certain period of 'calendar' time. During this interval of time the conditions that characterize the equilibrium position will certainly undergo significant changes, so that, in this context, the position of a fully fledged equilibrium risks appearing as a notion devoid of concrete meaning.

Various ways of tackling this problem have been suggested in the literature, but none appears a satisfactory solution. Some are expedients that have taken the problem out of historical time and thus have simply hypothesized its solution: for example Walras's *tâtonnement*; Edgeworth's 'renegotiations'; Hicks's 'Monday of equilibrium exchanges'.[18] Others are hypotheses which, in order to keep the problem within historical time, have made the solution of the conundrum dependent upon the *rapidity* of the adjustment process (for example, Hicks 1939, 1965) or the *slowness* of the process of change of the equilibrium position through time (for example, Garegnani 1979).

These apparently insoluble problems become more tractable if the adjustment process is conceived in *logical* terms, instead of in strictly chronological terms. The tendency towards equilibrium could then be understood as a process of *potential* convergence towards the equilibrium position that corresponds to a given set of predetermined values for the fundamental variables of the model.[19]

To clarify this point, it is worth noting that the first logical step should be the definition – with reference to the model chosen as a stylized representation of the economic system – of the equilibrium position that corresponds to the basic elements of the model.[20] Clearly this situation cannot represent an unchanging reference point, as the passing of time implies a modification in the data on the basis of which the equilibrium position has initially been defined. However, this circumstance does not prevent each equilibrium position from exerting a strong attraction over the real variables in each period of time. The fact that the system will never be able to reach the equilibrium position (which is in continuous movement, through actual calendar time) does not deprive this position of its importance as a meaningful point of reference, as a centre of gravity for the system. On the contrary, it represents a mirror of the actual reality of contemporary economies, in their perennial unrest, in their continuous process of change – a reality which does not convey the image of a state of rest. In this perspective, the convergence process should be seen, not as an analysis of the path followed by the variables through time until the attainement of the equilibrium position, but rather as the identification of the variables' *direction of movement* towards the predefined equilibrium position. The equilibrium position would exert its effective force of attraction on the real values even if it were to live only *l'espace d'un matin*, the space of one morning, immediately making way for a new centre of gravity (corresponding to the new values taken up by the relevant magnitudes). This latter would exert its own force of attraction and then disappear in its turn; and so on, in a sort of chase, incessant and vain, but nevertheless not devoid of legible meanings for economic theory.[21]

It is worthwhile stressing some differences (however, implicit in what has been said so far) between the approach suggested here and the 'traditional' conception of equilibrium as a long-period position in the chronological sense.

With the 'traditional' conception, the correctness of the construction depends not only on the possibility of supplying an analytical demonstration of the system's tendency to reach an equilibrium position, but also on the capacity to demonstrate that the economic system *actually reaches* such a position.

In the approach suggested here, the need to demonstrate the latter does not exist any longer (it is on this ground – as has been said above – that insoluble problems arise); but the need does remain to supply the proof of convergence, because this proof coincides with the demonstration of the existence of the *attraction* exerted by the equilibrium position over the actual variables of the model, and therefore, of the direction of movements of the variables towards equilibrium. It is thus necessary to prove that *if the conditions corresponding to the predefined equilibrium position were to hold for a sufficiently long-period of time*, the system would be able to reach that position.

2. This point is delicate and deserves special attention because the differences, with respect to the chronological conception of the Marshallian type, *seem* to dwindle and disappear. In reality this is not so.

It is well known that Marshall defines as the normal or 'natural' value of a commodity, 'that which economic forces tend to bring about in the long run': 'It is the average value which economic forces would bring about if the general conditions of life were stationary for a run of time long enough to enable them all to work out their full effect' (1966: 289). Marshall is perfectly aware of the fact that the 'general conditions of life' do not remain unchanged through time and that, therefore, the long-period position can never be reached. The consideration of this circumstance – which would risk making equilibrium, as long-period position, lose much of its significance – seems to lead Marshall close to considering the suitability of shifting the analysis outside a strictly chronological conception: '[W]e cannot foresee the future perfectly. The unexpected may happen; and the existing tendencies may be modified before they had time to accomplish what appears now to be their full and complete work' (p. 289).

However, Marshall's reflection on this methodological knot does not go beyond recognizing that this fact 'is the source of many of the difficulties that are met with in applying economic doctrines to practical problems' (ibid.), and his theoretical construction remains firmly anchored to the conception that 'the nature of equilibrium itself, and that of the causes by which it is determined, depend on the length of the period over which the market is taken to extend' (1966: 274). On this ground, the analysis Marshall conducts of the various possible cases that can be identified in correspondence with possible supply conditions obviously leaves unanswered the incisive methodological question he himself had raised.

It is worth while stressing again that the logical conception of the long-period position suggested here appears capable of solving the problem of the continuous change in the 'general conditions of life' without doing away with the possibility of a meaningful reference to the equilibrium position. This position, in fact, remains the fundamental concept for interpretations of the economic system – even in the awareness that this latter will, presumably, never succeed in actually reaching the equilibrium position, continuously changing through calendar time

3. The line of argument developed above deals with changes that have an exogenous nature with respect to the model, i.e. variations in economically significant parameters or data on the basis of which the equilibrium

position, that represents the initial reference point of the analysis, is defined. It is worth stressing that, in the approach suggested here, new values concur to define a new equilibrium position for the system, hence a new potential centre of attraction.

These variations can derive either from events that are not of a strictly economic nature (for example, population changes stemming from new ethical, religious or social values, changes in the state of expectations linked with political change) or from economic events which are not taken into consideration in the functional relations that make up the theoretical model. An example of an event of the latter type could be offered, in an income determination model, by the *exogenous* assignation of a new value to the saving propensity. This value – different from the initial one used to calculate the equilibrium income and with respect to which one can think that a movement of potential convergence has been set in – could in principle be thought of as a 'reflection' of the new values which income gradually assumes during the movement of potential convergence. In reality, however, the model would not include a functional relationship – which, it may be repeated, could in principle be specified – between the variable in question and the solution of the model in the value of income.

On this ground, the difference between the chronological and the logical approach emerges clearly. Whereas in the *chronological* conception the changes under discussion create the unsolvable problems for which the literature has had recourse to the devices mentioned above (which leave the problem totally unsolved), in the *logical* conception of the long-period position this possibility does *not* – as has been said – represent an obstacle to the use of this position as a reference point for analysis. In other words, the fact that the 'point of attraction' moves through time does not prevent each single actual situation in the economic system from being interpreted with reference to its corresponding situation of equilibrium, i.e. to the situation the system is tending to move towards at that moment. The concrete configuration of the decision-making mechanism that sets the adjustment process in motion is *irreversibly* defined in each period with reference to the situation of equilibrium corresponding to the fundamental data of that time period. Subsequent modification of these fundamental data gives rise to the definition of *new* equilibrium positions, *new* points of reference for *new* decisions that will be made by agents in subsequent periods. However, these modifications cannot in any way influence the initial equilibrium position whose fundamental data have constituted the reference point for the actual decisions initially made by economic agents. Those decisions have set in motion the process of potential convergence towards equilibrium, a process whose significance is not questioned by the subsequent, inevitable, changes in the reference point for the economic system.

A different, and delicate, matter relates to the way in which exogenous variations can be accounted for in the definition of a new reference framework based on the new value of the fundamental data. There are no obvious general rules to perform this task. However, what can be excluded is that the choice of the new values (the ones that are to be considered as given for the identification of the new solution) can be made on a totally arbitrary basis. This choice must have at least some minimum requirements. In the first place, it must respond to a criterion of reasonableness with regard to the model's framework of reference (for example, assigning a new value to the labour content of wheat must reflect the need to analyse, in a model of the Ricardian type, the effects of the decreasing returns in agriculture on the economic system's rate of growth); but, above all, the choice must respond to the criterion of logical coherence with regard to the economic phenomena examined. In particular, a new value exogenously attributed to one of the fundamental variables of the model cannot be accompanied by a hypothesis of *ceteris paribus* that conflicts with the logic of the recognized functional relationship between the variables of the model. An assortment to be carefully avoided is, for instance, the choice of a new value for the exogenous distributive variable, which presumably implies a change in the quantities demanded and produced in the system, accompanied – in the general case of non-constant returns – by the hypothesis of the invariance of the matrix of technical coefficients (on this point see Caravale 1988).

The general idea around which the whole argument pivots is that in each period the economic system is more 'readable' as a stylized representation of the dominant and systematic forces at work in that period. From this point of view, reference to a situation of equilibrium seems to lose its significance if the change in one of the fundamental data of the model generates 'recursive' effects. These may be thought of as the phenomena resulting from the interaction between data and variables to be determined, which can be specified within the model in terms of a precise functional relationship, for which, however, the outcome of convergence towards the new position of equilibrium is not proved (i.e. that corresponding with the new value of the variable which has undergone the change). A variation in one of the initial data would in fact cancel the original equilibrium position, while – because of their 'permanently iterative' character – the recursive phenomena would not allow the identification of the new equilibrium position, i.e. of the new stylized image of the system for which the system itself should experience an attraction that would 'substitute' for the one exerted by the initial situation.[22]

4. The logical, not chronological, character of the conception of the process of adjustment towards the equilibrium of the system must be carefully distinguished from the ahistorical nature of the conception of time in neoclassical theory. While the latter appears to be a tool implying abstraction from reality, the notion of equilibrium to which the present argument refers does not carry similar implications. It is conceived in fact in terms of a framework, with both classical and Keynesian characteristics,

which refers to a context that is long-term in the logical sense but remains a short period in the Marshallian sense – in that a series of variables are considered *given* as a result of past history (in particular the decisions made in the past by economic agents) – and is, therefore, deeply embedded in a historical perspective.

Equally important is the distinction between the conception of potential convergence towards natural equilibrium mentioned above and that idea of 'history' which at times has been suggested, for example by Joan Robinson (1979), as an alternative to the conception of atemporal neoclassical equilibrium, on the basis of the (unproved) hypothesis that only a single concept of equilibrium be given: the neoclassical one. The notion of 'history', which evokes effectual reality and concrete problems, may perhaps appear as a seductive proposal for the general approach to the study of economic problems; it, however, represents an extremely confused notion and as such cannot be used in economic theorizing (Caravale 1987). This latter is not merely meant to describe facts, but aims to identify interpretative frameworks capable of helping to understand real economic systems. In other words, the weakness of the atemporal neoclassical conception of equilibrium must not lead us to reject entirely the concept of equilibrium and to begin a dangerous journey into the unknown (and non-existent) territory of 'history', understood as a ground alternative to that of equilibrium, for the development of economic analysis. We should instead have recourse to an approach founded on a more reasonable notion of equilibrium – a stylized reflection of the reality observed – to be structured in order to represent the central idea for economic theorizing, in the sense indicated above.

SOME CONCLUDING REMARKS

The critical conclusions that emerge from the analysis conducted in the first part of this chapter of the main approaches to the problem of economic equilibrium are rooted in the use of the concept of equilibrium as either an apologetic or a critical tool. This assessment is the premiss of the following attempt to identify some fundamental properties of a different approach to equilibrium that stresses its role as a tool for the understanding of the working of economic systems, freed from the constraints of both the 'apologetic' and the 'heretical' views.

If these properties (equilibrium as a meaningful position, as an expression of rationality on the part of agents under conditions of uncertainty, as a long-period position in the logical sense) prove to be a sufficiently firm basis, they could provide the starting point of an attempt to construct a theoretical framework capable of representing an analytically solid and realistic alternative, built on more adequate microeconomic foundations than those that have traditionally represented the 'scientific' approach in economics.

Some positive indications of possible uses of this different notion of equilibrium are inferable from certain characteristics that may be identified even at this stage of the discussion: (1) its compatibility with the systematic presence of phenomena of unemployment; (2) its compatibility with phenomenon of incomplete utilization of production capacity; and (3) its compatibility with an analytical framework in which the equilibrium prices are explained by the rational behaviour of economic agents under conditions of uncertainty.

1. From the first point of view, it seems important to stress that the systematic presence of non-transitory or frictional unemployment does not, in principle, constitute an element that can alter the economy's equilibrium position (to use Vercelli's expression, mentioned above, unemployment does not represent an 'endogenous dynamic force' capable of moving the system away from equilibrium). Obviously this is true only if the presence of unemployment emerges in the theoretical model as an expression of 'dominant' forces working in the system.

The notion specified above can be used to interpret Keynes's *General Theory* in terms of unemployment equilibrium – i.e. of a reading where unemployment is *not* interpreted as the result of market 'imperfections' with regard to the abstract conditions of competitiveness, or as the mirror of transitory phenomena of disequilibrium which the system spontaneously tends to cancel. On the other hand, this notion seems to respond to the need, increasingly felt in the neoclassical field, for a new definition of economic equilibrium – different from the one traditionally used – that includes, specifically, the phenomenon of unemployment.[23]

2. From the second point of view, reference to the condition of equality of the profit rates *expected* by economic agents in the various sectors allows the definition of economic equilibrium to free itself from the constraints of the close association between equilibrium and complete (or, which is the same, uniformly distributed) utilization of the existing production capacity that would result from the choice of the condition of equality of the *realized* profit rates in the various sectors – emphasized for example, in some analyses also of classical inspiration (Garegnani 1979; Eatwell and Milgate 1983) – as the essential characteristic of the economic system's position of rest.

In effect, if reference were made to this latter condition, equilibrium could be reached only if the production capacity were perfectly 'adjusted' with regard to the structure of the demand, and that would imply either the complete utilization of existing equipment, or – and the differences do not appear to be considerable – the existence in the various sectors of a same degree of non-utilization of the production capacity.

Reference to the condition of equality in expected profit rates enables us instead to avoid these disadvantages, and at the same time to 'recover' an interpretation in terms of equilibrium of the typical Keynesian situations characterized not only by unemployment of labour but also by the wide (and not uniformly distributed) non-utilization of existing plant (on these points, Caravale 1992a,b).

3. The recognition that profit expectations play a crucial role in the definition of the equilibrium position could represent the missing link in an explanation of equilibrium prices founded on the rational behaviour of economic agents under conditions of uncertainty. From this point of view, the notion of equilibrium could provide a tool capable of bringing to light the nexus of continuity between the theory of classical economists and that of Keynes.

That role, in fact, may on the one hand constitute the basis for the explanation of investment decisions in the various sectors, corresponding to an equilibrium position that is not necessarily one of full employment (Caravale 1987). It can also represent on the other hand the point of reference for a reinterpretation of the classical relationship between market prices and natural prices in terms of a logical sequence that leads, in each period, to the identification of the equilibrium point through a process that goes from the agents' expectations of quantities and prices, to the production decisions assumed by them on the basis of those expectations, to the comparison between the results of the decisions and market reactions, up to the identification of natural prices, combined expression of demand and production conditions (Caravale 1994a).

The link between Keynes's methodology regarding investment and employment theory and that of classical economists regarding price theory could perhaps be developed in the direction of a search for a systematic relationship between the set of prices expected by economic agents and the set of equilibrium prices. The former are the prices at which those agents expect that products will be sold on the market, and which are implicit in the profit expectations forming the basis of their decisions.[24] The equilibrium prices, on the other hand, are ultimately connected with the classical notion of production prices as potential centres of gravity of the economic system – defined on the basis of given demand conditions and given technical conditions.[25]

These aspects of the approach suggested here could bring the interpretative tool closer to the reality of modern economic systems, in which unemployment of the labour force, the incomplete utilization of existing production capacity and the decisive influence of decisions made under conditions of uncertainty are the rule.

If verified, this circumstance would justify, as I pointed out above, the commitment to proceed along the line of research that I have just outlined. *Per se*, it does not justify less than cautious conclusions. Because, if it is correct to say, with Einstein, that 'the content of truth of the [theoretical] system consists of the verification of the propositions . . . through sensorial experiences (1960: 355), it is none the less true, as Fausto Vicarelli has pointed out, that 'the comparison between logical conclusions and the reality of the facts . . . cannot supply . . . a decisive element of evaluation of a theory [in that] an illogical way of reasoning could lead to conclusions that coincide with reality' (1983: 303).

What counts, in the end, is the critical judgement on the significance of the model and on the correctness of the method of analysis.

NOTES

1 This 'minimal sense' is moreover disputed in the literature. See Vercelli (1987, 1991).
2 This latter type of approach characterizes the analysis conducted in Caravale (1969).
3 The notion of incomes policy has recently undergone a change which is at the same time radical and theoretically weak. See on this point Caravale (1997).
4 The thesis that the modern general theory of economic equilibrium is able to define a situation of order in a decentralized economic system whose information mechanism is exclusively represented by price signals is frequently accompanied by the qualification (for example, Hahn 1982) that 'this does not mean that any real economy has been described . . . It is a considerable intellectual conquest, but . . . a lot more is required for practical activity.'
5 The demonstrably suboptimal outcomes of Nash equilibrium – a logical construction with purely neoclassical connotations – are essentially linked with hypothetical market imperfections (as opposed to the hypothesis of free competition) and the level of information available to economic agents.
6 Some authors stress (see, for example, Chapter 5 below) that criticisms of the logical coherence of the construction do not touch on the modern disaggregated version of intertemporal general economic equilibrium. This thesis does not in any way touch upon the question of the realism of the hypotheses and hence of the capacity of this formulation of general economic equilibrium to supply an interpretative tool of reality (see the following point 3 in the text).
7 Kornai (1971: xvi) speaks of his 'exasperation' with (the) inadequate and unworkable character (of neoclassical general equilibrium theory).
8 Likewise Hahn (1973, 43): 'The Marxian analysis of values and prices, in so far as it is comprehensible to me, seems to be describing an economy in equilibrium.'
9 On this point see below my 'Reply' to Lunghini's 'Comment' (p. 38–40).
10 There is no lack of examples in the history of economic thought, or in contemporary economic theorizing. A case of institutional framework far from the observable reality is certainly constituted by Walras's *tâtonnement* mechanism, which is, substantially, an economic system that functions as a particular stock exchange – that in Paris at the end of the nineteenth century where transactions out of equilibrium were excluded (see Jaffé 1981). On the other hand, an example of agents' behaviour far from the concrete reality of economic systems, characterized as they are by a continuous and high degree of uncertainty, is constituted by the hypothesis of infinite and perfect ability to forecast, on which so-called New Classical Macroeconomics is based (see, for example, Rodano 1987, Torr 1988). With theories based on institutional contexts of this type one may well wonder – even without taking problems of internal logical coherence into consideration – whether the elegance of the representation can

constitute a justification sufficient to compensate the vast distance from the real world and hence the choice (conscious or not) in favour of the irrelevance of the model as an interpretative tool. It is obvious that in such cases any attempt to use the theoretical model as a logical basis for conclusions regarding economic policy would be paradoxical.

11 The presence of hypotheses of rationality also in non-neoclassical contexts is stressed by Hahn: 'The idea of the calculating rational agent . . . of course is not peculiar to any school: it occurs in Marx and Ricardo as centrally as it does in the work of, say, Professor Hicks and it is used by Professor Robinson, in her study of the choice of techniques, as much as by Professor Solow in his' (1973: 57).

12 As is known, according to Keynes, each agent constructs, so to speak, his or her own distribution of probabilities, assigning to it a 'weight', a degree of trust, that can vary depending on the quantity of available information.

13 Within the Keynesian framework, the distinction between different categories of economic agents can be grasped in the area of the differentiation between the role of consumers (substantially passive, in that consumption depends on realized income) and the role of investors (whose decisions represent the active factor in the system as a whole) (Carabelli 1982a, b), both in terms of the difference between the position of these latter and that of workers who, to use Torr's effective expression (1988: 32), 'are not in a position to change matters which do not suit them'. This difference, which is deeply rooted in Keynes's work, becomes particularly evident in the distinction (to which the first drafts of the *General Theory* referred) between a 'co-operative economic system' and an 'entrepreneurial economic system'. In the first type of system, agents are all self-employed craftsmen and therefore, unlike what happens in 'entrepreneurial economies', to which Keynes wants to refer, the problem of drawing a role distinction between entrepreneur-capitalists and workers does not arise.

14 The complexity of contemporary economic societies – linked with the presence of other economic subjects (the State, unions, ecology movements, consumers' associations, etc.) – does not seem to detract from the distinction drawn in the text. In fact, either these other subjects are capable of deciding and realizing investments (then they play the role of 'active' economic agents, even though the criteria followed in the decision-making process can be different with regard to those of entrepreneurs-capitalists) *or* they do not have that capacity, and their role is limited to conditioning the investment decisions of 'active' economic agents.

15 Unlike that which occurs when the point of reference is constituted of *current* profit rates in the various sectors, the condition of equality in the *expected* profit rates seems capable of accounting not only for unemployment but also for the phenomenon of incomplete utilization of the production capacity in a situation of Keynesian equilibrium (Caravale 1992a,). The point is briefly discussed in the concluding section.

16 For the validity of this criterion the hypothesis of perfect competition does not seem necessary. In fact, also in the case of barriers to entry in the single sectors, or other kinds of constraints, investment decisions respond to the criterion indicated in the text, since the anticipation of profit incorporates the weight of the constraints or the barriers, provided that, obviously, financing is available under the same conditions throughout the economic system.

17 The neoclassical analysis of the microfoundations is the expression of so-called 'methodological individualism', i.e. the assumption 'that the economic mechanism can be explained commencing from the analysis of the single

individual without in any way passing through the concept of social group or of class' (Graziani 1992: 369). On these aspects Dow (1985: 97–107); and Chick (1983, *passim*). See also Hahn (1973: 64–5).

18 The exclusion of transactions out of equilibrium represent – as is known – the essential tool for the logical construction of various hypotheses.

19 The notion of 'virtual equilibrium at a point in time' proposed by Vicarelli (1984) for the interpretation of Keynes's contribution runs very close to this conception.

20 An example is supplied by the position which, in Keynes's theoretical framework, corresponds to a particular given value of all the elements specified in detail at the beginning of chapter 18 of the *General Theory*, to which should be added the state of the long-run expectations.

21 J. Viner appears fully aware of the limits of the chronological conception of long-run equilibrium and the necessity of a conception of a *logical* type: 'The only significance of the equilibrium concept for realistic price theory is that it offers a basis for the prediction of the direction of change when equilibrium is not established. Long before a static [long-run] equilibrium has actually been established, some dynamic change in the fundamental factors will ordinarily occur which will make quantitative changes in the condition of equilibrium. The ordinary economic situation is one of disequilibrium moving in the direction of equilibrium rather than of realized equilibrium' (1932: 103).

A conception analogous to that suggested in the text seems to be implicit also in Keynes's analysis of 'long-run expectations': 'If we suppose a state of expectations to continue for a sufficient length of time for the effect on employment to have worked itself out so completely that there is, broadly speaking, no piece of employment going on which would not have taken place if the new state of expectation had always existed, the steady level of employment thus attained may be called the long-period employment corresponding to that state of expectation. It follows that, although expectation may change so frequently that the actual level of employment has never had time to reach the long-period employment. corresponding to the existing state of expectation, nevertheless every state of expectation has its definite corresponding level of long-period employment' (1973: 48). It seems particularly important to stress that, in the perspective of the *logical* conception of equilibrium as a long-period position, the contradiction disappears – emphasized recently by Goodwin – between the 'dynamic' nature of the multiplier and the 'static' nature of the analytical structure of the *General Theory*. According to Goodwin, '[t]he central pivot of the Keynesian revolution is Lord Kahn's multiplier, which is a sequential dynamical process. Keynes *perversely transformed* this essential conception into a statical proposition, one which makes little sense. "The" multiplier does not exist at a point of time: one cannot multiply instantaneously; it takes time, and so one is immediately and inevitably involved in dynamics. In the *General Theory*, Keynes talked about change, even long-period change, but the concepts are not integrated into the analytical structure' (1992: 106, italics added). Freeing the concept of equilibrium from the fetters of the chronological conception, the problems pointed out by Goodwin disappear and the 'perverse transformation' dissolves, evincing how Keynes's use of the notion of the multiplier represents an essential element of a solid and coherent analytical construction. These aspects are more amply examined in Caravale (1992a, b; 1994b).

22 From this general methodological viewpoint, the 'iterative' procedure suggested – in a strictly chronological context – by Garegnani (1983; 1990 and

recently taken up by Mongiovi (1991) gives rise to serious perplexities as an analytical framework adequate for the analysis of the crucial relationship between prices and quantities in the context of classical theory. In effect, in the definition of the various 'separate logical phases' on which the interpretative proposal is pivoted, Garegnani explicitly stresses the circumstance that the adjustment mechanism, in its concrete operation, determines (in the general case of non-constant returns) significant variations in the matrix of the technical coefficients as well as in the independent distributive variable, i.e. in the two elements on the basis of which the equilibrium position was initially defined. In this regard, see also Vercelli's (1991) observations on the necessity to prove that the equilibrium position *does not* depend on the 'dynamic path followed' as one of the conditions for the correctness of the analysis.

23 Particularly significant from this point of view are the stands taken recently by F. Hahn and R. Solow in a theoretical perspective close to that of the so called school of 'New Keynesian Economics'. (For a review of the literature of this theoretical stream see Gordon 1990.) Hahn points out that – contrary to what the so-called 'search theory' maintains (i.e. that 'the unemployment which we observe is to be explained by the search for the best wage offer and by the preference for leisure') 'involuntary unemployment is well defined, compatible with rationality and not inconsistent with an equilibrium of the economy' (Hahn 1987: 1). On the other hand, Solow stresses how comprehension of the phenomenon of unemployment 'will almost certainly involve an equilibrium concept broader, or at least different from, price-mediated market clearing' (1986: para. 34). In spite of the caution that at times comes through, and the resistance to drastic 'breaks' with respect to the neoclassical tradition of thought (for example, immediately following the sentence quoted above, Solow writes: 'I say 'almost' to allow for the possibility that slowly self-correcting disequilibrium may turn out to be a better idea'), these positions represent an undoubted manifestation of the discomfort felt by neoclassical economists and their concern that – sticking to the traditional neoclassical equilibrium concept (with its features of optimality, efficiency and full employment) – economic analysis may lose the possibility of representing a tool for the interpretation of the reality of contemporary economic systems. Lastly, it seems worth pointing out that 'new' theories of involuntary unemployment (substantially the so-called 'New Keynesian Economics') explain the unemployment equilibrium on the basis of a microeconomics analysis of the rigidities of wages and prices, and presuppose that in the absence of 'imperfections' the system would be capable of recovering its full employment equilibrium – thus neglecting the fundamental argument developed in detail by Keynes in chapter 19 of the *General Theory* to show how a general reduction in wages would *not* lead to full employment, especially because of the negative effects it would have on the 'state of confidence'.

24 These decisions would constitute part of the price adjustment process.

25 Simultaneously with these equilibrium prices – which could represent the potential centre of gravity of the economic system – would be coincidence between expected profit rates and realized profit rates (still on the absolutely abstract hypothesis that the 'basic' situation of the economic system remained unchanged for a sufficiently long-period of time to enable the adjustment process to develop fully).

REFERENCES

Arrow, K.J., and Hahn, F.H. (1971), *General Competitive Analysis*, Amsterdam, North-Holland.

Carabelli, A. (1982a), 'Consumo', *Dizionario di Economia Politica* 2, Turin, Boringhieri.

Carabelli, A. (1982b), 'Investimento', *Dizionario di Economia Politica* 3, Turin, Boringhieri.

Carabelli, A. (1988), *On Keynes's Method*, London, Macmillan.

Caravale, G. (1969), *Fluttuazioni e sviluppo nella dinamica di squilibrio di un sistema economico*, Rome, Iscona.

Caravale, G. (1987), 'The Neo-Keynesian School: Some Internal Controversies', *Atlantic Economic Journal*, December.

Caravale, G. (1988), 'Condizioni di domanda ed equilibrio naturale nelle teorie classiche e di tipo classico', *Rivista di Politica Economica*, December.

Caravale, G. (1992a), 'Keynes, Equilibrium and Modern Economic Systems', *Perspectives on the History of Economic Thought*, ed. R.F. Hebert, Aldershot, Elgar.

Caravale, G. (1992b), 'Keynes and the Concept of Equilibrium', in *Keynes and the Notion of Equilibrium*, ed. M. Sebastiani, London, Macmillan.

Caravale, G. (1994a), 'Demand Conditions and the Interpretation of Ricardo', *Journal of the History of Economic Thought* 16, fall.

Caravale, G. (1994b), 'Prices and Quantities – Walras, Sraffa and Beyond', *Studi Economici* 52.

Caravale, G. (1997), 'On a Recent Change in the Notion of Incomes Policy', in *New Keynesian Economics/Post-Keynesian Alternatives*, ed. R. Rotheim, London, Routledge, forthcoming.

Chick, V. (1983), *Macroeconomics after Keynes*, Oxford, Philip Allan.

Dore, M.H.I. (1984–85), 'On the Concept of Equilibrium', *Journal of Post-Keynesian Economics*, winter

Dow, S.C. (1985), *Macroeconomic Thought*, Oxford, Blackwell.

Eatwell, J. and Milgate, M. editors (1983), *Keynes's Economics and the Theory of Value and Distribution*, London, Duckworth.

Einstein, A. (1960), *Ideas and Opinions*, New York, Crow.

Garegnani, P. (1979), *Valore e domanda effettiva*, Turin, Einaudi.

Garegnani, P. (1983), 'The Classical Theory of Wages and the Role of Demand Schedule in the Determination of Relative Prices', *American Economic Review*, Papers and Proceedings, May.

Garegnani, P. (1990), 'Sraffa: Classical versus Marginalist Analysis', in *Essays on Piero Sraffa*, ed. by K. Bharadwaj and B. Schefold, London, Unwin Hyman.

Goodwin, R.M. (1992), 'The General Theory: Critical and Constructive', in *The Notion of Equilibrium in the Keynesian Theory*, ed. M. Sebastiani, London, Macmillan.

Gordon, R.J. (1990), 'What is New Keynesian Economics?', *Journal of Economic Literature*, September.

Graziani, A. (1992), *Teoria economica: Macroeconomia*, Naples, ESI.

Hahn, F.H. (1973), *On the Notion of Equilibrium in Economics*, London, Cambridge University Press.

Hahn, F.H. (1981), 'General Equilibrium Theory', in D. Bell and I. Kristol (eds), *The Crisis in Economic Theory*, New York, Basic Books.

Hahn, F.H. (1982), 'The Neo-Ricardians', *Cambridge Journal of Economics*, June.

Hahn, F.H. (1987), 'On Involuntary Unemployment', *Economic Journal* 97.

Hicks, J. (1939), *Value and Capital*, London, Macmillan.
Hicks, J. (1965), *Capital and Growth*, London, Oxford University Press.
Jaffé, W. (1981), 'Another Look at Léon Walras's Theory of Tatonnement', *History of Political Economy*, Summer.
Keynes, J.M. (1973), *The General Theory of Employment, Interest and Money* VII, *Collected Writings of J.M. Keynes*, London, Macmillan.
Kornai, J. (1971), *Anti-equilibirum*, Amsterdam, North Holland.
Lunghini, G. (1989), 'Equilibrio', in *Dizionario di Economia Politica*, Turin, Boringhieri.
Lunghini, G. (1991), 'Almeno Keynes!', Introduction to J.M. Keynes, *La fine del laissez-faire e altri scritti*, Turin, Bollati Boringhieri, 1991.
Marshall, A. (1920), *Principles of Economics*, eighth edition, London, Macmillan.
Mongiovi, G. (1991), 'The Ricardo Debates: a Comment', *Canadian Journal of Economics*, August.
Pasinetti, L. (1981), *Structural Change and Economic Growth*, Cambridge, Cambridge University Press.
Robinson, J. (1979), 'History versus Equilibrium', in *Collected Economic Papers* V, Oxford, Blackwell.
Rodano, G. (1987), 'Introduzione', *Ascesa e declino della nuova macroeconomia classica*, Bologna, Il Mulino.
Solow, R.M. (1986), 'Unemployment: Getting the Questions Right', *Economica* 53.
Torr, C. (1988), *Equilibrium, Expectations and Information*, Cambridge, Polity Press.
Vercelli, A. (1983), 'Dall 'equilibrio alla probabilità: una rilettura del metodo della "Teoria Generale"', in *Attualità di Keynes*, Bari, Laterza.
Vercelli, A. (1987), *Keynes dopo Lucas*, Rome, La Nuova Italia Scientifica.
Vercelli, A. (1991), *Methodological Foundations of Macroeconomics. Keynes and Lucas*, Cambridge, Cambridge University Press.
Vicarelli, F. (1984), *Keynes: the Instability of Capitalism*, Philadelphia, University of Pennsylvania Press.
Viner, J. (1931), 'Cost Curves and Supply Cirves', *Zeitschrift fur Nationalöekonomie III*.

COMMENT

Giorgio Lunghini

Giovanni Caravale reproaches me with: (1) lumping the classical and neoclassical schools together in terms of the orthodox notion of optimal equilibrium; (2) limiting myself, regarding Marx, to Marxian schemes of reproduction; (3) not recognizing in Keynes any notion of equilibrium other than the apologetic one. Regarding the first point, Caravale grants that I acknowledge that either approach has its own irreducible essence. However, what I maintain is that both approaches take for granted a concept of natural order, *à la* Pangloss: 'All events are linked together in the best of all possible worlds.' This raises the question of history, which can be put briefly as follows. There was history in classical economics (*e.g.* the 'early and rude state of society') but it will end up in a stationary state. History does not count, for neoclassical economists, and this is the difference between the two epochs of economic thought. It is, however, a negligible difference as far as belief in a natural order is concerned. For the heretics, on the contrary, analysis *systematically* has a historical relevance, since its subject is historically determined.

Caravale's second criticism is that, regarding Marx, I have limited myself to Marxian reproduction schemes and failed to deal with the so-called transformation 'problem'. The reason is that 'transformation' is not a mathematical problem, as Marx himself erroneously (in a Ricardian sense) sustained, but a historically determined *process*, as Marx himself maintained later. What is more historically determined than a joint-stock company? According to Caravale this 'problem' can be understood only 'in the logical context of a concept of equilibrium correctly seen as a centre of gravity, and devoid of the relative implications of value judgments.' But it is precisely this Sraffian suppression of value judgements, implicit in the analytical equivalence of the different units of measurement ('values' or 'physical quantities') that is dangerous, because it distracts from analysing events in the sphere of production.

Caravale's third criticism is that I tend to preclude the possibility of interpreting Keynesian unemployment as a non-transitory phenomenon, but 'as a true equilibrium'. In view of Caravale's apparent concept of 'true equilibrium', I can understand his perplexity, but I had in mind (and wrote) that 'an intermediate situation which is neither desperate nor satisfactory is our normal lot', and that optimum equilibrium can occur only *by accident or design*. My interpretation according to Caravale 'risks conflicting with an interpretation of Keynesian unemployment as a non-transitory phenomenon'. An interpretation with which I fully agree – not because Keynesian equilibrium is a centre of gravitation but because the 'conditions of stability' for Keynes act in ways which contradict the summary of the *General Theory* and prevent the system from being violently unstable. Admitting the existence and operation of conditions of stability is the tribute analysis owes to history. Orthodox economists are defaulters here.

REPLY

Giovanni Caravale

E00, D00,
B41

Regarding Lunghini's first point, I should like to reply with three remarks.

1. The designation 'natural' classical economists used to identify some essential components of their analysis does not have, as Marx (1969: 214) points out, 'anything to do with nature' – and thus it does not indicate either conformity to a spontaneous state, or a characteristic of intrinsic goodness, but simply constitutes the way classical economists chose to refer to the forces they considered 'dominant' and 'systematic'.

2. Attributing to classical economists a view of the world '*à la* Pangloss' is clearly contradicted by the 'active' conception of economic policy that is typical of both Smith and Ricardo. The point is well exemplified by Adam Smith's ('Keynesian') thesis according to which one of the fundamental tasks of the State is that 'of erecting and maintaining those public institutions and those public works, which, though they may be in the highest degree advantageous to a great society, are, however, of such a nature, that the profit could never repay the expence to any individual or small number of individuals, and which it therefore cannot be expected that any individual or small number of individuals should erect or maintain' (Smith 1776: book V, cap. 1, p. 244).

3. The characteristic of the 'historical dimension,' i.e. the circumstance that the object of the analysis is historically determined, does not represent an adequate criterion for the identification of the two schools indicated by Lunghini (the 'orthodox' on one side and the 'heretics' on the other). If by 'historical dimension' we mean attention to the conditions of the historic reality, it is certainly present in Keynes; but *it is also present* in the classical school. If, on the other hand, it indicates consideration of the institutional framework as a reality that is neither eternal nor necessary, it is certainly absent in classical economics; *but it is also absent* in Keynes – to whom it is difficult to attribute, for example, the auspices of an 'exit' from the system in order to establish an institutional framework inspired by the doctrine, 'so illogical and so dull' (Keynes 1927: 34), of Marxist socialism. The criterion of 'historical dimension' could thus serve, in its first meaning, to 'isolate' (negatively) neoclassical economists and, in its

38

second meaning, to 'isolate' (positively) Marx and Schumpeter – certainly not to make the distinction suggested by Lunghini.

As to the second point, I should like to note that my critical observation has not so much to do with the 'sin of omission' of not having treated the problem of transformation, but rather with the 'sin of commission' of having attempted to uproot Marx's analysis from the concept of equilibrium. This operation would, in my opinion, make it impossible to understand the meaning of essential parts of his analysis. In the first place, the passage from values to prices, which is 'fundamental' at a logical level in order to provide a demonstration (which could not be provided, as we know today) of the 'reality of exploitation', also for the general case of the non-validity of the labour theory of value. It is in this perspective that the problem arises of where to place Sraffa, who is excluded from both the orthodox and the heretical groups, a 'victim' of Lunghini's rejection of a notion of equilibrium freed from value judgements. On the contrary, Lunghini considers Sraffa's 'suppression of value judgements' as 'danger-ous, as it distracts from the analysis of what happens in the sphere of production'. A thesis that would be plausible only if it did *not* refer to the Sraffian framework of the general determination of production prices and alluded instead to the lack, in Sraffa, of a Marxian-type analysis of the 'essence' of phenomena, as opposed to capitalist 'appearances'. In that case, however, in avoiding the Sraffian 'distraction', the analysis would encounter insurmountable difficulties regarding the transformation of values into prices – difficulties which cannot be exorcised with the emphasis – of a dubious exegetic and especially dubious logical solidity – on the 'transformation' as a *historical process*.

Concerning the third question, Lunghini confirms the thesis – which he has taken up again in another paper (1991: 10) – according to which in Keynes 'equilibrium is not dictated by a natural order, but occurs only by *accident or design* (as for Marx, by chance or as a consequence of a plan); when *this* [italics added] equilibrium occurs, it normally is not of full employment and therefore it is not optimal'. Two distinct, deeply incom-patible notions of equilibrium seem to be overlaid here. One is the notion of equilibrium as an optimal position; the other is that of equilibrium as an important position, an expression of the dominant forces operating within the system, but devoid, *per se*, of apologetic or critical connotations. The expression 'by accident or design' implies that the equilibrium being discussed is optimal. The other equilibrium, the one which in Keynes 'occurs' – at times, according to the excerpt just quoted; 'always' accord-ing to the thesis expounded by Lunghini (1989: 73) – is something else, not 'this one' (i.e. the optimal one).

Analysis, concludes Lunghini, must pay history the tribute of recogniz-ing the systematic contrast between an inherent tendency towards instabil-ity and the operation of 'factors of stability'. One can only agree with the necessity of explicitly admitting the complexity of the forces at work in real economies; but one should not be deceived into thinking that reflection on this complexity can attain the status of *analysis* – and thus go beyond the level of mere description – by negating or eluding of the notion of equilibrium.

REFERENCES

Keynes, J.M. (1927), *The End of Laissez-faire*, ed. Leonard and Virginia Woolf, London, Hogarth Press.

Lunghini, G. (1989), 'Equilibrio', in *Dizionario di Economia Politica*, Turin, Boringhieri

Lunghini, G. (1991), 'Almeno Keynes!', introduction to J.M. Keynes, *La fine del laissez-faire e altri scritti*, Turin, Boringhieri.

Marx, K. (1969), *Theories of Surplus Value*, London, Lawrence and Wishart.

Smith, A. (1776), *An Inquiry into the Nature and the Causes of the Wealth of Nations*, London, Oxford University.

2

EQUILIBRIUM, REPRODUCTION AND CRISIS

Giorgio Lunghini

It is as though the fall of the apple to the ground depended on the apple's motives, on whether it was worth while falling to the ground, and whether the ground wanted the apple to fall, and on mistaken calculations on the part of the apple as to how far it was from the centre of the earth.

(J.M. Keynes 1937)

The word 'equilibrium' has the same normative value in economic theory that it has in everyday language, somewhere between the consolatory and the intimidating. It implies a state of universal calm. The system tends to move, or to gravitate naturally, towards this state – either from structural necessity or as a result of appropriate behaviour on the part of individuals – when it is not already there, or when it has been upset by unforeseen events, or by some, albeit curable and removable, defect or conflict.

This notion, although largely authorized by economic theory, is not a good historiographic or epistemological guide, since, by affirming equilibrium as a law of composition or an elementary assumption of the system, it concentrates theory and the history of theories on presumed, 'natural', essentially static and atemporal determinations of equilibrium, rather than on the historical conditions of processes and conflicts. Identifying a given state of a given system as that which must be produced and reproduce itself suggests a general opinion that equilibrium, in that it is necessary, is desirable if not optimal for everybody, and thus prohibits change in analysis and action. The myth of equilibrium is the expedient whereby dominant agents and theories in the economy and in society convert history into nature and set the past up as the only admissible future, by treating the outcomes of previous revolutions as data and as forces that can and must balance contradictions that have survived or emerged or are feared.

MODELS AND VISIONS OF THE WORLD

Strictly speaking, there are as many notions of equilibrium in economic theory as there are theories, and for each theory there are as many configurations of equilibrium as there are solutions to models within the same theory. The minimum content of the concept of equilibrium (the concentration of its possible meanings, as Alessandro Vercelli puts it) is that of the solution of a model. This is the only unambiguous, if albeit drastically reductive, meaning, because it is restricted to those theories that can be formalized without grey areas and which presuppose the possibility of distinguishing 'endogenous' from 'exogenous' variables. The solution of a model is that configuration of endogenous variables which respects the system of propositions the model itself consists of, given the values of the variables set as exogenous to it and therefore treated as parameters.

Thus a curious inversion occurs. Since variables that are assumed to be so important as to be inexplicable are treated as parameters, the true unknowns turn out to be the parameters. For Keynes (1937) 'it is usual in a complex system to regard as the *causa causans* that factor which is most prone to sudden and wide fluctuation'. In effect, any analysis assumes the definition of its own limits. 'Boundary' variables that save the theoretical construct's link with external history are possible (the vague Keynesian concept of 'animal spirits', for example). However, in general, treating the sub-set of a system's state variables as parameters implies a hypothesis of structural invariance in the system itself, admitting only mechanical phenomena of passive adaptation in endogenous variables. Any equilibrium is relative to the institutional, technological or even 'economic' circumstances the theory assumes as given.

The equilibrium conditions set by theory are the conditions thought to be necessary for the existence and the reproduction of a given system. Since they control the course of events to ensure the existence and preservation of this system, they refer immediately to a vision of the world. Thus, in the concept of equilibrium, the method and the substance of political economy are one.

EQUILIBRIUM AND REPRODUCTION

The current expectation that a scientific theory must be, first and foremost, formally rigorous, i.e. translatable into mathematical language, establishes the conditions of equilibrium with which a theory begins and ends as the sole proof of the existence of the theory itself. If the conditions of equilibrium are interpreted as those necessary for the reproduction of the system, that is true in general and not only for purely deductive theories: without some notion of equilibrium, any theory (as opposed to a description) would be impossible, because it would be impossible to evaluate its importance. A theory is measured according to the variables it does *not* explain.

Not all economic theories are ideological theorizings of equilibrium or mechanistic metaphors. The Marxian critique of political economy is the most exemplary, as it directly analyses the conditions for the production and reproduction of capital and, rather than assuming economic equilibrium as a fact of nature, it explains it as accidental. Not all theories that admit the practical possibility of equilibrium affirm the necessity and the normality of equilibrium itself, let alone of its uniqueness, stability and optimality for all. Keynes' general theory is an example, as are some versions of the neoclassical theory of general economic equilibrium, even if pointlessly complicated and much *too* general.

Every discussion of the existence and the characteristics of equilibrium that is not purely formal is an (ultimately political) wager on the reproducibility of the system isolated in the theory. Therefore the importance of the theory differs according to where the surgical division is made between the outside and the inside of the theory, between that which is given as known and that which the theory promises to calculate. The conditions of equilibrium are the boundary line between common and economic knowledge in a theoretical system, where the vision of the world characteristic of a given economic theory is sought, i.e. the vision of the capitalist mode of production that it produces or repeats. To treat one or more variables as data, to which the others must logically adapt, or to which they will have to conform, means taking for granted, against the evidence, that the system in question is eternal. Furthermore, it usually obliges the invention of, and imposes as a norm, behaviour that progressively reduces the differences (the deviations) between the terms of the conditions of equilibrium, thereby excluding truly important phenomena from positive theoretical respectability because they are contradictory, as well as seemingly irrational visions and behaviour that explain them.

This is a consequence of the reductionism prevailing in economic theory, practised as if its subject, which is capitalism, could be reduced to a mechanism or a solid crystal: as if uncertainty could be reduced to risk, money to *numéraire*, capital to a set of means of production, historical time to logical time, history to a reversible process, and as if power and institutions were unimportant in the determination of reproduction, equilibrium and crisis in the capitalist mode of production.

In so far it is a theoretical construct, equilibrium is artificial and it can only be protected 'by repressing innovations and by artificially keeping the parameters constant. Only organized and authoritarian repression can maintain the static harmony of equilibrium' (Prigogine and Stengers 1978). According to Hahn (1973), 'an economy is in equilibrium when it generates messages which do not cause agents to change the theories which they hold or the policies which they pursue'.

The stability of the system, while it lasts, 'rests upon a convention: the tacit general agreement to *suppose* it stable. This stability, once doubted, is destroyed, and cascading disorder must intervene before the landslide grounds in a new fortuitous position' (Shackle 1967).

43

PARAMETERS AND UNKNOWNS

Which variables are considered parameters for the purposes of reproduction and which are regarded as unknowns whose equilibrium values the theory serves to calculate reveals the main difference between the various theories and enables a summary distinction to be drawn (to the point of excluding all the innovating heretics, Marx and Keynes included) between two great classes of models. For expository purposes these could be labelled the classical framework of a natural order which governs production, distribution and surplus accumulation and the neoclassical framework of individual rationality which governs the allocation of scarce resources (Walsh and Gram 1980).

A SCHEME OF 'CLASSICAL' AND 'NEOCLASSICAL' THEORIES

Classical political economy (from Petty to Ricardo) analyses capitalism as a historically determined mode of production, but determined by history which is supposed to be past. In fact, its essential characteristics, its class structure, its technology and its ability to produce surplus are assumed as given. Class structure and technology determine the distribution of surplus. Capitalists' decisions on how to spend profits condition the process of capital accumulation and consequently the conditions of reproduction. In the classical framework the following are assumed as parameters: a viable technology (able to generate surplus), a subsistence wage, the composition of the social product and the scale of production. Conversely, endogenous variables are: profit rate, relative prices, and the rate of accumulation.

Neoclassical economic theory (the predominant one since 1870) can be understood not as an analysis of a given mode of production, but as a technique for solving the economic problem that is assumed as general and eternal: to what extent should individuals, by means of exchange, redistribute the goods and services initially at their disposal to obtain the best outcome, according to their preferences. In this framework, class structure becomes analytically unimportant, as does the concept of surplus. The former is suppressed and replaced by the given structure (just as class structure is given in the classical framework) of the initial endowements of goods and services of individuals (or groups). A similar weakening in defining the circumstances (with a consequent increase in generality and loss of importance) occurs with technology.

In the neoclassical framework technology is also assumed as given, the only condition being the ability to transform scarce resources into exchangeable goods. The parameters are therefore the following: initial endowment of resources and efficient technology (as supply determinants), the tastes or preferences of individuals and the distribution among these of

44

the ownership of resources (as demand determinants). Endogenous variables are: the quantities of productive services allotted to the production of each commodity and the quantities of each commodity or service allotted to each consumer, the prices of productive services (hence the incomes of the resource owners) and the prices of final goods (the transformers' incomes). These prices ensure the equilibrium of the system, in that they ensure that the demand for any commodity or productive service does not exceed the supply, and that all incomes are determined simultaneously, because fate and the market intervene and correct privileges and balance of powers.

In the classical system the price theory is an intermediate stage in the analysis of value, distribution and accumulation; in the neoclassical system economic theory and practice are wholly resolved in the theory and practice of exchange relations. In the former, dominated by the need for action, equilibrium prices are a necessary condition for reproduction of the capitalist relationship and its own growth capacities. In the latter, dominated by the need for choice, equilibrium prices are a sufficient condition for maintaining the *status quo ante* (whereas, in Marx, the so-called 'transformation problem' of values into prices is the true question inherent to capital).

ORTHODOXY AND HERESY

In view of any possible didactic usfulness of this schematic counterpositioning, at least two warnings are needed. The first risk is to think that the opposing parties are so simple and clear-cut as to reduce the innumerable theses and arguments of economic theory to two and to prevent the greatest contributions – with a minimum of philological respect – to the critique of economic theory as an ideology of equilibrium (from Marx, Schumpeter and Keynes, above all) being included among them.

If one looks at the question from another more essential point of view (the normal or random nature of equilibrium), one could hold that the switch from the classical vision to the neoclassical vision is marked not so much by a revolution as by a transformation in the concept of equilibrium, and that the elements of continuity prevail over the opposing elements. This is true, if the price theory is placed at the centre of economic theory and the rational reconstructions of its history, which in both 'paradigms' would end up having an allocative function (explicitly in neoclassical theory and as a condition of uniformity of the profit rate in classical theory, if one accepts its neo-Ricardian lesson).

The real conflict then turns out to be the continually recurring – not only chronologically – clash between the two extreme visions of the capitalist system. The prevailing orthodox one, first of the classical then of the neoclassical school, would have the system upheld by a natural order, or by moral principles which make it gravitate towards a unique, stable and optimal configuration of general equilibrium. The structure of the system and the way its agents act ensure that any shift from equilibrium can only be random and is therefore temporary. Orthodox economists (the 'classical economists', according to the Keynesian solecism) view this mode of production as if production were production for use and as if money and machines were the neutral tools of the relationship between man and man and man and nature. Possible 'disequilibria' would be automatically corrected; the structural stability of the system is a duty of its elements. Faith in the existence of a natural order, ensured by the market's capacity for self-regulation, has an immediate political implication (political economy is a blend of economic theory and the art of government). If the immanent natural order is greater than any artificial order, the laws established by humanity and the State can only prove to be useless or harmful to the reproduction of the system, then: *laissez faire, laissez passer!*

The situation is the opposite from the heretic's point of view: like any other system, the capitalist system is not natural but historically determined ('artificial'). A capitalist economy is a monetary economy of production, in which production is production for profit. The capitalist system is also capable of some equilibrium, and in fact it exists. That equilibrium, however, can occur only by accident or by design. Crisis, not equilibrium, is the capitalist norm. (For Marx 'equilibrium itself – given the primitive character of this production – is an accident', 1948; just as for Keynes 'classical' equilibrium can only come about 'by accident or design', 1936.)

Since neither viewpoint (political economy and the critique of political economy) is unaware that not only is the law taken as such, but the exceptions are strikingly regular, each will need theories and models capable of affirming the first and tolerating the second – in short, of explaining what by law constitutes a case considered normal. Classical and neoclassical economists therefore have to explain what allows crisis to come about, and this they do by identifying its cause in imperfections and conflicts which hinder the natural order – if things were left to the natural order: if all artificial obstacles were removed – equilibrium would dominate and remain, immobile and perfect. History, at last, would have ended.

The opposite seems true to the critics: in history, the structural stability of the system is a possible case, but known not to be necessary. Rather than being hindered, disturbed or corrupted by presumed imperfections or occasional conflicts, it is made possible, caused and preserved precisely by the institutions in which the antagonistic causes, the conditions of stability, are crystallized. In the first situation any institution placed over the Market, the supreme helmsman, will drive equilibrium away and only temporarily permit bad equilibria; only in the second situation will these artificial elements of the system make its existence and reproduction possible. Those who adopt the first standpoint believe that we already live in the best of all possible worlds; others think it would be possible to live otherwise.

MONEY AND MACHINES

There is a second, but more important, risk in an approach that presumes the subject can be adequately dealt with by dividing it into classical and neoclassical schools, rather than orthodoxy and heresy. This is the conviction that money and machines are variables which are necessarily and unanimously treated as neutral with respect to equilibrium. However they become its principal determinants when money and production techniques are conceived as the variables which are most easily moulded to suit the needs of equilibrium and capitalist reproduction.

The heretics mentioned above (Marx, Schumpeter, Keynes and others), but also simple observation and disenchanted thought, are enough to convince us that money and machines are the mirror-image of production relations and therefore a focal point in the reproduction process. Capitalist-entrepreneurs' expectations as to *their* future are fixed in machines, in the design and use of machines, just as they are in the command and the use of money, thus establishing the characteristics of the present equilibrium.

REFERENCES

Hahn, F.H. (1973), *On the Notion of Equilibrium in Economics*, Cambridge, Cambridge University Press.

Keynes, J.M. (1936), *The General Theory of Employment, Interest and Money*, London, Macmillan.

Keynes, J.M. (1937), 'The General Theory of Employment', *Quarterly Journal of Economics*, February.

Marx, K. (1948), *Das Kapital. Kritik der politischen Ökonomie* II, Berlin, Dietz.

Prigogine, I., and Stengers, I., (1978), 'Equilibrio/squilibrio', in *Enciclopedia Einaudi*, 5, Turin, Einaudi.

Shackle, G.L.S. (1967), *The Years of High Theory: Invention and Tradition in Economic Thought, 1926–39*, Cambridge, Cambridge University Press.

Walsh, V., and Gram, H. (1980), *Classical and Neoclassical Theories of General Equilibrium: Historical Origins and Mathematical Structure*, Oxford University Press.

ACKNOWLEDGEMENT

This is a general outline of the chapter 'Equilibrio' in the *Dizionario di economia politica*, 14, Bollati Boringhieri, Turin, 1988.

E9°   3

EQUILIBRIUM, DISEQUILIBRIUM AND MACROECONOMIC THEORY

Alessandro Vercelli

In recent decades, macroeconomics has increasingly concentrated on equilibrium positions and paths, totally (or almost) excluding the analysis of the dynamics of the economic system in disequilibrium. This partly depends on the diffusion of methods of analysis that favour the analysis of equilibrium (such as game theory and the theory of stochastic processes) and partly on the dominance of lines of research that have justified exclusive attention to the analysis of equilibrium (in particular 'new classical economics' and 'atheoretical econometrics').

In the meantime, the concepts of equilibrium (and disequilibrium) utilized in macroeconomic models have multiplied without a sufficient effort being made to explain the links between them and to examine the meaning and limits of the various types of equilibrium analysis. This is why we see concepts of equilibrium and disequilibrium crop up in the controversies among different theoretical lines in macroeconomics. The debate has often become sterile because of confusion over insufficiently explained terms. For example, the position Keynes calls 'underemployment equilibrium' is interpreted by Lucas as a position of disequilibrium; and, vice versa, if we adopt Keynes's meaning of equilibrium, what is called by Lucas 'equilibrium business cycle', it necessarily implies a dynamic mechanism that operates in disequilibrium (see Vercelli 1991: chs 8, 9, 13). This example should be sufficient to suggest that there can be no serious and constructive debate between the different lines of research in macroeconomics until the different meanings of the concept of equilibrium have been clearly defined and their reciprocal relationships sufficiently investigated.

I shall try to tidy up this intricate tangle of problems by distinguishing between three fundamental concepts of equilibrium of which all others can be seen as particular cases: the syntactic (or logical) meaning, briefly discussed in the next section, the dynamic meaning, analysed in the following one, and the family of particular semantic meanings, briefly dealt with in the fourth section. In the fifth I review some basic reasons that explain the crucial role of equilibrium positions in economic analysis. Then in the sixth I discuss the relativity of the distinction between equilibrium and disequilibrium. Although this distinction depends on the theoretical and formal assumptions of the model, we cannot forgo the analysis of both categories, equilibrium and disequilibrium, without distorting the semantic implications of analysis. A model of pure equilibrium, like that suggested by Lucas and the other 'new classical economists', raises insuperable paradoxes that I shall mention in the seventh section.

In the eighth, I mention the basic reasons why the analysis of the dynamic stability of the compared equilibria is considered a fundamental prerequisite of comparative statics. In the ninth, I argue that this is also substantially true of comparisons between stationary stochastic processes that characterize models of equilibrium under conditions of uncertainty. Although these comparisons are the basis of the appraisal of alternative rules of economic policy in new classical economics, this fundamental prerequisite is generally neglected.[1]

In Appendix 3.1, I outline a semantic interpretation of the procedure for solving functional dynamic equations in order to explain the relationship between the syntactic and semantic implications of equilibrium and disequilibrium concepts. Appendix 3.2 contains a brief discussion of Nash's concept of equilibrium, a particularly widespread concept of equilibrium today, that confirms the need for a rigorous dynamic foundation for the equilibrium concepts utilized in macroeconomics. In Appendix 3.3 I briefly deal with some elementary concepts of the ergodic theory to explain why and in what sense stochastic equilibria can and must be subjected to an analysis of behaviour 'in disequilibrium'. In the future the ergodic theory may contribute to the analysis of the 'dynamic stability' of stochastic processes.

THE SYNTACTIC CONCEPT OF EQUILIBRIUM

Often an equilibrium is defined as the solution to an equation or a system of equations. There are many examples in macroeconomic literature.[2] Nevertheless this meaning of equilibrium is unacceptable as it cannot, *per se*, supply a criterion that enables us to discriminate between a position of equilibrium and one of disequilibrium, in that both must be conceived as solutions to a formal system (see Appendix 3.1).

From a strictly syntactic point of view, the solution of a system of equations is the set of values of the endogenous variables that makes the system's equations logically compatible. From this purely logical point of view, the distinction between equilibrium and disequilibrium has no possible empirical content. In fact, every set of values that does not satisfy the system of equations implies a logical contradiction within the system and cannot be accepted as an object of scientific analysis. Therefore the distinction between equilibrium and disequilibrium within a formal system can be accepted only if both correspond to different solutions to the system.

49

This is possible within a formal dynamic system on the basis of semantic considerations that lie beyond a strictly syntactic point of view.

Accordingly, every time the solution of a system of equations is interpreted as an 'equilibrium' we must adopt a criterion of distinction that is not syntactic but semantic. In most cases, there is an explicit or implicit dynamic model at the root of this criterion[3]. An example is given by Walras's model of general economic equilibrium: the parabola of *tâtonnement* serves, among other things, to introduce a dynamic context that justifies using the term 'equilibrium' to indicate the solution of the model.

THE DYNAMIC NOTION OF EQUILIBRIUM

According to the dynamic concept, a system is in equilibrium whenever it is not characterized by an 'endogenous' dynamic process (i.e. its state would persist even if the system were isolated from the environment).

The concept of equilibrium in its dynamic meaning can be explained by an appropriate interpretation of the procedure for solving a dynamic functional equation (see, for example, Gandolfo 1983). Let us consider the simplest case: a first-order linear difference equation with constant coefficients. The general solution is obtained by adding a particular solution to the general solution of the homogeneous form. The particular solution is found immediately, in the hypothesis that the known terms are constant, by assuming that the unknown function is stationary. If, on the other hand, the known terms are a function of time, the textbooks suggest 'proving' as a solution a function of time qualitatively similar to that which characterizes the known terms. We thus obtain the general solution of the homogeneous form, by excluding the known terms (i.e. the exogenous influences) and by studying the dynamic behaviour of the solution that is interpreted as a deviation from equilibrium or 'disequilibrium'.

The rationale of this solving procedure becomes transparent as soon as it is considered from a semantic point of view. The particular solution represents the equilibrium path which, by definition, represents the exogenous dynamics of the system. The equilibrium is revealed to be stationary or mobile, depending on whether the known terms that represent the environment's influence on the system are a constant or a function of time. In the second case, the system's dynamic behaviour depends strictly on exogenous impulses in that, by definition, a system in equilibrium is passive, i.e. devoid of endogenous dynamics.

On the other hand, the general solution of the homogeneous form is obtained by completely excluding the known terms, i.e. the environment's influence on the system. This makes it possible to analyse the endogenous dynamics of the deviation from equilibrium and hence the properties of the system's dynamic stability.

The general solution, then, describes the dynamic behaviour of the system as the sum of the exogenous dynamics in equilibrium with respect to external coordinates (the particular solution) and the endogenous dynamics in disequilibrium with respect to the equilibrium path (general solution of the homogeneous form).

This semantic interpretation of the solving procedure for a dynamic functional equation has a wide area of application. It is also applicable to a first-order linear differential equation with constant coefficients that can easily be obtained by a difference equation with the same characteristics by means of simply taking a limit which does not alter the semantic properties of the solving procedure. It is also applied to difference or differential equations of a higher order (n^0) which – as we know – can be ascribed to systems of n equations of the first-order.

This dynamic interpretation suggests possible criteria for the use of concepts of equilibrium and disequilibrium. These criteria can ultimately be stated, depending on the context and the particular application, but they cannot be violated without jeopardizing the coherence and transparency of the analysis.

THE SEMANTIC NOTIONS OF EQUILIBRIUM

The dynamic notion is the 'lowest common denominator' of various concepts of equilibrium, specified from the semantic point of view, related to the dynamic forces that characterize a certain system according to a particular theory. Thus for example, rational mechanics defines equilibrium as a state characterized by the compensation of virtual 'works' that determine the potential endogenous dynamics of the system. Likewise, according to the Walrasian theory of general economic equilibrium (which, originally, was greatly influenced by rational mechanics), equilibrium is defined as a state in which there are no excesses of demand or supply, which are considered the only possible sources of endogenous dynamics.

As far as macroeconomics is specifically concerned, I shall briefly mention the concepts of equilibrium of Keynes and Lucas. Keynes's notion is fundamentally of the dynamic type: underemployment equilibria are defined in this way, by contrast with the 'classical' tradition, in that Keynes maintains that in these positions there are no endogenous dynamic mechanisms that tend to modify the *status quo*, given that 'there is no incentive for employers as a whole to contract or expand employment' (1936: 27). Keynes's notion of equilibrium is therefore fully coherent from the dynamic point of view (contrary to widely held opinion). One of the sources of this prejudice is Don Patinkin, who has repeatedly maintained that the Keynesian concept of underemployment equilibrium is incompatible with the assumption of flexible money wages in that the concept of equilibrium would imply that 'nothing changes in the system' (1965: 643). Nevertheless, variations in money wages do not, *per se*, imply variations in the state variables that characterize the labour market: real wages and employment. Keynes maintains that prices could vary in the same direction as money wages, leaving real wages unchanged. Furthermore, the dynamic notion of equilibrium adopted by Keynes does not in the least imply that 'nothing changes in the system'. There are cases in which, as in the previous example, variables different from those of state vary with effects that reciprocally compensate each other. Furthermore, equilibrium can be mobile, as in growth models.[4] Patinkin's reasoning has been resumed by the new classical economists, who counter it with a different concept of equilibrium.

According to Lucas there is equilibrium when: (1) economic agents act in their own interests, (2) all markets are cleared. This notion of equilibrium is applied to stochastic versions of general economic equilibrium. When the above-mentioned requirements are satisfied, the fundamental sources of endogenous dynamics typical of general equilibrium models (excesses in demand and supply) are excluded by hypothesis. The stochastic versions of the model, however, allow a further type of exogenous dynamics induced by stochastic shocks that are compatible with 'equilibrium', since the latter is conceived as a stationary stochastic process. The use of stochastic functional dynamic equations accentuates the similarity between the behaviour of the model and the behaviour of the reality represented, as has often been stressed by Lucas and Sargent. Nevertheless, this modifies some semantic details of the concept of equilibrium, but does not substantially modify the dynamic concept of equilibrium.

THE REASONS FOR EQUILIBRIUM

It is no accident that equilibrium is at the heart of analysis in economics and other scientific disciplines, since the concept performs a series of extremely useful epistemological functions. Nevertheless an abuse of the concept of equilibrium can be dangerous in that it may lead to profoundly erroneous conclusions. This can be avoided by gaining a critical awareness of its functions, of which I shall mention the following.

1. It serves as a favoured reference in analysing the dynamics of a system. As we have seen, the endogenous dynamics of a system are typically studied in relation to coordinates centred on the equilibrium position. The exogenous dynamics are analysed as the dynamics of the equilibrium position in relation to coordinates outside the system that are, in turn, considered in equilibrium *vis-à-vis* the observer. This is not surprising: the degree of permanence of an equilibrium position is, by definition, greater than any other position the system can assume, since outside equilibrium endogenous causes are added to exogenous causes.[5]

2. It serves as a criterion on the basis of which the dynamic behaviour of a system can be divided into two components: one endogenous in relation

to the equilibrium position; the other, exogenous, that determines the dynamics of the equilibrium position itself. In the case of linear systems, in particular, the concept of equilibrium allows an additive separation between the two components. The subdivision of a complex problem into a plurality of simpler problems is a problem-solving strategy that often proves effective.

3. The hypothesis of equilibrium enables considerable simplifications to be made to the functional structure of the model. In particular:

1 Feedback is represented in equilibrium by a single relationship (for example, the interaction between income and expenditure can be represented by a single relationship, the multiplier).
2 Some variables become equal (for example, demand and supply, income and expenditure, etc.), thereby reducing the number of unknowns.
3 Certain terms become nil (for example, the derivatives when equilibrium represents a maximum or a minimum).
4 The equilibrium often corresponds to the maximum or minimum value of a certain function and is thus an important point of reference for the explanation or the forecast of the behaviour of a rational economic agent.[6]

For these reasons and others, if we compare the analysis of equilibrium position with the analysis of the 'global' dynamic behaviour of the system, studied both in equilibrium and disequilibrium, we can immediately verify that the first is much simpler and this facilitates the analysis considerably.[7] However, it should never be forgotten that the analysis of equilibrium is much poorer in information than a full dynamic analysis. Therefore any conclusion drawn from the sub-set of information characterizing the analysis of equilibrium can be gravely misleading unless it can be demonstrated that the system will never abandon the equilibrium position.

The above-mentioned properties that endow equilibrium analysis with its methodological appeal are strictly linked with the dynamic notion of equilibrium. This is not necessarily true of the last property listed (3 (4)), because it is not certain that the equilibrium trajectory would be the optimal trajectory of the system. Nevertheless, this is certainly not the reason why definitions of equilibrium that are not quite coherent with the dynamic notion are sometimes adopted (as in the case of the new classical economists: see Vercelli 1991: chs. 8, 9, 10). It should therefore be concluded that in general the dynamic concept of equilibrium is the one that guarantees the greatest methodological advantages.

We should avoid confusing the different notions of equilibrium. From a semantic point of view equilibrium is a particular case of dynamic behaviour, but from the syntactic (or logical) point of view each form of dynamic behaviour, even out of equilibrium, must be reduced to formal timeless structures in order to be intelligible. Genetic epistemology interprets these structures as equilibrium structures of the epistemic subject that guarantee the coordination of the operative structures of a rational agent and its adaptation to the environment. This has nothing to do with the type of dynamics (in equilibrium or not) of the empirical referent of the model,[8] and in any case, it has induced undue forms of 'reification' of equilibrium, i.e. projection of the formal characteristics of equilibrium on the empirical reality.

The reification of equilibrium has characterized some currents of philosophical thought (in particular the 'rationalist' current, criticized by Voltaire in *Candide*), and has influenced scientific thought in many disciplines, including economics. Keynes often criticized 'rationalist' positions in the theory of probability and in economics, positions he deemed typical of 'classical' economists. Similar positions are still found, particularly in the contributions of new classical economists.[9] The reification of equilibrium can be avoided only by being fully aware that disequilibrium positions are plausible, relevant and intelligible and can irreversibly modify a rational agent's set of available options.

THE RELATIVITY OF THE DISTINCTION BETWEEN EQUILIBRIUM AND DISEQUILIBRIUM

The definition of disequilibrium is no less problematic than that of equilibrium. In its case, however, the syntactic definition is clearly unacceptable. A set of values of the endogenous variables that do not correspond to one of the solutions of the model would imply a logical contradiction.

As for the semantic definitions, there are – obviously – as many as there are definitions of equilibrium. In this case too, the dynamic definition proves to be the 'lowest common denominator' of the semantic definitions.

In terms of the dynamic point of view, there are still ambiguities in the distinction between equilibrium and disequilibrium which depend on the fact that this distinction can change if so much as a single detail of the theory or model is varied.[10] A well-known example is the distinction between 'periods' of different length, which often occurs in economic analysis. In this case we find a succession of models that differ from each other only because, in passing from one to the next, a constant becomes a variable. For example, in the Keynesian distinction between short and long-periods (which derives from the more complex and structured Marshallian classification) the capital stock is assumed as a constant in the short-period and as a variable in the long-period. In general, a short-period equilibrium is a position of disequilibrium with regard to long-period equilibrium. This is a possible source of misunderstanding. For example, the so-called theoreticians of disequilibrium (Benassy, Malinvaud, etc.) use the term 'disequilibrium' to indicate positions that other economists prefer to call 'temporary equilibrium' or 'non-Walrasian equilibrium'. Both definitions are correct from their own standpoint. Short-period equilibria generally are disequilibria from the long-period perspective.

Dynamics in disequilibrium can be conceptualized as a succession of short-period equilibria such that short-period equilibrium dynamics depend on the gap between short-period equilibrium and long-period equilibrium, while long-period equilibrium dynamics do not generally depend on short-period equilibrium dynamics. This description does not support the idea expressed by Lucas (1981) and by other new classical economists (see Klamer 1984) that the analysis of dynamics in disequilibrium is none other than 'a more complex analysis of equilibrium'. This argument, if it were correct, would justify adopting a method of pure equilibrium that completely neglects the explicit analysis of positions of disequilibrium. Nevertheless, the above holds strictly only from the syntactic point of view, not from a semantic point of view. By adopting a method of pure equilibrium we would lose track of the distinction between endogenous and exogenous dynamics, in that all dynamics, by definition, depend on exogenous impulses, which is not necessarily true from the empirical point of view. This could in turn influence value judgements concerning the desirability of changes in the system's structure. In fact, given that the dynamics occur in equilibrium, we are led to believe that those dynamics represent the system's optimal response to external shocks.[11] Furthermore, if something wrong is identified in the dynamic behaviour of the system, we are led to attribute the responsibility to exogenous factors (for example, the rules of economic policy). A method of pure equilibrium could therefore be dangerously misleading.

PARADOXES OF THE METHOD OF PURE EQUILIBRIUM

In the history of philosophical and scientific thought, intelligibility has often been linked with equilibrium. According to the 'rationalist' tradition, which dates back to the beginnings of Greek philosophy, the essence of phenomena is defined by unchanging structures of equilibrium (*logoi*) and reason (*logos*) is seen as a faithful 'reflection' of them. Any phenomenon that cannot be reduced to these equilibrium structures is considered as mere appearance and not fully intelligible. In the extreme version, time and every type of movement are considered as mere illusions (as in the celebrated paradoxes of Zeno).

This point of view has re-emerged repeatedly in the history of thought. In particular, the so-called 'rationalists' of the seventeenth and eighteenth centuries (such as Descartes, Spinoza and Leibniz) elaborated an extremely sophisticated and influential version of this concept of rationality.[12]

This point of view has also influenced modern sciences. A telling example in modern physics is the theory of general relativity, which reduces time and dynamics to topological structures interpretable as equilibrium structures.[13] Nevertheless, in recent decades the natural sciences have progressively liberated themselves from the umbilical tie between rationality and equilibrium, devoting increasing attention to disequilibria, irreversible processes, phase transitions, qualitative changes, etc. (see, for a review of these new developments, Prigogine and Stengers 1984).

On the contrary, the link between rationality and equilibrium has become progressively more inseparable from macroeconomic orthodoxy. An extreme case is that of Lucas, who has repeated on various occasions that equilibrium positions are not intelligible and has advocated adopting the method of pure equilibrium. This point of view should be firmly rejected. Any method that concentrates analysis exclusively on equilibrium positions seems to be intrinsically unilateral and inevitably leads to paradoxes that cannot be overcome within that method.[14] I shall briefly mention three particularly relevant ones.

Quite some time ago Arrow (1958) noted that the standard definition of competitive equilibrium is contradictory in that the assumption that all markets are cleared requires a rapid adjustment to prices at the equilibrium level, while the assumption that agents are unable to influence prices individually (in that they are price-takers), makes it impossible to understand how prices can adjust to equilibrium values. To understand the working of a competitive market we are in reality obliged to abandon the hypothesis of equilibrium and study how economic agents react to situations of disequilibrium. Only in that way can a competitive market become intelligible, in the sense that we can explain its genesis, working and persistence.

A second example, closely linked with the first, is the paradox pointed out by Grossman and Stiglitz (1980). To the latter we owe the observation that the hypothesis of efficient competitive markets is contradictory if formulated in the usual way in a perspective of pure equilibrium. If markets are efficient, asset prices fully reflect the available information. However, if that were so, no economic agent would have any incentive to gather and elaborate information[15] and it could not be understood how prices could modify to account correctly for the available information.

The third paradox, pointed out by Sims (1987), is linked with the previous one. If the hypothesis of rational expectations implies that agents perfectly forecast the systematic part of the future,[16] then, under this hypothesis, it would not be possible to modify its course by means of economic policy interventions. This reasoning is intended to demonstrate the impossibility of economic policy in the hypothesis of rational expectations.

These and other paradoxes that derive from the application of a method of pure equilibrium are not logical but semantic paradoxes. In general we can infer from an analysis of the paradoxes that there are semantic implications of equilibrium that remain unintelligible if we do not interpret the equilibrium as the limit of a dynamic process.[17] Arrow's paradox points out that the standard definition of competitive equilibrium would not explain how agents adjust prices to equilibrium values, which is a crucial semantic characteristic of the competitive market. Similarly, in Grossman and Stiglitz's paradox it is pointed out that the standard definition of equilibrium in 'perfect' financial markets would not explain how prices manage to reflect fully the available information on *market fundamentals*. Lastly, Sims's paradox clarifies how the hypothesis of rational expectations, in its extreme version, does not lend itself to the study of the effects of economic policy.[18]

These paradoxes suggest the observation that equilibrium is not fully intelligible unless we interpret it in terms of a dynamic analysis. Therefore we cannot avoid studying the dynamic behaviour of the economic system not only in equilibrium but also in disequilibrium. The new classical economists claimed that macroeconomics must have an equilibrium foundation. In any case, we cannot do without a dynamic foundation of macroeconomics.

THE DYNAMIC BEHAVIOUR OF THE ECONOMIC SYSTEM IN DISEQUILIBRIUM

I will now discuss why an accurate analysis of the behaviour of the economic system in disequilibrium cannot be avoided. First of all, in many cases a preliminary analysis of the behaviour of the economic system in disequilibrium is indispensable for legitimizing the use of equilibrium models. This is true, for example, of models involved in exercises in comparative statics. As Samuelson (1947) explained long ago, comparative statics has no meaning if we cannot prove that the compared equilibrium positions are dynamically stable. If the equilibria were not stable, the dynamics in disequilibrium could no longer be considered transitory and therefore would have to become the main object of the analysis. Furthermore, even if the compared equilibria were stable, the discussion of comparative statics would scarcely be meaningful if the convergence towards equilibrium, following a change in one or more parameters, were not reasonably rapid.

Dynamic stability and rapidity of convergence are necessary but not sufficient conditions for the correct use of comparative statics. The following circumstances would also have to be excluded:

1 *Path dependence*. In general, the equilibrium towards which the system tends depends not only on the initial conditions but also on the dynamic path travelled. Dynamics in disequilibrium often modify the structure of

parameters (for example, the availability of production factors) and therefore modify the characteristics of the set of potential equilibria.

2 *Indeterminacy.* If there is a plurality of equilibria, only the analysis of the dynamic behaviour of the system in disequilibrium can clarify the equilibrium to which the system tends to converge. Unfortunately, it should by now be clear that the existence of a plurality of equilibria is the rule rather than the exception (see Arrow and Hahn 1971).

In each of these cases, comparisons between different systems need to be based on a model of comparative dynamics that does not exclude analysis of dynamics in disequilibrium. It cannot be denied that currently we do not have sufficiently general and effective methods of comparative dynamics, but that is not a good reason simply to assume that the complicating factors which make comparative statics unreliable do not exist. We are obliged to prove that in the case under consideration the above-mentioned effects are negligible for the purposes of analysis. The new classical economists, on the other hand, often simply content themselves with excluding the presence of the above-mentioned complicating factors. Furthermore, given that they consider disequilibrium non-intelligible (Lucas 1981), we do not understand with which method they could analyse its presence and importance. On the contrary, Keynes prefers to maintain constant awareness of these problems even if he is not able to analyse them and solve them with strictly analytical methods.[19] This, however, enables us to draw qualitative indications of a probabilistic type on the system's dynamic behaviour to avoid the errors of evaluation which we would otherwise make.

The economist must attribute full awareness of the importance of disequilibrium paths to the economic agents themselves. Given that a state of disequilibrium offers opportunities of arbitrage, there is no reason to exclude that rational agents are not able to discover and exploit those opportunities in their individual interests. Under these hypotheses, there are no *a priori* guarantees that the economic system converges towards a Walrasian equilibrium. The economy could converge, for example, towards an equilibrium with rationing, such as the Keynesian underemployment equilibrium.

It has recently been demonstrated that the dynamic stability of a Walrasian equilibrium is ensured only if the number and the intensity of the favourable surprises do not exceed a certain threshold.[20] Consequently, the stability of the general economic equilibrium depends, above all, on objective factors, such as technological innovations that create new opportunities for economic agents.[21] This demonstrates the relevance today of Schumpeter's (1911, 1939) intuitions. A Schumpeterian swarm of innovations implies a set of favourable surprises which is likely to destroy the stability of the 'circular flow', i.e. general economic equilibrium. Furthermore, instability also depends on subjective factors, i.e. on the perception of the existence of favourable surprises unforeseen by economic agents. If this perception varies in a discontinuous way on the basis of conventional criteria, as suggested by Keynes, the stability of equilibrium cannot be taken as granted even in the absence of objective favourable surprises of sufficient intensity.

The hypothesis of perfect foresight, typical of traditional formulations of general economic equilibrium, like the rational expectations hypothesis, typical of some recent reformulations,[22] implicitly excludes the possibility that agents can perceive favourable surprises of a systematic type which produce instability. The problem of the dynamic instability of equilibrium is thus eliminated by definition in these sets of models, but it is not eliminated in reality. The problem is merely shifted and it reappears in the form of an extremely limited sphere of application of the model.

THE DYNAMIC INSTABILITY OF EQUILIBRIUM IN A STOCHASTIC CONTEXT

Some economists have recently been under the illusion they can elude the problems analysed in the previous sections by simply reformulating the equilibrium models in stochastic language. But even if the language is different and partly obscures the analogies, the problems remain substantially the same.

As we have seen (pp. 51–2), the 'equilibria' of the stochastic models elaborated by new classical economists are typically identified as stationary stochastic processes. According to the new classical economists, this 'new' concept of (stochastic) equilibrium breaks the bounds of the 'old' concept of (deterministic) equilibrium. In their opinion, while the old concept of equilibrium is static in the sense that in this state 'nothing changes in the system', the new stochastic concept is dynamic in the sense that it is compatible with a wide variety of dynamic paths of the economic system (Lucas 1981). We cannot share this point of view – above all because it is not true that in the 'old' concept of equilibrium 'nothing changes in the system' (see pp. 51–2), and then because, on closer inspection, the two concepts are more or less identical. In both cases a certain degree of invariance is assumed that is higher than that of the alternative states or processes.[23] In the 'new' concept, the systematic part of the process does not vary in time in perfect analogy with a stationary deterministic equilibrium; the only conceptual difference is the fact that the stationarity of the systematic part of the process is compatible with a wide variety of dynamic behaviour of the realizations of the stochastic process as a consequence of exogenous impulses.

In any case, the correct use of a stochastic equilibrium requires a solid dynamic foundation, precisely as in the case of a deterministic equilibrium.

This implies, above all, an accurate analysis of the 'dynamic stability' of the equilibrium. In other words, we have to analyse to what extent the distribution of probabilities that characterizes the stochastic process converges towards the original one following a perturbation. Knowledge of the properties of the Gaussian distribution would have scant practical relevance if the central limit theorems had not proved that this distribution is the limit distribution of a stochastic variable under quite general hypotheses. Likewise, we are obliged to appraise the properties of stability of the stationary stochastic process assumed as equilibrium in order to evaluate its soundness, analytical implications and economic policy. This is particularly important for comparisons between alternative stochastic equilibria when evaluating the impact of different economic policies. These comparisons, which we could describe as 'stochastic comparative statics' and are at the centre of the analysis of the new classical economists, make sense only if the equilibria under comparison have an analogous degree of robustness with regard to exogenous shocks. It is thus necessary to prove that, following a disturbance, the moments of the distribution converge rapidly towards the original stationary values. Furthermore, if we can succeed in identifying a stationary stochastic process different from the one in which we live, no less robust and preferable, before trying to change economic policy we should make sure that the transition takes place with sufficient rapidity and that the costs justify the change. This requires an accurate analysis of the behaviour of the stochastic process 'in disequilibrium'. These requirements are generally unknown,[24] although the analysis of them is not entirely beyond the range of existing techniques. Stochastic convergence has been systematically studied in particular by the ergodic theory that has found vast applications in the natural sciences (see Appendix 3.3). It is surprising but significant that this fast-developing branch of mathematics has been applied so rarely to the field of economics. It may be further evidence of the uncritical use of the concept of equilibrium in economics.

The systematic introduction of stochastic methods in economics is certainly useful, but it should not be used as a pretext for failing to provide a rigorous dynamic foundation of the stochastic equilibria which explains their meaning, soundness and implications.

CONCLUSIONS

The attention of macroeconomics has progressively shifted towards the exclusive analysis of equilibrium positions and has increasingly neglected the analysis of the positions of disequilibrium and their dynamics. In spite of this (or perhaps because of it) the meaning and the limits of the analysis of equilibrium have yet to be sufficiently examined.

I have tried to show that the syntactic definition of equilibrium, although increasingly more widespread in the recent literature (in particular among new classical economists), is not acceptable because, *per se*, it is not capable of discriminating between equilibrium and disequilibrium. The growing set of semantic definitions is based upon a dynamic definition of equilibrium that is useful to adopt as a common reference point.

Analysis of the dynamic behaviour of a system in disequilibrium is inescapable if we wish to lay solid foundations for macroeconomics. Every economist should be aware of the crucial role of dynamics in disequilibrium in determining aggregate economic activity and should attribute this awareness to rational economic agents.

APPENDIX 3.1 SEMANTIC INTERPRETATION OF THE PROCEDURE FOR SOLVING FUNCTIONAL DYNAMIC EQUATIONS

In this appendix I intend to clarify some affirmations in the text. To this end, I shall refer to a dynamic system characterized by a feedback that is influenced by the environment by means of an input variable. I shall represent the system in terms which are equivalent from a formal point of view but hold different heuristic functions:

1 linear algebra as a bridge to modern mathematics;
2 algebra of block diagrams, which may be inferior to linear algebra as far as manipulation and calculation are concerned, but which favours the intuitive perception of the semantics of the formal relationships.

The combined use of these two languages that can easily be translated one into the other, provides a useful bridge between the syntactic and semantic aspects of the dynamics of economic systems.

Let us assume that x and y are the state variables of the system. They represent the polarity of a feedback, that is, a couple of functional relations that are not inverse of one another:[25]

$$y = ax$$
$$x = by + u \qquad a \neq 1/b, \, a > 0, \, b > 0, \, u > 0 \qquad (3.1)$$

This elementary system of equations can be represented in the language of block diagrams (see Fig. 3.1). The input variable u represents the influence exerted by the environment on the system. In the block the transformation is indicated which, given the value of the input variable, enables one to obtain the value of the output variable. The circle represents the 'summation node' that operates the algebraic sum of the input variables with their sign, and the point represents a bifurcation point after which the same variable that precedes the point is represented by different branches of the circuit.

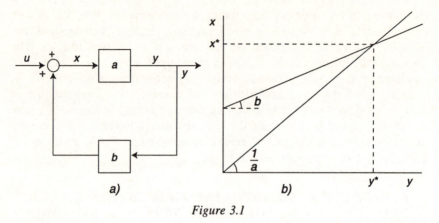

Figure 3.1

Generally, in a system of simultaneous equations, any set of values different from those that solve the system implies a logical contradiction. This appears intuitive if we look at Fig. 3.1*b*. Assuming that the first function can be inverted, we can obtain the value of *x* from both the first and the second equation. Nevertheless the values obtained are different, except for the values that correspond to the intersection of the two functions, i.e. the values that represent the solution of the system. The two functions cannot both be 'true' at one and the same time unless they assume the values that solve the system.

So, in statics, the solutions to the system are the only admissible values for the endogenous variables because they are the only values that do not violate the principle of non-contradiction. If we define the set of solutions as an equilibrium, all the other values, which we would be tempted to call disequilibrium, would be non-intelligible.[26] The conclusions vary radically, however, if we pass from statics to dynamics.

The simplest way of making the system dynamic (3.1) is to introduce a lag in one of the two functions. That way we obtain, for example, the following system:

$$y_t = ax_t$$
$$x_t = by_{t-1} + u \qquad a \neq 1/b, \, a > 0, \, b > 0, \, u > 0 \qquad (3.2)$$

The new system can be represented in the language of block diagrams by introducing a new block that contains the lag operator L whose function is that of delaying the time subscript by a number of units equal to the exponent (see Fig. 3.2*a*).

It is easy to verify that in this case the gap between the two functions does not imply any logical contradiction, because the values of the same variable obtained by the two equations refer to different periods of time

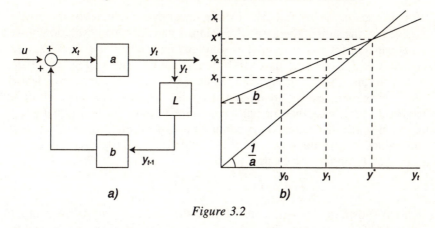

Figure 3.2

(see Fig. 3.2*b*). A situation of this type implies the existence of an endogenous dynamic process and therefore implies dynamics in disequilibrium. However, the introduction of the delay makes the system indeterminate in every instant. The order of the lag determines the number of degrees of freedom. (In our example the lag is of the first-order and there is a degree of freedom.) It is possible to eliminate the degrees of freedom and make the system determinate by fixing the value of the delayed variable (or of the delayed *n* variables if the order is *n*). This latter, on the other hand, is determined in a system of equations identical to the previous one except that the time subscript is delayed by a period.

Thus we obtain a succession of systems of simultaneous equations from the initial period to the period considered:

$$y_0 \rightarrow \begin{cases} y_1 = ax_1 \\ x_1 = by_0 + u \end{cases} \rightarrow \begin{cases} y_2 = ax_2 \\ x_2 = by_1 + u \end{cases} \ldots \rightarrow \begin{cases} y_t = ax_t \\ x_t = by_{t-1} + u \end{cases} \quad (3.3)$$

Each of these systems of simultaneous equations is *per se* indeterminate, but the entire succession of simultaneous systems can be rendered determinate by simply fixing the value of y_0, i.e. of the unknown function in the initial period. Each of these systems has a set of solutions that cannot be considered in equilibrium because each period is characterized by an endogenous dynamic process. We could say that in general the set of solutions represents a situation of disequilibrium unless the initial conditions place the system exactly on the equilibrium path, and there are no ensuing disturbances that keep the system away from equilibrium.

What has been said can be further specified with reference to the theory of functional dynamic equations (see, for example, Gandolfo 1983). The succession (3.3) can be expressed in a reduced form by a difference equation (linear, of the first-order and with constant coefficients):

$$y_t - aby_{t-1} = au \quad (3.4)$$

63

As is known, the general solution of a linear dynamic functional equation is given by the sum of the particular solution and the general solution of the homogeneous form. The particular solution that can be interpreted from the semantic point of view as equilibrium is found immediately when the known terms (that represent the exogenous variables by means of which the environment exerts an influence on the system) are constant. It is assumed in this case that the particular solution (equilibrium) is stationary in the absence of exogenous dynamic impulses. Therefore, by equalizing the values of the unknown function with different time subscripts, we immediately obtain the desired solution:

$$y^* = au/(1 - ab) \qquad (3.5)$$

If the known term is a function of time, the textbooks suggest 'proving' a function of time that has the same qualitative characteristics as the known term as a solution. This should not be surprising in the light of the semantic interpretation suggested above: the dynamic behaviour of a system in equilibrium depends exclusively on the characteristics of the exogenous dynamic impulses.

The general solution to the homogeneous form is easily found, leaving aside the effects of the exogenous variables, i.e. by cancelling the known terms. The dynamics described by the general solution of the homogeneous form are therefore purely endogenous and refer to the deviation from equilibrium $(y'_t = y_t - y^*)$. The general solution of the homogeneous form is easily found by means of the iterative method. In fact, from (3.4), we obtain:

$$\begin{aligned} y'_1 &= aby'_0 \\ y'_2 &= aby'_1 = (ab)^2 \, y'_0 \\ &\cdots \\ y'_t &= (ab)^t \, y'_0 \end{aligned} \qquad (3.6)$$

The general solution of the homogeneous form enables one to study the properties of dynamic stability of the system. It is easy to verify that in this case the system is stable if $|ab| < 1$, unstable if $|ab| > 1$, and neutral if $|ab| = 1$. (The trajectory in disequilibrium is 'oscillatory'[27] if $ab < 0$, and 'monotonic' if $ab > 0$.)

The general solution of our dynamic functional equation is therefore given by the sum of the particular solution and by the general solution of the homogeneous form:

$$y^*_t = au/(1 - ab) + (ab)^t \, y'_0 \qquad (3.7)$$

The semantic interpretation of (3.7) should be clear. The dynamic behaviour of a system like that described by (3.2) and by Fig. 3.2 is given by the additive composition of the equilibrium path reconstructed in relation to external coordinates and the path in disequilibrium described in relation to coordinates that originate in the value of equilibrium.

APPENDIX 3.2 THE CONCEPT OF NASH EQUILIBRIUM

Nash equilibrium is used with increasing frequency in macroeconomics and is considered by many authors as the paradigmatic example of economic equilibrium (this is the case in Lucas 1987).

According to the intuitive definition, one has the Nash equilibrium of a game when the strategic choice of each player is an optimal response to the strategic choices of the other players (see, for example, Binmore 1986: 15).

The prevailing interpretation of Nash equilibrium is of a syntactic type. A Nash equilibrium is considered as the only position of the game in which all the players' actions are reciprocally *coherent*,[28] given the assumption that all the decisions are rational. The syntactic nature of the concept in the interpretation of many economists is also revealed by the fact that the numerous refinements of the concept of Nash equilibrium are often called *solution concepts.*

In spite of the fact the it is becoming more and more widespread, the concept of Nash equilibrium is the object of growing criticism. In particular, the concept of rationality that lies at the foundation of Nash equilibrium has been evaluated as very narrow. Rationality, as understood in game theory, requires each agent necessarily to select a strategy of equilibrium, even choosing privately and independently (see, for example, Binmore and Dasgupta 1987: 8). Rationality typical of Nash equilibrium is therefore consistent with substantive rationality, but completely neglects procedural rationality,[29] as well as broader conceptions of rationality (see Vercelli 1991: ch. 6).[30] Furthermore, the orthodox tradition of game theory is limited to exploring the existence of a Nash equilibrium but has almost completely neglected its stability.

The existence of a Nash equilibrium has been demonstrated for a wide variety of games under weak assumptions. Nash himself managed to prove, a long time ago (1950, 1951), that all finite games have at least one Nash equilibrium with mixed strategies. The attention of scholars has been almost exclusively concentrated on the attempt to generalize the proofs of existence and, especially, on the attempt to identify a single NE, or at least to reduce the number of possible Nash equilibria. It soon emerged that in many cases the solution of a problem (model) in terms of Nash equilibrium is indeterminate. A process of 'refining' the concept of Nash equilibrium began immediately, to solve, or at least attenuate the problem. This has given rise to an extremely prolific set of concepts of equilibrium. Selten (1975) introduced 'subgame-perfect' and 'trembling-hand perfect' equilibria, Myerson (1978) introduced the 'proper equilibria,' Kreps and Wilson

(1982) defined 'sequential equilibria', Banks and Sobel (1985) have defined 'divine equilibria', etc.

On the other hand, the problem of the stability of Nash equilibrium has been little examined. Furthermore, the most recent results are anything but encouraging. It has been demonstrated, for example, that in almost all finite games characterized by generalized gradient processes, the Nash equilibrium based on mixed strategies is unstable (Stahl 1988). Unfortunately most authors share the opinion that unstable Nash equilibrium cannot be utilized in economic analysis (Dasgupta and Binmore 1987: 6). Furthermore, even if an equilibrating process exists and takes shape in the minds of the players, as in the theory of rational agents, or in real time, as in evolutionary game theory, it does not mean that the current version of game theory founded on the concept of Nash equilibrium is an adequate tool, if the environment were to change too rapidly to enable the game to reach equilibrium.

The present lively debate on the adequacy of the concept of Nash equilibrium confirms that it is necessary to abandon the interpretation of equilibrium in syntactic terms in favour of an interpretation in dynamic terms.

APPENDIX 3.3 ERGODIC THEORY AND MACROECONOMICS

Ergodic theory studies the behaviour of 'long-period' dynamic systems. By 'long-period behaviour' I mean the tendential characteristics of a system's behaviour as it emerges from a large number of subsequent observations. (The time unit can even be very brief: for example, in statistical mechanics, molecular collisions are so frequent that only the tendential 'long-period' effects can be observed.)

Some of the fundamental problems of ergodic theory refer to conditions in which historical time 'does not count'. These conditions enable one to simplify the analysis of real systems, ensuring their observability and predictability.

The term 'ergodic' is a neologism introduced at the end of the last century by the eminent physicist Ludwig Boltzmann, who was the first to formulate what he called the ergodic hypothesis. (The etymology of the word comes from the Greek and has the meaning 'path of energy'.) This hypothesis substantially maintains that the time mean of a stochastic process should coincide with the spatial mean, i.e. the long-period time mean that characterizes a single realization of the stochastic process should correspond with the mean of all possible realizations. This enables one to estimate the parameters of the real stochastic process through observations of a single realization, and to forecast the mean characteristics of possible future realizations.

The original ergodic hypothesis was revealed to be false in general as a factual hypothesis but stimulated analysis of the conditions in which the hypothesis is true. The first theorems on the nature of these conditions were demonstrated in 1931 by Von Neumann and Birkhoff. When a system verifies the above-mentioned conditions it is called ergodic. A large part of contemporary physics is applied only to ergodic systems. Samuelson (1968) justly observed that this is true also in economic theory, at least as far as neoclassical theory is concerned.

Let us assume that X is the state space of the system. The evolution of the system is represented by the transformation $T:X \to X$, where Tx defines at time $t + 1$ the state of a system which at time t finds itself in state x. In order to provide a formal analysis of the behaviour of the system, the mathematical nature of X and T must be specified. The three cases that follow have been examined by special branches of mathematics:

1 X is a differentiable manifold and T is a diffeomorphism: the case of differential dynamics.
2 X is a topological space and T is a homeomorphism: the case of dynamic topology.
3 X is a metric space and T is a transformation that maintains the measure: the case of the ergodic theory.

Obviously the three cases mentioned above face similar problems. Often, it is the same problem analysed from different points of view that can be complementary. It is therefore surprising that the ergodic theory, unlike differential dynamics and topological dynamics, has hardly ever been applied to economics. (Among the very few exceptions are Champernowne 1953, Steindl 1965, Samuelson 1968, Davidson 1982–3 and Sargent 1984.) This partly depends on the fact that economic theory has only recently begun to be expressed systematically in probabilistic terms. Furthermore, some of the currents of thought that have contributed the most towards introducing models of stochastic processes into macroeconomics have simply assumed the ergodicity of the economic system studied, without attempting to analyse or prove its empirical plausibility. This is particularly the case with new classical economics and the 'new' econometrics based on vector autoregression. More generally, the rational expectations hypothesis in its prevalent interpretation assumes the ergodicity of the economic system.

Let us assume that (X,β,μ) is a space of probability and that $T: X \to X$ is a univocal transformation such that T and T^{-1} are both measurable and $T^{-1}\beta = T\beta = \beta$. Let us also assume that $\mu(T^{-1}E) = \mu(E)$ for every $E \in \beta$. A transformation T that satisfies these conditions is called a transformation that keeps the measure. The systems defined by (X,β,μ,T) are fundamental objects of study of the ergodic theory.

The $\{T^n x: n \in z\}$ trajectory of a point $x \in X$ represents a complete realization of the system, from the infinite past to the infinite future. We can interpret the σ-algebra β as a set of observable events, with the measure μ unchanging with regard to T, characterized by a quite precise probability of occurrence (independent of time). If a measurable function $f{:}X \to R$ represents the measurement of any characteristic of the system, we can interpret $f(x)$, $f(Tx)$, $f(T^2x)$ ... as values of a certain variable y observed in succession. We can now briefly consider the two fundamental problems of the ergodic theory: stochastic convergence and recurrence.

A fundamental problem of ergodic theory concerns the conditions in which the long-period time mean of a high number of subsequent observations of the variable $y_t = f(T^kx)$ converge towards a central value $f^*(x)$.

Every time we have

$$f^*(x) = \lim (1/N) \sum_{k=0}^{N-1} f(T^k x)$$

$f^*(x)$ can be interpreted as an equilibrium value of the variable y.

A convergence of this type was proved long ago in particular cases. In 1909 Borel succeeded in demonstrating the so-called 'law of large numbers' in the case where the observations are independent and identically distributed. Theorems of general convergence were not demonstrated until 1931, when Von Neumann succeeded in demonstrating the general convergence of the least squares of the deviations from the mean ('ergodic mean theorem'), and when Birkhoff succeeded in demonstrating the hypotheses under which convergence occurs 'almost everywhere'.

Another problem of notable importance analysed by the ergodic theory is the study of the properties of 'recurrence', i.e. the qualitative characteristics of the dynamic behaviour of a system. In particular, the study of the properties of recurrence enables us to ascertain whether a certain system is ergodic or not. Birkhoff demonstrated that a system is ergodic if, and only if, the orbit of almost every point 'visits' every set of positive measures: this is implied by the property of strong mixing, which is a very demanding property of recurrence.

The ergodic theory would be very useful for studying the soundness of stationary stochastic processes that are interpreted as equilibria of the economic system. Let us assume that a certain stationary stochastic process is characterized by a stationary distribution $f^*(x)$. It would be extremely important to study the set H of perturbations $h_i \in H$ such that $h_i(T^k)$ continues to converge towards the stationary distribution $f^*(x)$; it would also be important to study the rapidity of the process of convergence and its possible alterations following the above-mentioned perturbations.

Furthermore, in order to correctly carry out exercises of comparative statics (of a stochastic type), if we find ourselves operating within a process characterized by T_0 and $f_0^*(x)$, a preference for an alternative process characterized by T_1 and $f_1(x)$ would be founded only if the two stochastic processes compared had substantially similar properties of stability.

Lastly, we should prove that a possible transformation T' exists such that $T'T_0$ ensures the convergence of the existing process towards the system that is deemed preferable, characterized by the transformation T_1. In order to demonstrate this, we have to study whether the system (X, β, μ, T', T_0) is ergodic and converges towards the system (X, β, μ, T_1) This analysis would also enable an accurate study of the characteristics of the process of transition and of its implications for the well-being of economic agents. This type of analysis is, in my view, indispensable if we are to make meaningful comparisons of economic policy.

NOTES

1 One of the few exceptions is Sargent (1984), who recognizes the need to postulate the ergodicity of compared stationary stochastic processes (see Appendix 3.3). Nevertheless, the ergodicity of stochastic processes cannot be simply assumed in the empirical applications: there is the onus of proof, which is never really supplied.

2 Some significant examples are found in the works of Lucas that define equilibrium as the solution of a system of differential stochastic equations or as finite differences (see, for example, Lucas 1981: 178, note 14), or as Nash's solution of an economic game (Lucas 1987).

3 Recently, Hahn (1984) and F. Fisher (1983) have insisted convincingly on this traditional requirement.

4 This is recognized by Sargent (1979: 3): 'A model is said to be in static equilibrium at a particular moment if the endogenous variables assume values that assure that equations (1) are all satisfied. Notice that it is *not* an implication of this definition of equilibrium that the values of the endogenous variables are unchanging through time. On the contrary, since the values of the exogenous variables will in general be changing at some nonzero rates per unit time, the endogenous variables will also be changing over time.'

5 More generally, it can be said that equilibrium may be a useful conceptual reference for the analysis of the economic system. In this way its role may also be 'negative', as has been suggested by Hahn (1984: 65): 'Debreu and others have made a significant contribution to the understanding of Keynesian economies, describing so precisely what would be the state of affairs if there were no Keynesian problems.'

6 This is not to imply in the least that an equilibrium is always Pareto-optimal or that it is the most desirable state. As Machlup clearly pronounced a long time ago (1963: 59): 'Equilibrium used in positive economic analysis . . . should not be seen as a value judgment, or as a reference to a "desired state of things". Equilibrium is not a Good Thing and disequilibrium is not a Bad Thing.'

7 This explains why, in the history of sciences, not only in economics, equilibrium theory has often come before a fully developed dynamic theory. This is true of both the mechanics and the theory of value (see, for example, Schumpeter 1954).

8 This point has been clarified by the school of Piaget (see, for example, Piaget 1967).

9 This judgement was put forward by Buiter (1980). Sargent (1984: 409) main-

EQUILIBRIUM IN ECONOMIC THEORIZING

tains that the criticism applies to Sims's 'atheoretical econometrics' rather than to new classical economics. See Vercelli (1991: chs. 8–10).

10 Machlup (1963: 57–8, 65–72) insisted on the relativity of the distinction between equilibrium and disequilibrium years ago.

11 This is to assume that equilibrium is considered a position of optimum, which is not always true. Nevertheless, some representatives of the school of new classical economics often indulge in this identification. That is why, for example, the business cycle in equilibrium (both monetary and real) is typically considered an optimal reply to exogenous shocks.

12 An excellent synthesis of rationalist thought is to be found in Cottingham (1988).

13 For an interesting discussion of these aspects of the theory of relativity see Piaget and Garcia (1971).

14 I use the word 'paradox' here in the same sense as Machlup (1963: 269): 'A paradox is . . . at times merely an apparent contradiction . . . which dissolves following an inquiry or more careful thought, a statement or a phenomenon in conflict with preconceived ideas on what is reasonable or possible.'

15 Grossman and Stiglitz (1976, 1980) point out that this incentive derives from the possibility of obtaining extra profits in the course of arbitrage.

16 This is strictly true only in the case of the 'strong' interpretation of rational expectations that excludes not only *ex-ante* but also *ex-post* systematic errors (see Vercelli 1991: ch. 6).

17 Another relevant example has clearly been indicated by Hahn (1984: 4): 'to impose the axiom that the economy is in every instant in competitive equilibrium simply removes the actual operating of the invisible hand from the analysis. Postulating that all the moves that increase well-being in the sense of Pareto are realized instantaneously eliminates all the problems of coordination between agents. An economic theory conceived in such narrow terms renders any important discussion impossible.'

18 Sims's interpretation of the paradox is different. The contradiction between equilibrium with rational expectations and the Lucasian definition of economic policy is solved by defining a change in economic policy different from that of Lucas. I have argued in Vercelli (1991: ch. 10) that Sims's solution is unacceptable.

19 Before the General Theory, Keynes concentrated his attention on positions of disequilibrium and their implications, while in the General Theory his attention moves to the second problem (indetermination in connection with the existence of a spectrum of underemployment equilibria).

20 This can be considered as the position of dynamic stability more general than a Walrasian general economic equilibrium. This condition has been formulated and demonstrated by F. Fisher (1983) who extended and generalized the so-called 'Hahn's process' (see Hahn and Negishi 1962).

21 The same effect can be triggered by other types of objective surprise: unexpected variations in taste, the availability of factors of production, changes in the environment (also in its political, institutional and ecological aspects). Stability can also depend on the same behaviour in equilibrium that could alter the set of opportunities.

22 See note 16.

23 In the case of stationary stochastic processes, strictly speaking, all the distribution parameters are unchanging. In the case of the stationarity in the broad sense, the average is constant while the auto-correlation depends only on the time interval. See, for example, Papoulis (1984) or Sargent (1979).

24 The recent literature on the learning of an equilibrium with rational expectations is a partial exception. For a review see, for example, Bray and Kreps
  (1986).
25 If each of the two relationships were the inverse of the other, the system would
  be singular and would therefore be without solutions or indeterminate.
26 This is a possible source of the Lucasian conviction that a disequilibrium is not
  intelligible.
27 In this case it would be more correct to speak of 'improper oscillations',
  reserving the term 'oscillations' for those of a sinusoidal type that appear only
  in equations of order equal or greater than two (see Gandolfo 1983: 18).
28 This is not to imply that the beliefs of the players around the world must be
  coherent: we are discussing whether the players can agree to disagree (see
  Aumann 1976; Binmore and Dasgupta 1987: 2).
29 There are some isolated exceptions such as the 'tracing procedures' of Harsanyi and Selten (Harsanyi 1975) and Bernheim's rationalizing algorithm (1984)
  and Pearce (1984). See Binmore (1986: n. 5, 3).
30 At times considerations of rationality can be called to the defence of choices
  different from those of equilibrium in a game, but only by postulating that the
  players are in reality playing another underlying game (normally a repeated
  game, or a super-game) (see Binmore and Dasgupta 1987: 8). This affirmation
  confirms that in game theory only the equilibria are in reality analysed and that
  the dominant conception of rationality is the substantialist one. Nevertheless,
  since every disequilibrium can be interpreted from a formal point of view as a
  succession of equilibria interconnected in a particular way (see pp. 54–5), game
  theory could aim at founding some types of analysis of disequilibrium and
  studying the implications of procedural rationality. I mention, however, that the
  equivalence between disequilibrium and equilibrium is only formal and raises
  unsolved semantic problems. Furthermore, attempts of this kind would imply a
  degree of complexity that goes beyond present technical knowledge.

REFERENCES

Arrow, K.J. (1958), 'Toward a Theory of Price Adjustment', in *The Allocation of
  Economic Resources: Essays in Honour of B.F. Haley*, ed. M. Agramovitz,
  Stanford, Stanford University Press.
Arrow, K.J. and Hahn, F.H. (1971), *General Competitive Analysis*, San Francisco,
  Holden-Day.
Aumann, R. (1976) 'Agreeing to Disagree', in *Annali di Statistica* 4, 1236–9.
Banks, J. and Sobel, J. (1985), *Equilibrium Selection in Signalling Games*, MIT,
  mimeo.
Bernheim, D. (1984), 'Rationalizable Strategic Behaviour', *Econometrica* 52, pp.
  1007–28.
Binmore, K.G. (1986), *Remodeled Rational Players*, London, LSE, mimeo.
Binmore, K.G. and Dasgupta, P. (1987), *The Economics of Bargaining*, Oxford,
  Blackwell.
Bray, M.M. and Kreps, D. (1986), 'Rational Learning and Rational Expectations',
  in *Essay in Honour of K.J. Arrow*, ed. W. Heller, D. Starret and R. Starr,
  Cambridge, Cambridge University Press.
Buiter, W.H. (1980), 'The Macroeconomics of Dr. Pangloss: a Critical Survey of
  the New-classical Macroeconomics, *Economic Journal* 90(2), pp. 34–50.
Champernowne, D.G. (1953), 'A Model of Income Distribution', *Economic Jour-
  nal* 63, pp. 318–51.

Cottingham, J. (1988), *The Rationalists*, Oxford, Oxford University Press.

Davidson, P. (1982/3), 'Rational Expectations: a Fallacious Foundation for Studying Crucial Decision-making Processes', *Journal of post-Keynesian Economics* 2.

Fisher, F.M. (1983), *Disequilibrium Foundations of Equilibrium Economics*, Cambridge, Cambridge University Press.

Gandolfo, G. (1983), *Economic Dynamics: Methods and Models*, second edition, Amsterdam, North Holland.

Grossman, S.J. and Stiglitz, J.E. (1976), 'Information and Competitive Price Systems', *American Economic Review* 66, pp. 246–53.

Grossman, S.J., and Stiglitz, J.E. (1980), 'On the Impossibility of Informationally Efficient Markets', *American Economic Review* 70, pp. 393–407.

Hahn, F. (1984), *Equilibrium and Macroeconomics*, Oxford, Blackwell.

Hahn, F. and Negishi, T. (1962), 'A Theorem on Non-tâtonnement Stability', *Econometrica* 30, pp. 463–9.

Harsanyi, J. (1975), 'The Tracing Procedure', *International Journal of Game Theory* 5, pp. 61–94.

Keynes, J.M. (1936), *The General Theory of Employment, Interest and Money*, London, Macmillan.

Klamer, A. (1984), *The New Classical Macroeconomics: Conversations with New Classical Economists and their Opponents*, Brighton, Harvester Press.

Kreps, D. and Wilson, R. (1982), 'Sequential Equilibria', *Econometrica*, 50, pp. 863–94.

Lucas, R.E., Jr (1981), *Studies in Business-Cycle Theory*, Cambridge, Mass., MIT Press.

Lucas, R.E., Jr (1987), *Models of Business Cycles*, Yrjö Jannsson Lectures, Oxford, Blackwell.

Machlup, F. (1963), *Essays on Economic Semantics*, Englewood Cliffs, N.J., Prentice-Hall.

Myerson, R. (1978), 'Refinements of the Nash Equilibrium Concept', *International Journal of Game Theory* 7, pp. 73–80.

Nash, J. (1950), 'The Bargaining Problem' *Econometrica* 18, pp. 155–62.

Nash, J. (1951), 'Non-cooperative Games', *Annals of Mathematics* 54, pp. 286–95.

Papoulis, A. (1984), *Probability, Random Variables, and Stochastic Processes*, Auckland, McGraw-Hill.

Patinkin, D. (1965), *Money, Interest and Prices*, second edition, New York, Harper and Row.

Pearce, D. (1984), 'Rationalizable Strategic Behaviour and the Problem of Perfection', *Econometrica* 52, pp. 1029–50.

Piaget, J. (1967). 'Logique et connaissance scientifique', in *Enciclopédie de la Pléiade* XXII, Paris, Gallimard.

Piaget, J. and Garcia, R. (1971), *Les Explications causales*, Paris, Presses Universitaires de France.

Prigogine I. and Stengers, I. (1984), *Order Out of Chaos. Man's New Dialogue with Nature*, London, Fontana Paperbacks.

Samuelson, P.A. (1947), *Foundations of Economic Analysis*, Cambridge, Mass., Harvard University Press.

Samuelson, P.A. (1968), 'What Classical and Neo-classical Monetary Theory really was', *Canadian Journal of Economics* I, 1, pp. 1–15, reprinted in R.W. Clower (ed.), *Monetary Theory*, Harmondsworth, Penguin.

Sargent, T.J. (1979), *Macroeconomic Theory*, New York, Academic Press.

Sargent, T.J. (1984), 'Autoregressions, Expectations and Advice', *American Economic Review* 72, pp. 408–15.

Schumpeter, J.A. (1911), *Theorie der wirtschafilichen Entwicklung*, Leipzig, Duncker und Humblot; English translation *The Theory of Economic Development*, Oxford University Press 1934.

Schumpeter, J.A. (1939), *Business Cycles: a Theoretical, Historical, and Statistical Analysis of the Capitalist Process*, New York, McGraw-Hill.

Schumpeter, J.A. (1954), *History of Economic Analysis*, London, Allen and Unwin.

Selten, R. (1975), 'Re-examination of the Perfectness Concept for Equilibrium in Extensive Games', *International Journal of Games Theory* 4, pp. 22–5.

Sims, C.A. (1987), 'A Rational Expectations Framework for Short-run Policy Analysis', in W.A. Barnett and K.J. Singleton (eds), *New Approaches to Monetary Economics*, Cambridge, Cambridge University Press.

Stahl, O. (1988), 'On the Instability of Mixed-strategy Nash Equilibrium', *Journal of Economic Behaviour and Organization* 9, pp. 59–69.

Steindl, J. (1965), *Random Processes and the Growth of Firms*, London, Griffin.

Vercelli, A. (1991), *Methodological Foundations of Macroeconomics: Keynes and Lucas*, Cambridge, Cambridge University Press.

ACKNOWLEDGEMENT

This chapter is based on chapters 2 and 3 of Vercelli (1991).

Part II

EQUILIBRIUM IN THE NEOCLASSICAL CONCEPTION

4

'CATHOLICITY' OF GENERAL EQUILIBRIUM

Pier Carlo Nicola

It is sometimes useful to work with continuous time. But it is probably wise to regard the analysis by stages as more fundamental.

(John Hicks 1985: 24)

SOME PREMISSES

Copernicus superseded Ptolomy, Einstein incorporated Newton, but Walras neither superseded nor incorporated Smith. Probably this more or less peaceful cohabitation of alternative, if not altogether contrasting, theories is the salient characteristic that distinguishes economics from the so-called 'exact' sciences, according to a term which, in truth, has grown antiquated. It would be an almost desperate undertaking, certain suicide, to attempt a classification of economic theories at present practised in the area of academic research, but at least one can list those that constitute the more widespread paradigms of our science today. The two schools that seem to gain most favour and the attention of the profession are the classical school, inspired by Smith, Ricardo and followers, with its various neo-, neo-neo, neo- . . . offshoots and the school of general equilibrium, in substance descendant of Walras, Pareto and associates, it too with its neo-, neo- . . . offshoots.

It is probable that this classification appears unjustifiably lean to many; there is at least a third school that should be added: the Keynesian school. It was not indicated with the other two because, in my opinion, in many aspects it is the fruit of a hybridization. The Keynesian school in fact marks the official birth of macroeconomics, while the previous two are decidedly oriented towards microeconomy, the school of general equilibrium directly, the classical school more indirectly.

Where Italy is concerned at present, it is also necessary to explain a flourishing section in the sphere of the classical school, that is to say the Sraffian sub-school, which has been very active in the past twenty years. Its exponents have infused Smith's and especially Ricardo's thought with new vigour, mainly studying the problem of distribution when prices are 'production prices' and the fundamental variables, which they have reduced to the production structure, are stationary. The most representative and least dogmatic scholar of this current is Pasinetti (1977, 1981), who did not limit himself to analysis of the production structure but was aware that demand, except in quite unrealistic cases, also plays a fundamental role in the determination of endogenous variables.

The considerations that follow are not aimed at presenting the umpteenth synthetic panorama of current economic knowledge. More modestly they are intended as a discussion of the notion of equilibrium in the – more or less vast, depending on one's point of view – history of general equilibrium. The notions of equilibrium introduced with game theory will not be considered, given the writer's fragmentary knowledge of the subject.

Many sustain that general equilibrium is based on so-called 'methodological individualism', and it is true. It implies a sort of act of faith as far as its main consequence is concerned: the overall functioning of the economic system is none other than the result of individual behaviours and decisions.

ON THE CURRENT MEANING OF EQUILIBRIUM

The term 'equilibrium', applied to an 'evolutionary process', or 'dynamic system', as every modern economy is, is used substantially with the same meaning as that used by physicists: equilibrium means exact balance between the various forces that give rise to the process under consideration. Since every economic process takes place in time, one is obliged to choose whether to express time as a discrete or as a continuous variable. Bowing to the authority of Hicks, whose thought is faithfully reproduced at the opening of this chapter, time is conceived as a discrete variable; in keeping with a well established practice, time will be conceived of here as subdivided into periods, all of the same length.

Imagine filming with a movie camera (set up in a protected position!), an economy during a certain interval of time, shooting a frame in every period. When all the frames are equal – i.e. when it would have been sufficient to take a single photograph of the whole economy – we can state that the economy is in *stationary (and multi-period) equilibrium*. It is clear that if we limit ourselves to taking just one photograph, the economy shows that it is in a possible state which we shall call *single-period equilibrium*. Both notions of equilibrium are important, but the stationary notion of equilibrium, which we could call permanent (stationary) equilibrium when it is of unlimited length, would seem conceptually more significant than the other. Alongside to these two notions, we can also consider that of *multi-period equilibrium*, without further qualifications. It is a particular (and usually quite hypothetical) situation, not identifiable by filming, in which all agents know how to forecast correctly, for two or more periods, the future fundamental variables of the economy, so that a succession of single-period equilibria is recognized as a multi-period equilibrium. Naturally, it is possible to recognize a multi-period equilibrium only *a posteriori*.

At times the term *dynamic equilibrium* will be used with the generic meaning of 'sequence of single-period equilibria'. Evidently a multi-period equilibrium or a stationary equilibrium is a particular instance of dynamic equilibria.

In this chapter, all the above-mentioned notions of equilibrium will be considered. If no adjective is added to the term it means that the context in which the term is used clearly indicates which type of equilibrium is being discussed.

When is an economy in stationary equilibrium? Using a term that has recently entered the vocabulary of economists, a necessary condition for obtaining stationary equilibrium is that the so-called *fundamentals* – or those characteristics which the structural parameters of the economy depend on – remain unchanged in time. Except that economic fundamentals are not like universal physical constants (for example, the speed of light) that prove to be absolutely constant in time and space. Economic fundamentals are such only in a manner of speaking: they are simply variables (treated as exogenous) that characterize the process under consideration and which usually appear significantly 'less subject to variations' in time than the endogenous variables. It is therefore unlikely that an economy can repeat the same equilibrium for a long enough time interval. Is the discussion of the notion of stationary equilibrium therefore ephemeral? Yes and no. Yes, if there is a conviction that the notion of equilibrium can be used especially for forecasting purposes. No, if one is content to describe, analyse and interpret the working of the economy period after period.

The 'yes' part of the question is quite obvious. The 'no' part requires a little explanation. The notion of equilibrium is a powerful conceptual tool that is extremely useful for 'tidying up' ideas and for managing to explain the current state of an economy as the result of the simultaneous action of numerous forces, substantially set in motion by economic agents. When, in a given period, the activities they engage in are mutually compatible there is single-period equilibrium. If this equilibrium also reveals itself as multi-period, it means that most likely the fundamentals are stationary. With absolutely stationary fundamentals there is no time limit on the repetition of an equilibrium and permanent equilibrium is attained. In other words, the notion of equilibrium does not have intrinsic time limitations; it is the length of the fundamentals that determines for how many periods a certain configuration of equilibrium can be repeated. Thus the adjective 'multi-period' simply indicates that an equilibrium lasts as long as the fundamentals. An equilibrium can be single-period only for two reasons: when the fundamentals vary from period to period, or when the fundamentals are stationary but the initial values of the endogenous economic variables, being given, are not compatible with the fundamentals of the evolutionary process under consideration, which can be formally represented with a system of first-order difference (dis)equations. In the second case the problem of sequences of single-period equilibria converging to a stationary equilibrium often crops up.

After passing from economic theories in general to the notion of equilibrium (in economic theories), the considerations that are the subject of this chapter are further circumscribed by notions of equilibrium, without exhaustivity demands, in the sphere of the school of general equilibrium. Hence nothing will be said, for example, about the notion of partial equilibria elaborated by Marshall.

The above can be rapidly expressed in formal terms. Let x_t be the vector that represents the endogenous variables of an economy in period t and let $F^t(\cdot)$ represent the law, identified by the fundamentals characterizing the economy, which governs its time evolution. Then, in decreasing order of generality, we can express the evolutionary process with the following formulas:

$$F^t(x_t, x_{t+1}) \geqq 0$$

when the fundamentals change in time;

$$F(x_t, x_{t+1}) \geqq 0$$

when the fundamentals remain stationary. If these evolutionary processes have a solution, the *multifunction solution* $\emptyset^t$ can be introduced and we represent the solutions by writing, respectively, $x_{t+1} \in \emptyset^t(x_t)$ or $x_{t+1} \in \emptyset(x_t)$.

Given the initial state of the economy x_0, in these cases there is generally a succession (x_t) of single-period equilibria, that is, satisfying the previous conditions, expressing a multi-period equilibrium. In particular, when the abstraction is made from the initial state, x_0, there is a positive scalar α and a vector x^* such that

$$\alpha x^* \in \emptyset(x^*)$$

then the economy $F(\cdot)$ allows steady growth. Even more so, if $\alpha = 1$ a stationary equilibrium or, mathematically speaking, a fixed point of the multifunction is obtained.

CLASSIFICATION OF GOODS IN GENERAL EQUILIBRIUM

The specification of this classification will be of great help further on in correctly outlining the most recent developments. It is a plain fact that extremely numerous goods exist in every economy, practically finite in number. Originally, or as Walras and Pareto would have it, goods differ from each other by physical, chemical and biological characteristics. A step ahead in the classification is taken by adding, as Arrow and Debreu (1954) do expressly, the period of time and the (spatial) location of each good. As long as these further characteristics are finite in number, we remain in the sphere of finite dimensional spaces. Still tracing the footsteps of Arrow and Debreu, states of nature can also be added, for simplicity still in a finite number, thereby introducing uncertainty into the economy.

A further step can be taken that favours the inclusion of market forms, other than those of perfect competition, in the classification of goods, on the basis of who produces them. Two goods produced by different firms are considered different *a priori*, as Hicks (1939: 49) clearly saw. It is worth pausing at this subdivision, which scholars generally overlook, to see its explanatory potentiality. Let n be the number of goods, different from each other on the basis of all the classifications mentioned above, and let us suppose that, for a given consumer, goods 1, 2, 3 are considered identical in that, for example, they are produced by three different firms but all three satisfy the same 'need' of the consumer. Let us call the quantities of goods consumed c_i and p_i the respective prices ($i = 1, \ldots, n$), then the utility function index of the above-mentioned consumer is of type $u(c_1 + c_2 + c_3, c_4, \ldots c_n)$. Supposing that $u(\cdot)$ satisfies the usual hypotheses, in particular that it is differentiable, making it maximum under the traditional budget constraint $p_1 c_1 + \ldots + p_n c_n$ = income, the well known (necessary) condition for a maximum is obtained:

$$u_i - m\, p_i \leq 0, \quad c_i\,(u_i - m\, p_i) = 0 \quad (i = 1, \ldots, n)$$

where m indicates the Lagrange multiplier. In particular, for the first three goods, we always have $u_1 = u_2 = u_3$, so when p_1 is the lowest of the three prices the consumer acquires the first good but not the second or the third, and likewise when the lowest price is p_2 or p_3. If a_{123} represents the income share devoted to the purchase of these goods, the corresponding quantity acquired is $c_i = a_{123}$. income$/p_i$ for the good which has the lowest price of the three and $c_j = 0$ for the other two goods. Therefore, quite automatically, the consumer always knows which of the three goods to acquire in any circumstance. Evidently, similar passages can be carried out regarding factors of production deemed identical by the firm.

These considerations serve to confirm how, in many aspects that numerous economists have not failed to point out, almost always without having recourse to formalisms, the classification of goods can in part be a subjective fact, characteristic of each consumer and each firm.

THE NOTION OF EQUILIBRIUM ACCORDING TO THE FOUNDERS

For the most part, the founders of the School of Lausanne consider single-period models of equilibrium, i.e. those in which the mutual compatibility between the choices of all agents is considered limited to the current period of time only. There is not, in their work, any substantial clue that they conceive of the coordination of individual actions as relative to one or more future periods.

According to the terminology of p 78 above, the founders' notion of equilibrium is a single-period equilibrium. Nevertheless, single-period equilibrium does not mean stationary equilibrium. That equilibrium is single-period is fully compatible with the time progression of the considered economy. In this regard it is necessary to refer to the variables that are assumed as given. Walras and Pareto suppose, among other things, that the initial quantities of goods are given (quantities inherited from the past) and determine, together with the prices of current equilibrium, the final quantities of all goods, including capital goods. Evidently, so that the represented economy is stationary, the vector of the final quantities must be equal to that of the initial quantities (once the worn-out capital goods have been deducted in the course of time owing to decay). This equality is not, however, generically verified, if not by mere accident; so the representations studied by those authors are not of stationary economies. It is, however, relatively easy to fundamentally transform their models into models of stationary economies. It is sufficient to include the initial quantities of all goods as unknowns and to set the condition that all final quantities should be equal to the corresponding initial quantities: as many new conditions are added as there are new unknowns. The model proposed by Sraffa (1960) and further elaborated by his followers, confined to the aspects of production and distribution, is a particular model of stationary general equilibrium.

If, instead of setting the condition of equality among the final and initial quantities of goods, only their proportionality were set, we would obtain models of general equilibrium with steady growth, according to the ideas that emerged at the beginning of the 1930s with Von Neumann (1932). In any case, as has been said, the possibility of current coordination of future individual actions does not seem to have been conceptualized by Walras or Pareto.

Historically the present discussion of the notion of general equilibrium according to the founders would not be complete without mention of Cassel (1918), who worked hard – perhaps not altogether voluntarily – to spread the ideas of the school of general equilibrium in the English-speaking world. According to Hicks (1985: 9), Cassel was the first to show the possibility of analysing a steady growth model, using the same tools as those used for single-period models: perhaps Cassel is a precursor of Von Neumann.

EARLY MODERN FORMULATIONS OF GENERAL EQUILIBRIUM

It was not until the 1930s that, thanks to Wald (1933–5), the first rigorous demonstration of the existence of general equilibrium saw the light of day in a simplified model similar to that of Cassel. However, the modern theory of general equilibrium is the simultaneous work of Arrow and Debreu (1954) and McKenzie (1954). Of the two formulations, the one generally adopted is the Arrow–Debreu version. The equilibrium described in their work is both single-period and multi-period. It is single-period if the goods are not also distinguished relative to the period of time in which they will be made available. It becomes multi-period if the time dimension is introduced. However, also in this second case, equilibrium does not become dynamic: all fact, all economic agents decide *una tantum*, at the beginning of the first period, their optimum multi-period plan and the equilibrium implies the simultaneous determination of the prices of all goods in all periods, so as to make the set of individual plans compatible among themselves. It is not envisaged that in the course of time new facts can occur, or rather it is supposed that in the first period all the agents know the fundamental variables that concern them for each period perfectly well. Naturally, this is a rather violent forcing of reality, all in all not necessary in view of the notion of temporary equilibrium presented in the next section.

TEMPORARY EQUILIBRIUM ACCORDING TO LINDAHL AND HICKS

At the end of the 1920s the so-called Swedish school, especially under the influence of Lindahl, rendered the general equilibrium model fully dynamic (or, rather, multi-period) by introducing the notion of temporary equilibrium, which has been spread through the English-speaking world by Hicks (1939), with some refinements and extensions. The essence of the notion of temporary equilibrium, to use Hicks's words (1985: 64), is the following:

> Lindahl . . . reduced the process of change to a sequence of single-periods . . . Within the single-period, quantities and prices could thus be determined in what resembles a static manner. Everything is just the same as with the 'static' kind of process analysis . . . save for one thing: that expectations are explicitly introduced as independent variables in the determination of the single-period equilibrium.

In current terminology we could say that logically the passage from the single-period equilibrium (of Walras–Pareto) to Lindahl–Hicks temporary equilibrium is carried out by simply including the (individual) expectations among the fundamentals of the economy. The representation of the economy is thus the following. In every period of time the agents actually present decide which plans (generally multi-period) to undertake on the basis of their present knowledge and their subjective expectations of the state of the economy in all future periods. However, the market coordinates the individual plans only as far as the current period is concerned, in that generally markets for future goods do not exist (furthermore, the fundamentals are not very durable). Thus a 'temporary equilibrium' is attained, also because, in the next period, by changing some fundamentals or confirming that the expectations were not justified, the agents in general are induced to review the previously formulated multi-period programmes. Therefore: individual decisions are of a multi-period nature, but their realizations remain single-period, except in the quite fortuitous case where all the fundamentals remain unchanged and all expectations are fulfilled. Temporary equilibrium presents itself as a kind of single-period equilibrium but one which is notably enriched by subjective forecasts regarding a certain number of future periods.

Although, formally, temporary equilibrium has a time-ordered series as a solution, this circumstance should not lead us astray. In effect, every period generates its own temporary equilibrium, while all the unknown future is only reflected (by the expectations) in the current state of the economy. The veil that unfailingly masks the future is progressively raised only in historical time. In the meaning of p. 80 above, a sequence of temporary equilibria represents a dynamic equilibrium, much more realistic and rich in possibilities than a multi-period equilibrium.

Conceptually, if not operatively, it is important to distinguish between the way in which the expectations are conceived by Lindahl and how they are considered by Hicks. It is Hicks (1985: 69) who clears the point up. In Lindahl current expectations are a function of past variables, while in Hicks current expectations are a function of current variables. Symbolically, if t indicates the current period of time and x_t the vector of the endogenous economic variables referring to period t, according to Lindahl the expectations are expressed by a formula of the kind

$$x_t = f(x_{t-1}, x_{t-2}, \ldots)$$

while according to Hicks in *Methods of Dynamic Economics* the formula of the expectations is

$$x_t = g(x_t, x_{t-1}, \ldots)$$

For practical purposes, while the first formula establishes a true link between periods and thus generates dynamic models, according to Hicks the other formula only enables us to obtain 'almost dynamic models'. It is interesting to note how Grandmont, at present one of the principal scholars of temporary equilibrium, uses Hicks's formulation (cf., for example, Grandmont 1988: xvi, formula (4)). It is also interesting to observe how

Lindahl's formulation immediately leads to the notion of equilibrium with fixed prices and goods rationing, in that all current prices become given as a function of vectors of past prices.

Temporary equilibrium, as it has been considered so far, is born of the explicit recognition that expectations of the future influence current decisions and events. It does not take a position on the permanence in time of economic agents which are usually active only for a finite number of periods. This aspect, extremely important at a concrete level, is linked with the demographic structure of an economy and was introduced into general equilibrium by Samuelson (1958), by means of the formulation of some simple models, known today as overlapping generation models. In Samuelson's formulation the agents are uniquely consumers (therefore he essentially uses exchange models) whose economic life spans a finite number of periods. In each period there is an influx and exit of agents, each of whom formulates a multi-period consumption plan spanning his economic life. Probably Samuelson's immediate aim was to create a space, within the sphere of general equilibrium, for money with which each consumer can transfer purchasing power among periods and thus plan a consumption time sequence not strictly linked with the time sequence of his or her income. At a formal level the greatest merit of overlapping generation models is that they make use of an infinite dimensional space, indispensable in the theory of general equilibrium, since in each period there are individuals whose economic life extends beyond the current period, so that a last period does not exist. From an economic point of view, an infinite dimensional space introduces new properties compared with finite spaces. For example, in spite of the fact that it is supposed that markets are in perfect competition and that conditions of convexity (preferences and technologies) apply everywhere, (equilibrium) solutions can exist which are not efficient in the Paretian sense, contrary to what happens under the same circumstances in the sphere of economic models that can be represented in finite dimensional spaces.

SEQUENTIAL EQUILIBRIUM

Towards the end of the 1960s, initially thanks to Radner (1968, 1972), the concept of sequential equilibrium gained ground, especially with reference to economies with uncertainty. The concept is based on the hypothesis that in an economy exchanges take place sequentially in time but in the absence of a complete set of future markets. This incompleteness constrains agents, as in the temporary equilibrium, to make predictions about the future of the economy; but unlike in temporary equilibrium the truly heroic hypothesis is accepted that each agent is capable of forecasting his future environment correctly. Probably, by forcing things a little, it could be said that sequential equilibrium is temporary equilibrium with the addition of the hypothesis of rational expectations, introduced by Muth (1961) and spread by Lucas and associates. Naturally, the Achilles heel of this construct is that it appears that normally, i.e. out of stationary (or at least sufficiently repetitive) equilibrium – of which it should be relatively simple to discover the characteristics and ascertain the repeatability – agents do not exist with the capacity to forecast the future of the environment they operate in. It is even less realistic to suppose that all agents possess similar faculties of divination and that they always hit the bullseye. As Grandmont argues (1988), the notion of sequential analysis could prove to be important in analysing centralized economies. Probably the idea of sequential equilibrium is not far from the idea of *equilibrium over time*, explicitly introduced by Hicks (1939: 132) as that equilibrium in which the (equilibrium) prices of each period coincide exactly with the prices expected by agents in the previous period. According to the terminology of pp. 78–80, intertemporal equilibrium is the most typical representation of a multi-period equilibrium.

A notion of multi-period equilibrium, in some ways related to sequential equilibrium, has been suggested by the author (Nicola 1969, 1973).

EQUILIBRIUM WITH RIGID PRICES AND RATIONING

The notions of equilibrium mentioned above share the (often cited) hypothesis that all prices are always fully flexible, in other words, they can *a priori* assume any value (in general not negative) in the course of a single-period. Precisely because of this characteristic an equilibrium (either single-period or multi-period) is represented by the condition of equality between total demand and supply of each good in each period, the only exception being where the demand for a good can stay lower than the corresponding supply which manifests itself when the price of the good itself is reduced to zero.

The critics of general equilibrium have been in a favourable position sustaining that, given these terms, the notion of general equilibrium is unlikely to correspond to real economies, where the existence of some partially unused goods, in spite of the fact that the current price is positive, is more or less always present. The most determined critic is without a doubt Keynes (1936), whose *magnum opus* founded (according to its author!) a theory capable of including Walrasian–Paretian general equilibrium as a distinct case. Unfortunately the original Keynesian theory produced only single-period macroeconomic models which are too narrow to satisfy Keynes' high aspirations.

In any case, the revolution begun by Keynes has made a deep furrow through all economics of the past fifty years, especially concerning the critical aspects of the notion of equilibrium. There is no doubt that Keynes' change of mind was strongly inspired by the widespread unemployment that accompanied the Great Depression of 1929, which was felt to various degrees in all industrial countries. It is not surprising to see that it was above all unemployment that particularly concerned Keynes, who stated that he could not accept the explanation of the current economic theory according to which it would be sufficient to reduce real wage rates to secure full employment for workers. Keynes maintains that there are good reasons, not least of them the existence of trade unions, which in fact provoke downward rigidity in the (money) wage rate, thus hindering full employment (which, on the other hand, depends on the effective demand).

The theory of general equilibrium did not pay serious attention to this criticism of the practical rigidity of (some) prices for a long time. At most, it registered vague signs of embarrassment. Although the formula mentioned above regarding Lindahl leads directly to rigid prices in the short run, the modern mathematical representation of the theory of general equilibrium, namely that of Arrow and Debreu and McKenzie mentioned above (p. 83), is based entirely on the hypothesis that all prices are fully flexible, as if Keynes had never existed. Only in 1968, thanks to Glustoff, was the first formalized model of general equilibrium published, in which the price of only one of the goods (labour) is not so limited. Glustoff's model did not have much luck in attracting the attention of scholars. Success smiled, however, on the work presented a few years later by Drèze (1975) and Benassy (1975).

In this work all prices are considered rigid, in the sense that they belong to pre-established intervals (Drèze) or are exogenously given (Benassy). How, then, can the problem of balancing the demand for and supply of various goods be solved? By rationing the quantities of goods. If at exogenously given prices the demand for a good exceeds its supply then not all purchasers can procure all they have decided to buy, while ideally all producers are able to sell all they have available, and vice versa, when the excess demand is negative. It is often said that when prices are not in (Walrasian) equilibrium agents belonging to the long side of the market are rationed.

The most interesting aspect of models of general equilibrium with rigid prices and rationing is the fact that their solutions, depending on the circumstances, have different characteristics. There can be situations of Walrasian equilibrium (all notional demands are equal to effective demands, which are equal to the effective supplies which are equal to notional supplies), states of equilibrium with Keynesian underemployment (the downward rigidity of some prices provokes the partial unemployment of corresponding goods), and solutions in which there is inflation combined with stagnation in production activity.

An important question in equilibrium with fixed prices is what gives rise to the determination and especially, in a dynamic equilibrium, what are the forces capable of changing (fixed) prices from one period to another. If in

87

each period prices are exogenously assigned, do they perhaps become part of the fundamentals? No completely satisfactory answer to this question is directly contained in these models; according to Hicks (1985: 82), in this regard it can only be said that a good is produced only if it is profitable to produce it, i.e. when prices are such that they cover the unit production cost as well as an adequate profit margin.

Clearly, it is forbidden to overlook the previous question, at least if it is deemed that the primary task of any economic theory is that of explaining how, in each period of time, prices of all goods are determined. On the other hand, it is not forbidden to combine models of price determination, setting them, for example, in situations of monopolistic competition, with models specifically designed to study the problem of rationing. There are many significant works on this matter, for example, Benassy (1976), Hahn (1978) and Negishi (1979).

Once prices in the single-period are taken as given, the task of rendering the demands and the supplies mutually compatible is reserved for rationing, as has already been mentioned. In short, it can be stated that the working of any rationing scheme requires that the signals transmitted in the economy are not limited only to prices, but also include signals on the quantitative constraints perceived by each agent. This implies a notable complication in the elaboration and transmission of messages, compared with usual general equilibrium, in which signals exclusively concern prices. In fact, in the models under discussion, it is assumed that single agents are not capable of autonomously elaborating the messages necessary to obtain a rationed general equilibrium and that the intercession of a superindividual authority is required, as will be discussed in the next section.

THE AUCTIONEER IN GENERAL EQUILIBRIUM

The notions of traditional general equilibrium, temporary general equilibrium and sequential general equilibrium refer to models of economies in which (competitive) prices are not determined by any particular agent or set of agents. On the other hand, in general equilibrium with rigid prices and rationing it is the rationing schemes which are impersonally applied. Sooner or later the question must arise of how prices (of equilibrium, period after period) are determined and how rationing schemes are applied. Walras was perfectly aware of the situation. His reply was to introduce a meta-agent, whom he called the 'auctioneer', whose task it is to determine equilibrium prices by means of the well known 'law of demand and supply'. Smith also raised the question in a much less formal context and excogitated the 'invisible hand' as an almost celestial tool for determining current prices. With a lot less poetry, and probably no greater realism, modern economists say that it is the 'market' which solves this problem.

The truth of the matter is that, whatever the term used and the image behind it, one of the weak points of the theory of general equilibrium, brought to light by Arrow (1959), is precisely the lack of formalization of a mechanism, within the model, for determining equilibrium prices, or for applying a rationing scheme. On a logical-mathematical plane, the determination of an equilibrium (with or without rationing) requires the application, in all cases, of a fixed point theorem to demonstrate the existence of solutions. Obviously, it is not the economy that applies one of these theorems to the model that represents it, but the scholar who formulates and analyses the model. He or she promotes him or herself, more or less forcibly, to the rank of auctioneer. At the level of application, since it is necessary to use automatic computation to solve a model of general equilibrium, the auctioneer is represented by the association 'scholar + computer + programmes'. We could say that the modern auctioneer is Scarf, who, in 1967, was the first to present an algorithm for calculating the fixed points of a (multi-) function. Nevertheless, it would be important to be able to include a sub-model capable of explaining how (Walrasian equilibrium and non-) prices are determined in every model of general equilibrium.

Conceptually, to determine prices by appealing to the auctioneer is the same as centralizing this very important aspect of an economy's working. But then it would no longer be 100 per cent true that general equilibrium (with private ownership of the means of production) is the prototype of an economy capable of functioning in a completely decentralized way.

IMPERFECT GENERAL EQUILIBRIUM

A way of overcoming the question of the existence and the determination of prices, which the author is working on (Nicola, 1994), is that of combining (temporarily) fixed prices, rationing and the endogenous change of prices in the course of time by using the notion of imperfect general equilibrium. It could be said that this notion takes its moves from the pioneering work of Negishi (1961) on general equilibrium with firms in monopolistic competition. In imperfect general equilibrium, at the beginning of each period of time the single producers determine, on the basis of their past knowledge, the current prices of goods. Once these prices are known, each agent determines his or her current notional demands and supplies, and if, as is quite probable, the current prices are not at equilibrium for all goods, the producers themselves apply (random) rationing among all potential purchasers of the goods they produce with the aim of transforming incompatible demands into transactions that are compatible among themselves. In the simplest formulation, prices are changed from one period to the next by the producers involved, on the basis of the law of supply and demand. At the beginning of a generic period a producer increases the selling price of his/her products if he or she sees that in the previous period the (potential) demand was greater than the supply, and *vice versa* in the opposite case. Just as in traditional general equilibrium, the mechanism of Walrasian *tâtonnements* is used here too, but whereas in traditional general equilibrium *tâtonnements* are conceived in logical time and are manoeuvred by the hypothetical auctioneer, here price changes occur in historical time and are managed directly by single producers.

Naturally, the gain in realism offered by imperfect general equilibrium is not obtained at zero cost. While the previous notions of general equilibrium – as long as one operates under perfect competition, in conditions of convexity and in finite spaces – are efficient in the Paretian sense with regard to each period of time, it is unlikely that an imperfect equilibrium is efficient in the Paretian sense, unless it coincides with a Walrasian equilibrium by pure chance.

MARKETS AND MONEY

The notion of the market has never been specified in presenting the various notions of general equilibrium, whether single-period or dynamic. Generically, it can be sustained that the notion of the market is that described by Smith, i.e. an (ideal) meeting place for all agents who intend to buy or sell certain goods. Nowadays, however, we should be able to say something more precise, given the introduction of theoretical frameworks based on incomplete markets and missing markets and the considerable progress that has been made in the understanding of the phenomenon of money. In the meantime, it is not true, at least as far as present-day modern economies are concerned, that a market is characterized by the meeting of the buyers and sellers of a single good. Bartering is certainly not the usual form of economic exchange, but rather the purchase or the sale of goods for money, which in all non-primitive markets always represents the substance of one of the two sides of the exchange.

What significance does it have to state that a market is 'incomplete' or even that there are markets that are 'missing'? Literally, if the market in a good were missing there could be no exchanges centred on that good. We should limit ourselves conceptually to considering exclusively macroeconomic models. The mere fact of considering models containing a plurality of interacting agents necessarily means at least admitting the existence of a flow of information (or signals or messages) between them, and therefore an information structure. In modern terms, it is this structure that constitutes a market, even though in models of general equilibrium this is not explicitly formalized and we are limited to supposing that it functions without requiring resources.

The existence of models containing merchandise brokers and transaction costs, as well as the usual agents (consumers and firms), still does not constitute a complete formalization of markets. There is no recognition of the fact that every time a signal of price or quantity is transmitted between two agents, both must defray a cost, one in emitting the signal and the other in receiving it. There is no doubt that money, including its more recent electronic forms, considered in its role as a means of exchange, sustains and enormously facilitates the transmission of signals and significantly reduces their cost. But that cost is like friction in mechanics, it can never be eliminated.

In general equilibrium *à la* Arrow and Debreu money seems absolutely out of place, in that the decisions (both present and future) of all agents are definitive and all markets exist to determine all prices, both current and future. Uncertainty is exactly calculated here, and then there is the auctioneer, who determines all prices and implements all exchanges, on the condition that for every consumer the (present) value of all expenditure is equal to the (present) value of all his or her income. This situation is different from that of other definitions of equilibrium. In temporary equilibrium many markets are absent and the fundamentals can vary in an unforeseen way; in sequential equilibrium individual situations of credit and debit that have to be solved through the movement of money can occur during every period; in equilibrium with rationing exchanges are multilateral and thus are mediated with money – this is also true of imperfect equilibrium.

Various chapters of Friedman and Hahn (1990) can be consulted on the role of money in general equilibrium models.

CONCLUSIONS: 'CATHOLICITY' OF GENERAL EQUILIBRIUM

In the preceding pages the main notions of equilibrium adopted, from Walras to the present day, in the analysis of models of general equilibrium have been briefly illustrated. The unifying thought of this chapter, which I hope emerges clearly even at a hurried reading, is that conceptually all the notions of equilibrium reviewed seem to originate, as if by natural germination, from the original Walrasian idea of equilibrium. Yet, on a concrete level, we can say that for over a century the most powerful stimulus to the progressive broadening of the notion of general equilibrium has come about mainly thanks to its critics, the more ferocious ones in particular. Of all of them, the most fruitful is almost certainly Keynes, who, convinced that he had finally elaborated the 'general theory' of economics, stimulated economists interested in undertaking the task of continually perfecting models of temporary general equilibrium and general equilibrium with rationing, simultaneously promoting their integration.

If that means 'Be dissatisfied with the theory of general equilibrium', we can declare ourselves satisfied with such dissatisfaction. It means that the theory is alive and incessantly oriented towards vaster horizons, as should happen with all genuine scientific research that continually aims to surpass itself in order to represent the phenomena of reality in an increasingly improved manner. If a theory were to exist that was closed in on itself, directed exclusively to the contemplation of itself, the equilibrium it represented would be a 'mummified equilibrium'. But such a theory does not exist in current research and belongs by rights only to the history of economic thought.

At present, at least in the writer's view, the integration of models of temporary equilibrium with overlapping generations with models with rationing constitutes the most fertile ground for the analysis of economic dynamics. There is still a long way to go, and the only thing we know for sure is that we do not know how far we have yet to go. In any case, just as general equilibrium has managed to absorb all the criticisms levelled at it so far, it is also prepared to incorporate the future ones, imminent or not. It is, in fact, becoming a tradition that cultivators of the theory of general equilibrium are animated by a spirit which – unlike what appears to occur in other schools of thought – could be defined as genuinely catholic.

REFERENCES

Arrow, K.J. (1959), 'Towards a Theory of Price Adjustment', in *The Allocation of Economic Resources*, A. Abramovitz, Stanford, Stanford University Press.

Arrow, K.J., and Debreu, G. (1954), 'Existence of an Equilibrium for a Competitive Economy', in *Econometrica* 22, pp. 265–90.

Benassy, J.P. (1975), 'Neo-Keynesian Disequilibrium Theory in a Monetary Economy'. *Review of Economic Studies* 42, pp. 503–23.

Benassy, J.P. (1976), 'The Disequilibrium Approach to Monopolistic Price Setting and General Monopolistic Equilibrium', *Review of Economic Studies* 43, pp. 69–81.

Cassel, G. (1918), *The Theory of Social Economy*, London, 1923.

Drèze, J. (1975), 'Existence of an Equilibrium under Price Rigidity and Quantity Rationing', *International Economic Review* 16, pp. 301–20.

Friedman, B.M. and Hahn, F.H., (1990), *Handbook of Monetary Economics*, Amsterdam, North-Holland.

Glustoff, E. (1968), 'On the Existence of a Keynesian Equilibrium', *Review of Economic Studies* 35, pp. 327–34.

Grandmont, J.M. (1988), *Temporary Equilibrium*, San Diego, Academic Press.

Hahn, F.H. (1978), 'On non-Walrasian Equilibria', *Review of Economic Studies* 45, pp. 1–17.

Hicks, J.R. (1939), *Value and Capital*, Oxford, Clarendon Press, second edition, 1946.

Hicks, J.R. (1985) *Methods of Dynamic Economics*, Oxford, Clarendon Press.

Keynes, J.M. (1936), *The General Theory of Interest, Employment, and Money*, London, Macmillan.

Lombardini, S. and Nicola, P.C. (1975), 'Income Distribution and Economic Development in Ricardian and Walrasian Models', in *Applications of Systems Theory to Economy Managements and Technology*, Rome, mimeo, pp. 294–320.

McKenzie, L.W. (1954), 'On Equilbrum in Graham's Model of World Trade and other Competitive Systems', *Econometrica* 22, pp. 147–61.

Muth, J.F. (1961), 'Rational Expectations and the Theory of Price Movements', *Econometrica* 29, pp. 315–335.

Negishi, T. (1961), 'Monopolistic Competition and General Equilibrium', *Review of Economic Studies* 28, pp. 196–201.

Negishi, T. (1979), *Microeconomic Foundations of Keynesian Macroeconomics*, Amsterdam, North-Holland.

Neumann, J. von (1932), 'A Model of General Economic Equilibrium', *Review of Economic Studies* 13, (1945–6), pp. 1–9.

Nicola, P.C. (1969), 'Equilibrio economico generale di tipo concorrenziale in condizioni dinamiche', *L'industria* pp. 3–16, 197–207.

Nicola, P.C. (1973), *Equilibrio generale e crescita economica*, Bologna, Il Mulino.

Nicola, P.C. (1994), *Imperfect General Equilibrium*, Berlin, Springer.

Pasinetti, L.L. (1977), *Lectures on the Theory of Production*, London, Macmillan.

Pasinetti, L.L. (1981), *Structural Change and Economic Growth: Theoretical Essay In the Dynamics of the Wealth of Nations*, Cambridge, Cambridge University Press.

Radner, R. (1968), 'Competitive Equilibrium under Uncertainty', *Econometrica* 36, pp. 31–58.

Radner, R. (1972), 'Existence of Equilibrium of Plans, Prices, and Price Expectations in a Sequence of Markets', *Econometrica* 40, 289–303.

Samuelson, P.A. (1958), 'An Exact Consumption–loan Model of Interest with or without the Social Contrivance of Money', *Journal of Political Economy* 66, pp. 467–82.

Scarf, H. (1967), 'The Approximation of Fixed Points of a Continuous Mapping', *SIAM Journal of Applied Mathematics* pp. 1328–43.

Straffa, P. (1960), *Production of Commodities by Means of Commodities*, Cambridge, Cambridge University Press.

Wald, A. (1933–35), 'On the Unique Non-negative Solvability of the New Production Equations', I–II in *Precursors in Mathematical Economics: an Anthology*, ed. W.J. Baumol and S.M. Goldfeld, London, London School of Economics and Political Science (1968), (from the German).

Weinrich, G. (1997), (this volume).

5

EQUALITY OF THE RATES OF RETURN IN MODELS OF GENERAL ECONOMIC EQUILIBRIUM WITH CAPITAL ACCUMULATION

Domenico Tosato

1. The subject of this chapter is more specific than the broader methodological themes of the definition and use of the concept of equilibrium. It deals with the question of the existence of a uniform rate of return on capital goods in models of general economic equilibrium when we move from Walras's original formulation to that contained in the theory of intertemporal equilibrium. The subject may not be new, but it is still of unquestionable theoretical importance.

Providing further food for thought was the publication of Garegnani's (1990)[1] *The Quantity of Capital* in the series of compact volumes of reprints of *The New Palgrave*. It has afforded me a better appreciation of the issues involved and rendered my line of argument more precise, both constructively and critically.

In short, Garegnani appears to make the following two central propositions: (1) in Walras's model, the equality of the rates of return generally cannot be reconciled with the hypothesis of arbitrarily given initial quantities of heterogeneous capital goods; (2) this circumstance carries over to models of intertemporal equilibrium, given that – here too – a uniform rate of return could occur only under the quite particular hypothesis that the initial composition of capital should be 'appropriate', that is to say, 'adjusted' to equilibrium outputs and production methods. While the first proposition had already been formulated in prior work (cf., for example, Garegnani 1960 II: chs II–III; 1966), the second appears to be new and represents a further step in Garegnani's criticism of the neoclassical theory of capital considered as a set of heterogeneous goods.

In evaluating the range and limits of Garegnani's critique of Walras's theory of capital formation, I had in the past (Tosato 1969) stressed that, in a dynamic context of change in the composition of capital, the rate of

94

return should be defined taking the own rate of interest into account as well as the percentage rate of appreciation or depreciation of the various capital goods. While, on that occasion, I developed the analysis in the direction of examining the conditions for the existence of a balanced growth path, I now intend to consider the implications for the problem of the existence of a uniform rate of return on capital goods of the more general case represented by a model of intertemporal equilibrium in which the possibility of change in relative prices is admitted.

First, I intend to show that the inequality between rates of return in Walras's theory is the result not of an inappropriate composition of capital but of a systematic forecasting error made by Walrasian savers, an error that occurs every time current production determines a change in the composition of the initial capital stock. Second, I intend to show that the uniformity of the rates of return is re-established when – as occurs in intertemporal equilibrium models – agents can make maximizing choices on the basis of equilibrium prices for any given date. If correct, these statements have critical implications for the concept of an appropriate composition of capital, as well as for the classical notion of 'normal position', as tools for the analysis of situations of structural change.

2. In a competitive system the rate of return on a capital good can be expressed in two alternative ways. The first definition takes into consideration the entire useful life of the capital good and implicitly assumes that the investor remains in possession of the asset for this whole length of time. The net rate of return is then that rate of interest that equalizes the present value of the sum of the rental prices, net of the depreciation allowance (and possible other charges), with the current price of the good:

$$P_i(t) = \sum_{\tau=t+1}^{T} \frac{V_i(\tau) - \delta_i P_i(\tau)}{(1+r_i)^{\tau-t}} \tag{5.1}$$

where $P_i(t)$, $V_i(t)$, δ_i and r_i are respectively the supply price, the rental price, the constant depreciation rate and the rate of return on the capital good i. T and t indicate the given time horizon and the time period considered, while τ is a time index.

The second definition considers instead a time horizon made up of only two periods and takes into account the possibility of liquidating at the beginning of the second period the investment undertaken in the first. The rate of return, $\rho_i(t)$ – generally different from period to period – is then defined as the interest rate that renders the capitalized value of the sum $P_i(t-1)$ advanced at the beginning of period t to purchase one unit of capital good i equal to the rental price $V_i(t)$ paid for the use of the good during period t plus the residual value of the good at the end of the period, calculated with reference to the appropriate price $P_i(t)$

$$(1 + \rho_i(t))P_i(t-1) = V_i(t) + (1 -\delta_i)P_i(t) \tag{5.2}$$

95

where the meaning of the different symbols has already been defined and ($1 - \delta_i$) indicates the residual quantity of the capital good i at the beginning of period $(t + 1)^2$.

In both cases the determination of the rate of return requires the knowledge of variables that do not belong exclusively to the current period but also refer to future periods. The problems thus raised by the time dimension inherent in the determination of the rate of return on capital goods have been tackled and solved in different ways.

The first and more explicit type of answer is represented by models of intertemporal equilibrium, in which the assumption of the existence of complete future markets engenders the possibility of determining all rates of return from the knowledge of the prices for current and future deliveries. A second answer is provided by the hypothesis that, in the absence of future markets, agents formulate expectations of unknown future prices on the basis of their current equilibrium values.

As we know, this second answer was adopted by Hicks (1945: ch. X) and is currently referred to as the method of temporary equilibrium, i.e. equilibrium only for the current period and susceptible to change whenever the price expectations currently formulated by agents are not confirmed by future equilibrium values and are thus modified in the course of time. Hick's insistence on the concept of elasticity of expectations, and therefore on the influence that the specific formulation of the agents' expectations function exerts on the current equilibrium position, makes the intertemporal nature of the problem of determining the rate of return on capital goods quite manifest in the Hicksian context.

Although less explicit, Walras's approach is conceptually identical. It is precisely from this approach that it is appropriate to begin, respecting not only the chronological order but also the logical link between this and the subsequent theory of intertemporal equilibrium.

3. Without particular emphasis on the underlying hypotheses, Walras defines the rate of return of a capital good as the ratio between the rental price of the service – net of the depreciation allowance (and the insurance costs) – and the supply price of the good, *both inferred from the current market evaluation:*

$$r_i = \frac{V_i}{P_i} - \delta_i \qquad (5.3)$$

It is clear that, in order to arrive at this relation, departing either from definition (5.1) or from definition (5.2), it is necessary to make restrictive assumptions on the dynamics of prices in time. In particular, moving from (5.1), it must be assumed that both rental prices and commodity prices are constant in time and equal to current values. On the other hand, moving from (5.2), the condition must be set that the beginning of the period price of each capital good $P_i(t - 1)$ coincides with the end of period price $P_i(t)$.

Walras, in mentioning this second condition, seems to take it for granted ('the prices of existing capital goods proper *are* equal to the prices of new capital goods proper', (1874–7: 309, emphasis added); he thus attributes a hypothesis of static or stationary expectations regarding the sequence of prices in time to all agents, in spite of possible individual differences that may well exist (ibid., 310–11).

Note, at this point, the crucial role this hypothesis plays. Owing to its effect, the intertemporal problem of capital accumulation is in fact reduced to a question of seeking an equilibrium referred exclusively to the current period, a circumstance that is stressed from the formal viewpoint by the elimination of the reference to the time index in the formulation of equation (5.3). For this reason I had previously chosen to characterize Walras's analytical construct as a model that defines a 'single-period equilibrium' – i.e. an equilibrium relative to a single-period of time – rather than an 'atemporal' one (Tosato 1969). The indication of temporary equilibrium chosen by others – for example, Diewert (1977), Impicciatore and Rossi (1982: 32–3), Donzelli (1986: 266 and n. l) – appears equally appropriate for the purposes of pointing out this methodological aspect of Walras's theory of capital formation.

This preliminary consideration makes it possible to clarify the issue of the existence of equilibrium in Walras's model of capital formation, as well as the question of the economic meaning of the equilibrium solution, given the two competitive conditions that must be met: the first regarding the production of the new capital goods (the equality of equilibrium prices to the respective production costs) and the second concerning the willingness of savers-investors to hold the different capital goods in their portfolios (the condition of uniformity of the rates of return). Observe, incidentally, in support of a briefer terminology widely used here, that this double condition finds a convenient and compact formulation in the proposition that the price of each capital good calculated on the basis of the market rate of return (demand price) should be equal to the production cost (supply price) or, alternatively, that the rate of return obtained as the ratio of the rental price to the cost of production should be in line with the market rate of return.

The formal analysis of the problem of the existence of equilibrium has shown that this question can generally be given a positive answer provided that, as in the case of consumer goods, the possibility is admitted that the equilibrium prices of capital goods may be lower than their costs of production. Should this occur for any capital good i, the additional production of such a commodity would obviously be nil and the rate of return on its initial stock would be lower than the market rate (Morishima 1964; Gay 1967; Zaghini 1968; Tosato 1969; Montesano 1970–1; Diewert 1977).[3]

The formal reasons for substituting equations with inequality constraints are easily explained by referring to a specific case. Suppose that production takes place in a regime of fixed coefficients and with the sole use of capital goods, available in given initial quantities. Assume further that the initial endowment is so 'unbalanced' that only one capital good proves to be limitational in defining the set of feasible productions of both consumer goods and new capital goods. All initially given capital goods but one would then be in excess supply; their rental prices would be nil and consequently so also would be their rates of return. Only the single capital good, which turns out to be scarce in the equilibrium solution, would command a positive rental price and obtain a positive rate of return.

4. It has been observed that the transformation of Walras's condition of equality between price and cost of production into an inequality constraint admitting the possibility that the equilibrium price may be less than or equal to the corresponding cost of production assumes a substantially different meaning when applied to the case of newly produced capital goods as opposed to that of consumption goods. Suppose, in fact, that in the equilibrium solution the price of a commodity turns out to be less that its cost. In the latter case, the consequences are limited to the sub-system of the model determining which consumption goods it is convenient or not to produce, without any further repercussion on the initial conditions and therefore on the equilibrium prices and quantities. In the former case, on the other hand, the existence of a discrepancy between the demand and the supply price of a given capital good would imply that the rate of return calculated on the basis of the supply price would be lower that the market rate, so that investors who were to purchase that newly produced capital good would be unable to obtain the rate of return realized on all other physical assets, while owners of the initial stock of the same commodity would experience a sort of a loss on capital account. There would accordingly be a tendency among maximizing investors to concentrate their demand exclusively on the new capital goods, ensuring a return equal to the market rate. The composition of the initial stock would, therefore, prove to be modified, with subsequent effects on equilibrium prices and quantities.

From these elements Garegnani draws the conclusion that the modifications to be made to the general equilibrium model of capital accumulation in order to ensure the existence of a solution cause a departure from the notion of equilibrium that Walras had in common with all previous theory (the classical school and Marshall in particular) as well as part of the subsequent one. Such a notion is centred on the identification of 'normal' or long-period values for prices and quantities, values that are the result of the action of all the persisting forces of the system and therefore able to represent centres of gravitation for the observed values of the economic variables. Among the persisting forces of the system are naturally to be included those resulting from the rational behaviour of investors aiming to maximize the return on their capital stock. It is then argued that, since it is not possible to rule out the existence of meaningful equilibrium solutions to the Walrasian model (as modified by substituting inequality for equality constraints) in which the condition of a uniform rate of return may obtain only with reference to all demand prices, while failing to be fulfilled with regard to the supply price of some capital goods, the model itself is in general capable of identifying only a short-period equilibrium, contrary to Walras's intentions and contrary to the traditional tenets of economic theorizing. Garegnani writes:

> The new conception of equilibrium would in fact relate to a situation where all the forces for maximizing behaviour are at rest, except for those which tend to adjust the existing physical composition of capital to the prevailing conditions, and are therefore at work to modify the *data* of the equilibrium to which the remaining forces would tend.
>
> (Garegnani 1990: 22).

In conclusion, Walras's theory of capital formation – and therefore the explanation of prices and distribution according to the principle of supply and demand – would be affected by an internal inconsistency between the choice of representing capital as a set of heterogeneous goods available in a given quantity and the need to meet the competitive condition that the rates of return on all capital goods should be equal. The difference in the rates of return, resulting from the possibility of inequality between the price and the cost of production of some new capital goods, would then reflect, according to Garegnani, the fact that 'the composition of the capital stock is not adjusted to the equilibrium outputs and methods of production' (1990: 21).

5. Before examining the scope of this conclusion, it seems worthwhile to make an observation about the reading of Walras's *Eléments*.

As is the case with the works of nearly all the great economists, Walras's text contains observations – generally aimed at relating the theoretical arguments to specific realities that are difficult to accommodate in a formal model – which appear to contradict the main body of the work. In two passages of the fourth edition of the *Eléments* Walras writes that not all equations of capitalization need to be satisfied in the equilibrium solution. Garegnani interprets these 'unobtrusive' admissions as conveying the 'meaning of retraction' (1990: 20). The passages in question are: 'all the equations of system (8) [expressing the condition of a uniform rate of net income on all capital goods proper] will be satisfied *after the exclusion* of those new capital goods which it was not worth while to produce' (Walras 1874–7: 294; italics by Garegnani 1990: 20); and again 'it is not at all certain that the amount of savings E will be adequate for the manufacture of new fixed capital goods proper in just such quantities as will satisfy the last l equations [uniformity of the rate of net income] of the above system' (Walras 1874–7, 308).

I should like to suggest a more generous reading which is, in my view, more in keeping with Walras's work as a whole.

In discussing the existence of solutions Walras repeatedly gives proof of a capacity for analysis that goes beyond the formal writing of the model. The consideration of particular situations leads him to anticipate the themes of the debate developed thirty years later by Karl Menger in his *Matematisches Kolloquium,* without, however, grasping the possibilities of generalization offered by the systematic transformation of his equality conditions into possible inequality constraints.

This is also true for the theory of capital formation. The second of the two passages mentioned above goes on as follows:

> In an economy like the one we have imagined [i.e. with given quantities of capital goods proper], which establishes its economic equilibrium *ab ovo*, it is probable that there would be no equality of rates of net income. Nor would such equality be likely to exist in an economy which had just been disrupted by a war, a revolution or a business crisis. All we could be sure of, under these circumstances, is: (1) that the utility of new capital goods would be maximized if the first new capital goods to be manufactured were those yielding the highest rate of net income, and (2) that this is precisely the order in which new capital goods would be manufactured under a system of free competition. On the other hand, in an economy in normal operation which has only to maintain itself in equilibrium, we may suppose the last l equations to be satisfied.
>
> (Walras 1874–7: 308).

It really seems to be forcing the reading and the spirit of Walras's text to take as a retraction what is a simple recognition of a complex reality and a suggestion of the sense in which the model – with the particular hypothesis of stationary expectations adopted by the author – operates and is therefore to be used when situations inconsistent with this hypothesis are envisaged.

The principle that guides the competitive allocation of resources, for the purposes of this discussion, is the maximization of net income on the part of savers. The corresponding analytical condition is the equality of rates of return; and this is a condition of general validity.[4] When, however, in applying this principle the constraint of stationary expectations is imposed, the criterion of equality of rates of return constitutes a reasonable guide to the behaviour of agents only if the hypothesis regarding price expectations proves to be adequate. Walras clearly believes this assumption to be appropriate when conditions of normal operation of the economy are considered, but not in the situations listed in the passage quoted above. In the latter situations – which push the prices of capital goods and of their services some very high and others very low – the hypothesis of stationary expectations becomes unrealistic; the maximization of net income cannot, therefore, be identified with the allocation that equalizes the rates of return, since that is not a feasible allocation.

In terms that have now become common, we could say that Walras drew a distinction between 'corner' solutions and 'internal' solutions of the model and tried to indicate concretely their possible use as instruments for understanding the allocation decisions of a competitive economy.

6. Returning to the main stream of the discussion, it is now necessary to examine the implications of the statement that unequal rates of return may reflect a composition of the capital stock inappropriate with regard to equilibrium outputs and production methods.

I should like to point out that the logical link Garegnani establishes between the existence of a uniform rate of return and the notion of appropriate composition of capital cannot hold only in a negative sense, but ought to be applicable, *mutatis mutandis,* in a positive sense as well. In other words, just as an initial endowment of capital inconsistent with the realization of the condition of equal rates of return is judged inappropriate, so should an endowment that proves to be compatible with the realization of this condition be deemed appropriate. Furthermore, just as it is stated that the failure of a uniform rate of return to obtain necessarily leads to changes taking place in the composition of capital, so it must be considered that when the rates of return are equal any such change is to be excluded.

There is, however, no certainty that respect of the condition that the rates of return be equal should necessarily imply the absence of forces tending to modify the initial composition of capital as well as the absence of effects on prices and on the rates of return themselves. Uniformity of rates of return does indicate that all new capital goods can be produced without loss by the firms and held by investors without involving a sacrifice of net income, but it does not mean that the goods must be produced in the exact quantities that would keep the initial composition of capital constant in time.

Consider, for example, a model in which only new capital goods are produced using only old capital goods as factors of production. If the matrix of the technique is productive and indecomposable, then, by the Perron-Frobenius theorem (Pasinetti 1977: 267–77), there exists a unique equilibrium growth rate, equal for all sectors, and an associated composition of capital, unchanging in time, with components that are all positive. This particular composition of capital is naturally that which corresponds to the Von Neumann path of maximal growth.

It is clear that, in any given period, there are generally many initial compositions of capital compatible with the full employment of all the available capital goods and with equality of rates of return according to definition (5.3) adopted by Walras (Tosato 1969: 551). However, it is by no means certain that this condition may be maintained in the course of time, taking into account the changes that occur in the composition of capital as a consequence of the production of new capital goods.[5]

In fact the attainment of the condition of a uniform rate of return does not represent a sufficient anchorage for the notion of the appropriate composition of capital. When with this concept we intend to refer to a situation that excludes – for reasons endogenous to the model itself, i.e. the accumulation of capital – any change in the equilibrium solution (with the possible exception of the mere scale of the system), then only one composition of capital is appropriate and it is that associated with the Von Neumann path. Moreover, even this restrictive anchorage would fail when the system does not admit growth at a uniform rate, as would be the case with models which consider not only capital goods but also consumer goods (with not necessarily homothetic preferences) as well as non-reproducible factors of production.

7. The strongly reductive or even negative conclusion that is reached regarding the possibility of defining the concept of the appropriate composition of capital means that the inconsistency between the competitive condition of equal rates of return and the hypothesis of given quantities of capital goods cannot be overcome by abandoning one of the two terms of the problem, but only by a correct reading of the definition of the rate of return. At the heart of the problem is the assumption of the invariance of prices in the presence of arbitrarily given quantities of capital goods, which are bound to change in proportion because of subsequent decisions regarding accumulation. This assumption is clearly untenable.

The definition of the rate of return in Walras, based – as we have seen – on the expectation that prices will be invariant, is *ex post* confirmed only in the case of uniform growth. That definition is then inapplicable when, as a consequence of the maximizing choices of savers-capitalists, the composition of capital changes; in that case prices in each of the subsequent one-period (temporary) equilibrium solutions change too and thus expectations are *ex post* disproved. Since the failure to attain equality of rates of return occurs only in this second case, and not in the first, it is natural to suppose that it may depend on a systematic forecasting error attributed to investors rather than on other reasons.

It is thus necessary to consider the assumption of perfect prediction instead of Walras's hypothesis of stationary expectations. This can be done by moving from the context of temporary equilibrium to that of the intertemporal equilibrium of the Arrow–Debreu model, in which the condition of perfect prediction is realized thanks to the assumption of complete future markets for all goods and for all dates, a circumstance that allows agents to make maximizing choices at equilibrium prices known from the very beginning of the time horizon.

The theorem of the existence of economically significant solutions for this model ensures that – given the initial endowments of the various commodities (naturally including the physical quantities of the different capital goods), the intertemporal preferences of households and the consumption and production sets of consumers and firms, and with suitable assumptions of convexity and continuity – there exist discounted prices for all goods and services that simultaneously clear all the markets, both spot and forward (Debreu 1959). The ratio between the equilibrium prices of the same commodity in two successive periods defines the own rate of interest. The possibility that relative prices may vary in time gives rise to own rates of interest which are generally different from good to good and for the same good from period to period (Bliss 1975: 51–5).

It is therefore not legitimate to consider Walras's hypothesis of constant prices as generally valid, or to assume own rates of interest to be uniform, as that would occur only in the case where the structure of relative prices should remain invariant.

The circumstance that own rates of interest are in general not equal obviously does not imply that rates of return on capital goods should also diverge. Intertemporal prices, in fact, identically fulfil the non-arbitrage condition represented by the fact that the return of a loan operation in terms of good i must be equal to the return realized from the more complex operation of exchange in the current spot market of good i with good j, in the subsequent loan denominated in terms of good j, and in the further retrade in the spot market of the next time period of good j with good i:

$$\frac{p_i(t)}{p_i(t+1)} = \frac{p_i(t)}{p_j(t)} \cdot \frac{p_j(t)}{p_j(t+1)} \cdot \frac{p_j(t+1)}{p_i(t+1)} \tag{5.4}$$

where prices $p_i(t)$ are now present values.

Having then defined a unit of measurement such that its undiscounted price is equal to one at the various dates, from the non-arbitrage condition (5.4) a relation of equality of the net 'effective' rates of return can be derived

$$\sigma_i(t) + \pi_i(t) = \sigma_j(t) + \pi_j(t) \tag{5.5}$$

As shown by equation (5.5), the net effective rates of return are defined as the sum of the own rates of interest $\sigma_i(t)$ and the percentage appreciation or depreciation of each good $\pi_i(t)$ (Dorfman *et al.* 1958: ch. 12; Burmeister 1980: ch. 2).

It is evident that the level at which the effective rates of return are equalized depends on the choice of the *numéraire* commodity. This is neither surprising nor limiting for the purposes of the result that is of concern here, i.e. equality of the effective rates of return and not the level at which it is realized.

If we now go back to definition (5.2) of the rate of return on capital good

i – as the interest rate that is required to make the capitalized value of one unit of the capital good i equal to the sum of the current rental price and the residual value of the good in the subsequent period – with an approximation that is more precise the finer the subdivision of time into periods, from (5.2) we have

$$\rho_i(t) = \left(\frac{V_i(t)}{P_i(t)} - \delta_i \right) + \pi_i(t) \qquad (5.6)$$

The rate of return thus obtained exactly coincides with the effective rate of return previously defined, when the fact is taken into account that the term in brackets on the right-hand side of (5.6) represents the own rate of interest net of the physical wear and tear on the capital good. Note that the different ways of representing the own rate of interest in Walras's theoretical framework and in the intertemporal equilibrium model are explained by the different focus of the analysis inherent in the two approaches. In the first, the distinction is between capital goods proper and the services they supply in the course of a same period, in the second between capital goods available in subsequent periods.

Equation (5.5) leads us to conclude that, in the presence of complete forward markets, a competitive system realizes in equilibrium the condition of equality of the effective rates of return. As regards Garegnani's claim, we can say therefore that it is not the initial composition of capital that proves to be inappropriate with respect to the equilibrium solution defined by conditions of competition, but it is the formulation of those conditions *in the hypothesis of expectations that are in any case stationary* that appears inappropriate with respect to an arbitrary composition of the capital stock. When the appreciation or depreciation of the individual goods is taken into account, as is implicitly and necessarily done by the intertemporal equilibrium prices, the reason for the inconsistency between the condition of uniformity of the rates of return and the assumption of arbitrarily given initial quantities of capital goods disappears.

8. The relevance of this conclusion to the purposes of the debate between equilibria having only short-period validity and long-period positions requires some additional consideration, in particular regarding two aspects.

First, it should be stated that, for the purpose of determining the percentage appreciation or depreciation of the various capital goods – which, as we have seen, is essential in order to establish the existence of a uniform rate of return – a situation of asymmetry between the initial period of the horizon under consideration and all the others appears in the intertemporal equilibrium model. In periods subsequent to the first there is no difficulty in calculating inflation rates relative to the various capital goods, given that the variables required for the calculation are part of the equilibrium solution of the model. However, this is not so for the first period: through the condition of competition in the production of new capital goods the model determines the value of the capital goods available at the beginning of the second period, but does not supply a distinct price for the capital goods that are part of the economy's endowment at the beginning of period one, endowment that depends on decisions taken before the beginning of the time horizon under consideration. The asymmetry arises, then, from the fact that, unlike the initial capital goods of any period $t > 1$, whose values coincide with the prices of new capital goods produced in the course of the preceding period $t-1$, for capital goods available at the beginning of period one there is no previous production to refer to in order to determine their values.

In a general context of change in relative prices it would naturally be wrong to attribute to the capital goods available at the beginning of period one the same value as that of the corresponding goods available at the beginning of period two. To make sure that the rates of return on all capital goods are equal also in the initial period of the horizon under consideration, it must be supposed, in a way that is consistent with the substance of the hypothesis of complete markets, that distinct markets exist not only for the services supplied by these capital goods, but also for the capital goods themselves. It is clear that transactions in the initial capital stocks on these markets would lead to the formation of prices that would necessarily satisfy the condition of equality of the effective rates of return in period one too.

We could, in fact, conceive using the condition (5.5) of equality of the rates of return to 'impute' a price to the initially available capital goods as well and thereby overcome the above-mentioned asymmetry.[6]

Secondly, we should consider the statement that, in spite of the equality of the effective rates of return, the notion of a uniform rate of return in the traditional sense is generally not to be found in models of intertemporal equilibrium (Petri 1989: 227, n. 11).

If the statement under examination refers to the impossibility of expressing in an economically significant way the rate of return derived from an investment decision or from the ownership of a capital good with a single number, it is certain that in models of intertemporal equilibrium the traditional notion of a general profit rate is not to be found; it could not be otherwise. This is the consequence of the potential variability of the effective rates of return from period to period. However, that this is a generalization, rather than a limit of the analysis, is made clear by the consideration that the traditional notion is included in the wider definition, as the extreme case obtaining when balanced growth is feasible.

Criticism of the failure of the traditional notion of a uniform rate of return to apply could, however, refer to the fact that equalization of the effective rates of return would occur only with respect to market prices, which do not necessarily coincide with supply prices. In the hypothesis, for example, that a capital good is not produced, the condition of competition in the production *could* be satisfied as inequality instead of as equality.

105

This circumstance would imply an equilibrium price lower than the production cost. With this hypothesis there would be a divergence between the rate of return determined with respect to the equilibrium price and the rate of return calculated with regard to the supply price. Reference to the supply price appears, however, inexpedient for the determination of the effective rate of return when the variability of prices is admitted.

9. The limits and the difficulties that have emerged in the examination of the attempt to infer a definition of the concept of an appropriate composition of capital from the condition of equality of the rates of return in Walras's sense – i.e. as equality of the own rates of interest (in the terminology of intertemporal equilibrium) – as that composition of capital that remains unaltered after taking into account the consequences of the maximizing choices of agents suggest some very 'tentative' final considerations at a methodological level.

As has been said, in his defence of the method of long-period positions, Garegnani appeals to the fact that, until recent times, economic theory – classical and neoclassical – has taken the concepts of 'normal' prices and outputs as the reference point of the analysis, in that they are the result of the full operation of the forces of competition. According to this approach, the persistence of these forces ensures that changes in normal prices from one period to another can be considered sufficiently small to be ignored. This would make it possible to approach the analysis of change with the method of comparative statics rather than through the identification of a sequence of equilibrium positions in time. Notwithstanding the difficulty of establishing when a change is to be considered small and slow and when it is to be considered large and rapid, the problems that have previously emerged regarding the concept of the appropriate composition of capital have a direct impact on the choice of method, in the sense that the method of long-period positions comes up against logical difficulties in the presence of *any* change in prices. Thus with a problem like that of the accumulation of capital it seems that the method of analysis must necessarily refer to the sequence of equilibria, precisely because the possibility of change in relative prices should be borne in mind in general.

The appropriate reference for the notion of gravitation thus seems to move inevitably away from the consideration of single positions, which can be validly used only for the analysis of stationary or semi-stationary situations, to the study of the whole time path of the variables. Resort to this method of analysis in the presence of dynamic phenomena that give rise to changes in the structure of the system appears, in fact, to be essential.[7]

Some considerations contained in *Quantity of Capital* lead us to think that Garegnani's attention is now moving in this direction. He seems to admit the need to consider price variations as an element that contributes to the determination of the effective rates of return on capital goods as soon as changes in relative prices are allowed for in the definition of the traditional normal position. In principle, this could be done – he adds – without altering the essential characteristics of the normal position of the economy, represented by an appropriate composition of the stock of capital goods. The basic criticism of the neoclassical approach would therefore remain unaltered:

> In fact, within marginal theory, the condition of a uniform effective rate of return requires an adjusted capital stock *whether or not changes in relative prices are allowed for.* With an arbitrary composition of the initial capital stock, the condition will *not* be fulfilled, whether price changes over time are allowed or not. The existence of economically meaningful solutions will therefore require in this case, no less than it did in Walras's, that such a condition be dropped from the system of equations . . .
>
> (Garegnani 1990: 55; the first italics have been added, the second are in the original)

Apart from the novelty – and perhaps the contradictory nature, at least with regard to well established logical schemes – of a construction of the long-period position with relative prices undergoing change,[8] the greatest obstacle is once more to be found in the notion of a suitably adjusted composition of capital as a characterizing feature of this position.

If changes in the structure of relative prices are admitted within the definition of the normal position, it necessarily follows that the element of price variation cannot be ignored in the formulation of the condition of a uniform rate of return. By doing so, however, the very criterion on which we ought to base the judgement regarding the appropriateness or not of the composition of capital becomes inapplicable and with it vanishes the possibility of distinguishing between long-period positions and short-period equilibria.

On the other hand, if a composition of capital that fulfils the principle of a uniform rate of return – naturally including the percentage price variations – is considered appropriate, then, in the light of the above-mentioned results of the theory of intertemporal equilibrium, each composition of capital appears to be appropriate. It would follow, paradoxically, that every general equilibrium solution would also, from the point of view under consideration, be a long-period position.

NOTES

1 On this occasion Garegnani has systematically resumed and broadened his critique of the neoclassical theory of capital, both in the aggregate version and in the general equilibrium approach. For the sake of convenience I shall here refer almost exclusively to this work and, naturally, only to the aspects that

concern the general equilibrium theory of capital. I do not touch on the questions Garegnani deals with in the seventh part of the above-mentioned essay, where he argues that through the notions of saving and investment the concept of aggregate capital – with all the problems that derive from it – is inevitably introduced also in models such as those of intertemporal general equilibrium, which only apparently do not consider it. Since the notions of aggregate saving and investment – certainly definable in a model of intertemporal general equilibrium – do not seem in any way relevant to the purposes of determining the equilibrium positions, all identified by microeconomic conditions, i.e. by conditions relative to individual markets, Garegnani's thesis does not seem to be very convincing.

2 Note that the definition of equation (5.2) depends on the particular hypotheses regarding the moment in which payments occur and the way in which the prices are expressed. So, for example, Diewert (1977: 78–9) supposes that the remuneration for the service is paid at the beginning instead of at the end of the period, while Donzelli (1986, in particular 288, 306) defines all prices with reference to a single decision-making moment – the beginning of period t – and thus works with present value prices. In this regard, we have here followed the rule of indicating the prices of capital goods paid in the various periods of time with the capital letter $P_i(t)$ and the present value prices with the small letter $p_i(t)$ (cf. pp. 103–4 below). This holds also for the rental prices of capital goods which are considered as paid at the end of each period.

3 Critically re-examining the meaning and the implications of Morishima's proof of the existence of economically significant solutions, Eatwell (1990) observes that 'the only case in which there must necessarily be a solution to the system [of equations of capital formation] is that in which only one capital good is produced' (ibid.: 255) and concludes that 'Morishima's model is thus yet another example of the use in neoclassical models of the 'one-produced-input world' assumption; which input is to be the one produced is endogenous to the model' (p. 256).

If Eatwell's thesis aims at questioning the validity of Morishima's demonstration of the existence of economically significant solutions, it is clearly without substance. Eatwell's reasoning is itself the most immediate proof (apart from the usual, necessary *technicalities*) of the existence of solutions.

If Eatwell intends to show that the model of general economic equilibrium with capital formation admits solutions only on the condition of losing its characteristic of being a model with heterogeneous capital and thus on the condition of necessarily collapsing into a framework in which there is effectively only one capital good, in that case too his conclusion cannot be accepted. That the equilibrium configuration may imply the full utilization of a single capital good, among those initially available in arbitrarily given quantities, and the production of a single new capital good, certainly cannot be excluded, nor is it in any way excluded from the demonstration of the existence of solutions. But this circumstance does not at all limit the scope of the demonstration, which, together with this possibility, also envisages that of the full utilization of several capital goods – eventually of all initially available capital goods – and their production in positive quantities.

4 Cf. below, esp. pp. 102–4.

5 In reality it is possible to make a stronger statement. There are, in fact, perfectly acceptable linear technologies for which it is generally possible to exclude the possibility of maintaining the full utilization of all capital goods when the initial composition does not coincide with that of Von Neumann's path. This is easily

verifiable in the case of two goods and technical coefficients such as $a_{ii} > a_{ij}$ for $i \neq j$.

6 This aspect of the question is expressly formalized by Diewert (1975), who analyses the equilibrium of a Walrasian model of capital accumulation in the context of a temporary equilibrium approach with a general formulation of price expectations. The prices of capital goods available at the beginning of the period are distinct from the prices of the new capital goods produced in the period – investment goods in Diewert's terminology – and are determined precisely by using the condition of equality of the rates of return.

7 The point that the 'normal position' should be identified with the entire growth path rather than with single points on that path is argued by Caravale and Tosato (1980: 9–11), who, in stressing the basically dynamic nature of Ricardo's theoretical construction, take the concept of the 'natural equilibrium path' as the methodological reference point of their analysis. In the same sense, cf. also Caravale in Chapter 1 above.

8 In reality the possibility of taking a change in relative prices into consideration in the very definition of the long-period position, e.g. a change in relative prices occurring between the beginning and the end of the period, seems to undermine one of the strongholds of the distinction between the classical and the neoclassical theories of value (cf. Hahn 1982).

REFERENCES

Bliss, C.J. (1975), *Capital Theory and the Distribution of Income*, Amsterdam, North-Holland.

Burmeister, E. (1980), *Capital Theory and Dynamics*, Cambridge, Cambridge University Press.

Caravale, G., and Tosato, D. (1980). *Ricardo and the Theory of Value, Distribution and Growth*, London, Routledge.

Debreu, G. (1959), *Theory of Value: an Axiomatic Analysis of Economic Equilibrium*, New York, Wiley.

Diewert, W.E. (1977), 'Walras' Theory of Capital Formation and the Existence of a Temporary Equilibrium', in *Equilibrium and Disequilibrium in Economic Theory*, ed. G.S. Schwodiauer, Dordrecht, Reidel.

Donzelli, F. (1986), *Il concetto di equilibrio nella teoria economica neoclassica*, Rome, Nuova Italia Scientifica.

Dorfmann, R., Samuelson, P.A., and Solow, R.M. (1958), *Linear Programming and Economic Analysis*, London, McGraw-Hill.

Eatwell, J. (1990), 'Walras' Theory of Capital', in *The New Palgrave – Capital Theory*, ed. J. Eatwell, M. Milgate and P. Newmann, London, Macmillan.

Gay, A. (1967), 'Esistenza e caratteristiche dell'equlibrio in modelli di tipo walrasiano', *Rivista di politica economica* 57, pp. 1203–39.

Garegnani, P. (1960), *Il capitale nelle teorie della distribuzione*, Milan, Giuffrè.

Garegnani, P. (1966), 'Sulle equazioni walrasiane della capitalizzazione: una risposta', *Giornale degli Economisti* 25, pp. 327–35.

Garegnani, P. (1990), *Quantity of Capital*, in *The New Palgrave – Capital Theory*, ed. J. Eatwell, M. Milgate and P. Newmann, London, Macmillan.

Hahn, F. (1982), 'The Neo-Ricardians', *Cambridge Journal of Economics* 6, pp. 353–74.

Hicks, J.R. (1945), *Value and Capital*, Oxford, Clarendon Press, second edition.

Impicciatore, G., and Rossi, E. (1982), *Teoria neowalrasiana: una reinterpretazione del processo neoclassico e keynesiano di accumulazione*, Padua, Cedam.

Montesano, A. (1970, 1971), 'Il sistema teorico dell'equilibrio economico generale e la coerenza della teoria walrasiana della capitalizzazione', *Giornale degli Economisti* 29–30, pp. 704–45, 427–67.

Morishima, M. (1964), *Equilibrium, Stability and Growth: a Multisectoral Analysis*, Oxford, Clarendon Press.

Pasinetti, L.L. (1977), *Lectures on the Theory of Production*, London, Macmillan.

Petri, F. (1989), *Teorie del valore e della distribuzione*, Rome, Nuova Italia Scientifica.

Tosato, D. (1969), 'Sur la thèorie walrasanienne de la capitalisation', *Economie Appliquée* 22, pp. 533–95.

Walras, L. (1874–7), *Eléments d'économie politique pure*, Lausanne, Cobaz, definitive edition 1926.

Zaghini E. (1968) 'Il problema dell'esistenza di soluzioni economicamente significative nel modello walrasiano di accumulazione', *Giornale degli Economisti* 27, pp. 357–90.

COMMENT

Pierangelo Garegnani

1. In his essay Tosato criticizes the thesis I advanced in my *Quantity of Capital* (1990) whereby in an intertemporal analysis, just as in the original Walrasian equations, there is an inconsistency between the condition of a uniform 'effective' rate of return on the supply prices of the capital goods[1], and the treatment of those goods, as separate productive factors[2] (Garegnani, 1990, 54–5: the adjective 'effective' here attached to 'uniform rate of return' is meant to remind that in an intertemporal context that rate must take into account the changes of relative equilibrium prices over time[3] and that its numerical expressions will accordingly change with the numeraire we choose)[4].

In (1990) I have in fact argued that that uniform rate requires an 'appropriate' physical composition of the initial capital stock, and does not therefore allow taking the stocks of the several capital goods as given in the initial factor endowment, as required for treating them as separate factors.

Here I should perhaps begin by making clear that by 'appropriate' physical composition of the capital stock I meant then, as I do now, no more than a composition compatible with the indicated uniform rate of return – and that the corresponding equilibrium will generally be changing over time as a result, at least, of the endogenously determined capital accumulation.[5] Thus, contrary to Tosato's interpretation (123–25), no reference is made to conditions of stationarity or uniform growth – as evident from the fact that I apply the notion of an appropriate composition of capital to intertemporal equilibrium where changes in relative prices enter the very definition of an equilibrium.

(It is indeed question of an 'appropriate' *physical compositon* of capital and not, instead, of that 'appropriate' *size* which the capital stock should assume, relative to the primary factors in order to give incomes per head for which aggregate savings be zero or just sufficient for uniform growth. Tosato, pp. 101–2, refers to von Neumann's model for a uniform growth which, he seems to think, may depend purely on the *composition* of the capital stock: however that model, with its division of the product between

111

wages and profits, and hence relative prices, determined by worker's sub-sistence has little if anything to do with the marginal theories under discussion. In particular the condition of steady growth is there *assumed* and is not the result of the demand and supply functions of a general intertemporal equilibrium. Within marginal theory, the von Neumann results would in fact require that the sizes of the capital stocks relative to labour be such as to yield exactly the subsistence wage and also to ensure a uniform rate of profits which in turn happened to be somehow equal to the rate of population growth – besides of course requiring individual preferences for which net savings are equal to total profits).

2. We may return now to the thesis of an inconsistency between a given initial vector of capital endowments and the condition of a uniform effec-tive rate of return on the supply prices of those goods. Tosato's criticism of that thesis in an intertemporal context (he admits its validity in the original Walrasian context) seems to rely on the variability of the capital goods prices over time (*e.g.* Tosato 103, 105) which, inexistent in Walras, and present in intertemporal equilibria, would allow the condition of a uniform rate to be satisfied. In that argument Tosato seems however not to make the necessary distinction between two quite different kinds of inequality between rates of return on capital. The first kind, which is peculiar to intertemporal analysis, is an inequality between 'own' or *nominal* rates of return of the several capital goods which is due purely to the assumed changes of the equilibrium *relative prices* over time: the rates of return are there calculated over the *demand* prices of the capital goods whether or not these demand prices are equal to the corresponding *supply* prices. The second kind of inequality of rates of return is instead the one under discussion here, due to an inappropriate physical composition of the capital stock, in which the rates are all calculated on the supply prices of the capital goods. Now, the first kind of inequality of rates is certainly compatible with an equality of the effective rates, and is indeed the way in which arbitrage imposes that equality. Such an equality should however not be identified with an equality of the second kind which is an altogether different matter; and would require that the demand prices of the capital goods be equal to their supply prices. In fact the changes in those demand prices reflect the changes in relative scarcities of the different capital goods and cannot therefore be such as to equalize the respective supply prices, except in so far as those scarcities are affected accordingly.

Tosato seems thus to overlook that already in the original equilibria considered by Walras the essential expression of the second kind of inequality of rates of return (the first being inexistent there because of the assumed constancy of prices) lay in the impossibility to equalize with the respective supply prices, the demand prices resulting for some capital goods from the uniform rate imposed by arbitrage. Now, as Tosato himself admits (p. 105) the same impossibility, and the fact that some capital goods may therefore not be produced, is present in the intertemporal equilibria, revealing that the variability of prices over time does nothing to eliminate the difficulty.[6]

3. Before closing this comment I would however wish to add something concerning Tosato's interpretation in terms of 'static price expectations' of Walras's constant equilibrium prices[7]. That interpretation appears to attribute to Walras a contemporary way of theorising which is alien to him. The texts make clear that, like his contemporaries and predecessors, Walras assumes equilibrium prices which are *objectively* constant, in the specific sense of supposing the forces determining the equilibrium be be persistent enough to allow ignoring the variation of the *equilibrium* prices, during the time necessary for those prices to emerge as some average of the *observable* prices.[8] In fact, contrary to what is sometimes asserted today, Walras refers to the equilibrium as a centre towards which the system gravitates. In his words

'We are now in a position to see clearly what the mechanism of market competition is. It is the practical solution, reached through a rise or fall in prices, of the same problem of exchange to which we have just given a theoretical and mathematical solution . . . The rapidity and reliability of the practical solution leave no room for improvement'.

(Walras 1874–77, 106).

Now, it is clear that for this 'practical solution reached through a rise or fall of in prices' it will be necessary to suppose that the subjective price expectations are continually revised (and will therefore be all but 'static'), so as to make it be true that:

'the market is like a lake agitated by the wind, where the water is incessantly seeking its level without ever reaching it'

(Walras 1874–77, 380).

NOTES

1 For the Walrasian distinction between 'supply prices' and 'demand prices' cf. n. 6 below.

2 For that inconsistency within the original equations of Walras and Pareto, cf. Garegnani (1960) Part II, chs. II, III and Appendix G. In that connection, while quoting the passage in the fourth edition of the *Elements* in which Walras admits the inconsistency, Tosato (pp. 99–100) objects to my comment on it, in which the English copy-editor thought fit the use of the word 'retraction' (Garegnani 1990, p. 20; for the original Italian version see Garegnani 1960, p. 116). Tosato observes then that in such a passage Walras does no more than keep into account specific situations which are in turn the result of a complex reality. However the original inconsistency of Walras had to do with something which is general since it concerns a contradiction between data and equilibrium conditions. The complexity of reality on the other hand is obviously not independent of the

theoretical approach adopted: the classical economists, who did not refer to factor endowments as determinants of distribution, could face the same reality without encountering the difficulties met by Walras.

3 If the price of commodity A increased by 1% relative to commodity B during the year, the interest rate on a loan expressed in terms of A will have to be 1% below that on a loan expressed in terms of B.

4 Tosato does not however consider the question, central to these problems, raised in Garegnani 1990 (paras 51–61), and concerning the presence in the analysis of the saving investment market – and therefore, *also* within the 'intertemporal' or 'temporary' equilibria – of the known difficulties resulting from the impossibility to measure a 'quantity of capital' in terms of independent distribution. Thus, Tosato writes there that 'the notions of aggregate saving and investment . . . . . . do not seem in any way relevant for the purposes of determining the equilibrium positions, all identified by microeconomic conditions, *i.e.* by conditions relative to individual markets' (p. 94 n.).

There is however no difficulty in tracing the question of savings and investment in the markets for individual commodities. Let's take *e.g.* the markets for corn available, respectively, in the periods t and $(t+1)$, in an economy where corn is the only consumption good. To be significant, the equilibrium on those two markets would require that a possible excess supply on the corn market for period t and excess demand on that for $(t+1)$ – the expressions of additional decisions to save – should bring about an additional employment of capital goods *in assisting the same quantity of labour* for the production at t of the corn becoming available at $(t+1)$. Those additional capital goods should have been produced on the other hand in $(t-1)$ *in place* of the corn no longer demanded in t. And these changes should occur in response to a fall of the ratio P_t/P_{t+1} between the two discounted corn prices – in response, that is, to a fall in the 'own' interest of corn $r_t = [(P_t/P_{t+1}) - 1]$ in period t.

We have referred so far only to markets for individual dated commodities. But what has the question here been, if not that regarding the necessity of an inverse relation between investment in t and the corn own interest rate in the same period, *i.e.* between the latter, and the proportion of 'capital' to labour in the production of corn at t. And of the necessity of such an inverse relation if an equilibirum of those two markets, *i.e.* of the savings and investment market is to be achieved (and be achieved for positive level of both the interest rate r_t and the wage rate)? However this is the very inverse relation which we know to be falsified by the impossibility to measure the 'quantity of capital' in terms independent of prices. And the consequences of that on the connected equilibria of the two markets of corn available at t and $(t+1)$ are altogether similar to those which have been brought to light for the traditional versions of the theory (cf. *e.g.* Garegnani 1990, 61–71, and the bibliography indicated there).

5 On the reason why these changes of equilibrium prices do not appear in Walras's price equations and more generally in the traditional versions of the theory, cf; par. 3 below and n. 8.

6 This may become clearer if we refer to undiscounted prices p_i $(i = 1, 2, . . . n)$. The general price equation of a product i, obtained with an annual production cycle and available at the moment $t+1$, is

$$p_{i,t+1} = (a_{0i}w_t + a_{1i}p_{1t} + . . . + a_{ni}p_{nt}) (1 + r_t)$$

where the a's are the production coefficients, w_t is the wage (advanced at the beginning of the cycle) and r_t is the general rate of interest in period t (the numerical expression of which will of course depend on the chosen numeraire m). If we indicate with π_{jt} the gross price of the annual service of the (circulating) capital j we shall have $\pi_{jt} = p_{jt}(1 + r_t)$, from which we shall be able to obtain the 'demand price' ('prix de vente', in Walras 1874–77, 351) of each capital good j, as the discounted value of the price of its service.

$$P^d_{jt} = \frac{\pi_{jt}}{(1+r_t)} \quad \text{that is} \quad r_t = \frac{\pi_{jt}}{P^d_{jt}} - 1$$

When the demand price thus determined by arbitrage so as to yield the uniform rate of return r_t must fall below the supply price P^s_{jt} ('prix de revient' in Walras 1847–77, 351) we shall have

$$P^s_{jt} > \frac{\pi_{jt}}{(1+r_t)} \;, \; i.e. \; P^s_{jt} = \frac{\pi_{jt}}{(1+r_{jt})} \; \text{for} \; r_{jt} < r_t$$

and hence a rate of return of the supply price of the capital good below the level r_t obtainable on other capital goods. The numerical expressions of r_t and r_{jt} will of course change with the numeraire, but the order of the two rates will not change.

7 For this interpretation Tosato (1993 p. 37) quotes Impicciatore G., Rossi E. (1982), Donzelli (1986), Diewert (1977).

8 With respect to the endogenous variation of the capital endowment the hypothesis of a sufficient persistence of the equilibrium had its correspondent in the uniformity of the rate of return on the supply prices of the several capital goods – requiring (as Walras was to discover by the time of the 4th edition of the *Elements*) an 'appropriate' physical composition of the capital stock (Par. 1 above). Under that condition the changes of equilibrium prices over the relevant period could be assumed to be proportionate to the *comparatively small variation* which the net savings of the period, spread over the vast array of all capital goods, would cause in the *aggregate* capital (cf. *e.g.* Marshall 1920, 534). Those changes in equilibrium prices could then be assumed to be themselves small enough to be ignored when using the equilibrium conditions. The position is of course different when the rates of return being different, the change in the equilibrium price would be proportionate to the variations which the savings would cause on the one or few stocks giving the highest rates of return, to which all investment would be directed. (cf. Garegnani 1990, 52). As for the 'difficulty to establish when a change is small', rightly noted by Tosato (p. 129), it concerns, in the first place, the analyses of Walras, Jevons, Wicksteed, Wicksell, etc., besides those of the Marshall of the passage mentioned above. Within marginal theory however the only alternative to that assumption are the intertemporal analyses for which it is appropriate to remember the warning of Marshall when he wrote.

> 'Thus, then, dynamical solutions, in the physical sense, of economic problems are unattainable [. . .] statical solutions afford starting points for such rude and imperfect approaches to dynamical solutions as we may be able to attain to'
>
> (Marshall 1898, 39).

REFERENCES

Diewert, W.E. (1977), 'Walras' Theory of Capital Formation and the Existence of a Temporary Equilibrium', in *Equilibrium and Disequilibrium in Economic Theory*, ed. G.S. Schwodiauer, Dordrecht, Reidel.

Donzelli, F. (1986), *Il concetto di equilibrio nella teoria economica neoclassica*, Rome, Nuova Italia Scientifica.

Garegnani, P. (1960), *Il capitale nelle teorie della distribuzione*, Milan, Giuffrè.

Garegnani, P. (1990) 'Quantity of capital', in *Capital Theory*, ed. J. Eatwell, M. Milgate and P. Newmann, New Palgrave series, London, Macmillan.

Impicciatore, G. and Rossi, N. (1982) *Teoria neowalrasiana: una reinterpretazione del processo neoclassico e keynesiano di accumulazione*, Padua, Cedam.

Marshall, A. (1920), *Principles of Economics*, Variorum edition Vol 1, London, Macmillan, 1961.

Marshall, A. (1878), 'Distribution and Exchange', *Economic Journal* 8, pp. 37–59.

Walras, L. (1874–7), *Elements of Economics*, ed. Jaffé, London, Allen and Unwin, 1954.

p 94 ?   D 50   E 25   D 33

REPLY

Domenico Tosato

I wish to thank Pierangelo Garegnani for the attention he has paid to my work and for the opportunity he has thus offered me to elaborate further my ideas. In particular on the question of the equality of the rates of return in models of intertemporal equilibrium this comment contains considerations that go beyond the points made in the chapter. Garegnani's critical remarks focus on three issues. I shall briefly recall them and then make a few observations in reply to each of them.

1. According to Garegnani, I have confused the concept of the appropriate *composition* of capital necessary to ensure the existence of a uniform rate of return with that of the *entity* of capital capable of generating uniform growth in the economy.

I think that this observation arises from a misunderstanding, perhaps due to insufficient clarity of my purpose in the passage to which Garegnani refers. His criticism is related to considerations that I put forward about Walras's theory of general economic equilibrium (para. 6 above). In that context the variability of relative prices is excluded; the condition of a uniform rate of return implies, therefore, the equality of the own rates of interest. I noted that there exist compositions of capital compatible with the condition of a uniform rate of return in the period under consideration, that are, however, destined to generate rates of return – always defined exclusively in terms of own rates of interest – that diverge in the course of time as a consequence of the process of accumulation, which modifies the given initial composition of the capital stock. I then examined how the concept of an 'appropriate physical composition of capital' could be defined. To this end, it seemed to me essential that the condition of a uniform rate of return should be continually fulfilled through time, having taken into account the endogenous evolution of the economic system due to capital formation. I singled out such a possibility in the *physical composition of capital* that is compatible with Von Neumann's growth path, but I pointed out that this possibility might not exist, as in effect happens when structural changes occur in the economy. It is clear that in this context the *entity* of capital is not important: the existence of a uniform rate of return (which could be nil,

117

if all capital goods were in excess supply relative to the availability of, for example, labour) depends only on the physical composition of capital.

In his comment Garegnani moves, however, his analytical point of reference from the Walrasian single-period context to the intertemporal one in which he admits the possibility of a variation in relative prices; this brings us to the central issue under discussion.

2. I must not have noticed – according to Garegnani – that in intertemporal equilibria, as well as in the original Walrasian equilibria, the failure of a uniform rate of return to obtain is signalled by the impossibility of equalizing the demand price with the supply price. Thus the variability of price in time does not modify the nature of the difficulty that is to be found essentially in the hypothesis of an arbitrarily given composition of the capital stock.

Let us rewrite here, with the same notation used in the chapter, equation (5.2), which defines the rate of return on a capital good i available at the beginning of period one

$$(1 + \rho_i(1))P_i(0) = V_i(1) + (1 - \delta_i)P_i(1) \tag{1}$$

Let us suppose for simplicity's sake, though not very rigorously, that $P_i(0)$ and $V_i(1)$ are known. The market then attributes the value $P_i(1)$ to the capital good i available at the end of period one, so that the owner can in any case realize the average rate of return of the economy $r(1)$. Equation (5.6), set out again below, holds therefore in terms of the market or demand price $P_i(1)$.

$$r(1) = \left(\frac{V_i(1)}{P_i(1)} - \delta_i \right) + \pi_i(1) \tag{2}$$

Let us further suppose that the production cost (supply price), indicated by $C_i(1)$, is greater than the demand price, so that the new production of capital good i is nil.

In Walras, with the hypothesis $P_i(0) = P_i(1)$, which implies $\pi_i(1) = 0$, the consequence is that the rate of return calculated with respect to the supply price:

$$r'_i(1) = \left(\frac{V_i(1)}{C_i(1)} - \delta_i \right) \tag{3}$$

is lower than the average rate of return of the economy. Consequently, in Walras's original equilibria, a divergence between the demand price and the supply price $P_i(1) < C_i(1)$ implies that the rate of return calculated on the supply price is lower than the market rate $r'_i(1) < r(1)$.

Turning now to the intertemporal equilibria, owing to the assumption of arbitrarily given quantities of capital goods, the possibility that the production cost of certain capital goods may exceed the demand price in the initial periods of the horizon certainly cannot be excluded. But, unlike what occurs in Walras's model, it does not seem to me justified to infer from this circumstance the conclusion that the composition of the capital stock is inappropriate. Obstacles – in my view insurmountable – arise regarding the possibility of determining the rate of return on the supply price and the possibility, therefore, of defining the required term of comparison with the rate of return on the demand price.

The difficulty is connected with the presence of the price variation component in the definition of the rate of return. This component is, in fact, determined with reference to *market prices*, not with reference to supply prices. Consequently, for the purposes of the calculation of the rate of return on the production cost, the use of the inflation rate of good i calculated on the basis of market prices would imply the bringing together of non-homogeneous terms. Note further that the calculation of the inflation rate on the basis of production costs would be difficult to understand as an element of the rate of return and, in any case, not practicable in the first period of the horizon under consideration.

Garegnani (n. 7 of his Comment) apparently does not encounter any difficulty in determining the rate of return on the supply price in an intertemporal context as well and therefore considers the comparison between rates of return calculated on the demand price and on the supply price susceptible of immediate generalization from the static to the dynamic context. Since Garegnani does not present the complete model on which his considerations are based, I shall limit myself – while awaiting the possibility of a more thorough examination – to observing that the choice of a model with circulating capital only seems to lead, by definition, to the exclusion of the entire problem of the effect of variations in relative prices on the rates of return.

Let us assume, in fact, that circulating capital completes its contribution to the production process in the course of one period. In the notation I have used, this means that the coefficient of physical wear and tear is equal to one for all capital goods. Equation (1) therefore becomes

$$(1+r_i(1))P_i(0) = V_i(1) \qquad (1')$$

Thus the consideration that relative prices of circulating capital goods may change in time is irrelevant, because the calculation of the rate of return obtained from the investment of $P_i(0)$ units of the *numéraire* commodity in the purchase of one unit of the capital good i is independent of the circumstance that its relative price in terms of the *numéraire* may increase or decrease. Garegnani's considerations in the above-mentioned note 7, containing a relation similar to (1'),[1] consequently appear unable to establish the possibility of determining the rate of return calculated on the supply price when capital goods are liable to repeated utilization.

3. According to Garegnani, I have attributed to Walras, the hypothesis of

static expectations, while he assumes *objectively* constant equilibrium prices.

The question has two aspects: the first of method, the second of exegesis. From the viewpoint of method, it seems to me that when considering the process of capital accumulation one can no longer refer to the method of statics and should, instead, use the method of dynamics.[2] With the accumulation of capital the conditions of the economy are modified: in Walras's words, the *fixed* equilibrium is transformed into a *mobile* equilibrium (1874–7: 318). On the process of convergence towards a given equilibrium position (a point on a time path) is superimposed a process of evolution towards a new equilibrium; this latter process hinders the possibility of observing the convergence towards the given initial position. The hypothesis of objectively constant prices is no longer adequate, because prices are generally not objectively constant. We are therefore obliged to refer to expectations. In the dynamic context, the assumption of objectively constant prices thus translates into the analytical proposition of static expectations.

From the exegetical viewpoint, I shall limit myself to observing that Walras, precisely in order to approach reality, considers that the hypothesis of a one-year market period should be abandoned in favour of the continuous market hypothesis. This market, according to Walras, 'is perpetually tending towards equilibrium without ever actually attaining it, because the market has no other way of approaching equilibrium except by groping, and, before the goal is reached, it has to renew its efforts and start over again, *all the basic data of the problem . . . having changed in the meantime*' (1874–7: 380, italics added). The image, evoked by Garegnani, which immediately follows the passage quoted above, of the lake – agitated by the wind, but always with a well defined level of water depth – does not seem to reflect adequately the idea of a continuous market, which implies the idea of becoming, certainly not the idea of continuously perturbed oscillation around a given level which is on average observable. Here too, as in the discussion on the nature of the solutions of the model with capital accumulation, we are dealing with intuitions (mobile equilibrium) that go quite beyond the formalization of the model (single-period static equilibrium) and observations that reflect different aspects of Walras's thought.

4. Garegnani stresses the importance of the presence of the aggregate savings–investments market also in the context of intertemporal analysis. This is a question I have not dealt with, although I did express doubt regarding the possibility that problems of aggregate capital would arise in a model of general equilibrium. I am still of this opinion (in note 4 of his comment, Garegnani considers, in fact, a single-good economy and not a model of general equilibrium); but I shall postpone, not least because my reply has already become rather lengthy, an examination of this problem until another occasion.

NOTES

1 It should be observed that Garegnani assumes that the payment of the services delivered by the circulating capital goods occurs at the beginning of the period instead of at the end of it, as I had supposed. Assuming for convenience's sake $r_i(1) = r(1)$, equation (1') becomes $[1 + r(1)]P_i(0) = V_i(0)$, which is now difficult to interpret. It is not clear why the owner of capital good i, the value of which is equal to $P_i(0)$, should *at the same time* receive, in equilibrium, a greater price for it, i.e. a price increased by the application of the general profit rate. It must necessarily be $P_i(0) = V_i(0)$. A positive rate of return can derive only from the use of that capital good – together with the others – in productive processes capable of generating a net surplus with respect to the value of the resources used.

2 Garegnani reminds me, in this regard, of Marshall's invitation to modesty contained in the passage (1898: 39) where he states that, whenever 'operative' dynamic solutions of economic problems cannot be attained, statical solutions offer, as far as our capacities go, 'concrete' starting points for an approach – albeit rude and imperfect – for the study of the problems of change. But the issue is not about the difficulty of dynamic economics, nor about the suitability or the necessity of contenting ourselves with the approximations offered by comparative statics. The issue is one of method and of the validity of the *ceteris paribus* hypotheses introduced in the analysis (in the specific case, of the hypothesis of the constancy of equilibrium prices when there is an endogenous change in the quantity and composition of capital, during the time necessary so that these prices can assert themselves in the average of observable prices).

REFERENCES

Marshall, A. (1898), 'Distribution and Exchange', *Economic Journal* 8, pp. 37–59.
Walras, L. (1874–7), *Eléments d'économie politique pure*, Lausanne, Cobaz, (final edition 1926).

6

THE THEORY OF EQUILIBRIUM WITH STOCHASTIC RATIONING

Gerd Weinrich

The theory of equilibrium with stochastic rationing arose as a further development of the theory of temporary equilibrium with fixed prices and rationing of quantities. As such it is to be seen as an extreme attempt to overcome certain deficiencies in the theory of equilibrium with rationing at fixed prices. It is worth briefly recounting the genesis of this theory.

Around the beginning of the 1970s the theory of general equilibrium *à la* Arrow and Debreu had reached a complete and rigorously articulated form. At the same time it had become clear that it was decidedly inadequate in accounting for numerous economic phenomena of some interest. These included waiting lines, delays in delivery, oscillations in the intensity and in the use of the production capacity, inventory cycles, and, for sure, unemployment. These are examples which are difficult to reconcile with a fundamental hypothesis of the theory of general equilibrium, i.e. with the full and instantaneous flexibility of prices.

The basic hypothesis of the theory of equilibrium with rationing, on the other hand, was that prices were characterized by a certain rigidity, or at any rate, that they did not move as quickly as quantities. More precisely, the basic idea can be framed as follows. Time is divided into a sequence of periods. Then:

> At the beginning of every period, prices are announced by, for example, sellers on the basis of their observations of the past and their expectations of the future. Once enunciated, these prices cannot change any more, and therefore remain in force for the whole period. On the basis of these prices, the demands and supplies formulated – *ex-ante*, so to speak – by economic agents may very well not be compatible. In that case, quantitative constraints are introduced on the individuals' opportunities of exchange, or, in other words, a rationing mechanism is presumed to function. This implies new demands and supplies, this time 'effective', and naturally a new possibility of incompatibility. In that case the constraints introduced must be modified, and so on. If in the course of this process a state is reached that is characterized by a

122

system of signals – or constraints on the possibilities of exchange – for which aggregated demand and supply can be reconciled precisely by applying the constraints of rationing that have generated them, an *ex post* equilibrium has been obtained between effective demand and supply, which is called equilibrium with rationing and fixed prices. At this point, exchanges can take place, and we pass on to the next period, characterized by a new system of prices generated on the basis of further evidence provided . . . in the course of the period.

(Battinelli 1988)

Schematically, respectively indicating vectors of prices and vectors of transactions by p^t and x^t for the tth period, we have:

$$\underline{\quad\quad t-1 \quad\quad}\Big|\underline{\quad\quad\quad\quad t \quad\quad\quad\quad}\Big|\underline{\quad t+1 \quad}$$

$$\ldots \rightarrow x^{t-1} \longrightarrow p^t \longrightarrow x^t \rightarrow p^{t+1} \rightarrow \ldots$$

The above shows that the model requires the specification of two mappings, one that associates an allocation x^t to every p^t and another that associates a p^{t+1} to every x^t (and possibly p^t). As far as the first is concerned, the specification found is none other than the concept of equilibrium with rationing and fixed prices expressed above. Regarding the second, it was not possible (I shall endeavour to explain why further on) to find a satisfactory specification in the context of non-stochastic or deterministic rationing. This is the reason that has motivated scholars to deal with stochastic reasoning.

I shall try, further on, to demonstrate how stochastic rationing in fact solves the problem raised. It follows that, in the context of the theory of fixed-price rationing equilibrium, the non-deterministic formulation responds not simply to a legitimate desire for greater realism and generality but to particular necessities internal to the development of the theory itself, which without this type of formulation would be confined to a situation of impasse.

The presentation that follows is brief and intentionally not the most general formulation. (For a more general and in-depth treatment, see, for example, Weinrich 1988.) The justification lies in the fact that, by eliminating everything that is not absolutely necessary, the main ideas should emerge more clearly.

NOTATION

I shall begin by introducing the notation used in the following. I indicate economic agents with $i = 1, \ldots, I$ and (non-monetary) goods with $n = 1, \ldots, N$. $p \in \mathfrak{R}_+^N$ denotes the vector of prices and $z_i \in \mathfrak{R}_+^N$ the vector of demands/supplies on the part of i. z_{in} is positive if it is a quantity demanded and negative if it is a supply. $z = \{z_i\}_i \in \mathfrak{R}^N$ is the vector of all the demands/supplies on all markets.

WALRASIAN EQUILIBRIUM

Denoting the vector of the Walrasian or notional demands of agent i with $z_i(p)$ the *Walrasian aggregate excess demand* is $Z(p) = \Sigma_i\, z_i(p)$. p^* is a *general* or *Walrasian equilibrium* if $Z(p^*) = 0$.

RATIONING EQUILIBRIUM WITH CONSTRAINED EFFECTIVE DEMANDS

If p is different from p^*, $Z(p)$ is no longer zero. Consequently, we will have constraints or quantitative signals $s_i = (\underline{z}_i, \bar{z}_i)$, for every i. As a result of these, agents formulate the effective constrained demands $z_i(p,s_i)$, i.e. which satisfy $\underline{z}_i \leq z_i(p,s_i) \leq \bar{z}_i$. These in turn give rise to the *constrained aggregate excess demand* $Z\,(p,s) = \Sigma_i z_i(p,s_i)$, with $s = \{s_i\}_i$. Given that prices are fixed, it is up to the quantitative signals to equalize demands and supplies. Consequently s^* is called an equilibrium with rationing of quantities if $Z\,(p,\,s^*) = 0$.

RATIONING EQUILIBRIUM WITH GENERALIZED EFFECTIVE DEMANDS

It is true that an equilibrium with rationing with constrained effective demands describes a consistent allocation, but it is also true that it does not give indications of the 'intensity' of the rationing that are easy to observe, given that in equilibrium there are no excesses of demand or supply. But these indications are indispensable according to the general logic set out above to determine price adjustments for the subsequent period.

To overcome this difficulty further concepts have to be introduced, first of all that of a rationing mechanism. Such a mechanism associates a consistent vector of transactions x with every vector of demands z; more precisely, it is an application F defined as follows:

$$\mathbb{R}^{IN} \ni z = \{z_i\}_i \xrightarrow{\quad F \quad} \{x_i\}_i = x \in \mathbb{R}^{IN}$$

such that

$$\Sigma_i F_i(z) = 0 \text{ for each } z \in \mathbb{R}^{IN}$$

Since the rationing scheme summarizes the concrete opportunities of exchange for every individual for every vector of proposed transactions, it is clear that the agent will try to take this into account when he or she formulates his or her exchange proposals. A thorough evaluation of the possibilities is, however, linked, for every individual, to the possession of a certain amount of information regarding what other individuals are doing, that is, regarding z. In general, also admitting that the general law by which in the various markets the economy transforms proposed transactions into actual transactions is known, it is in any case not certain, but on the contrary will be rather improbable – at least in an economy with numerous agents – that the single individual will be in possession of the detailed description of the planned economic activities that z provides.

For this reason it is assumed that every agent receives certain signals $s_i \in S_i \subseteq \mathfrak{R}^{l(i)}$ that synthesize the state of his information at each instant; these can consist of statistics relative to z, of coefficients whose values are provided by the rationing scheme as (for example) lower and upper limitations on the possibilities of exchange, etc. Formally it is assumed that it is possible to define *signal functions* $\{G_i\}_i = G$ that associate with every z signals $\{s_i\}_i$:

$$\mathbb{R}^{IN} \ni z \xrightarrow{\quad G \quad} \{s_i\}_i = s \in S = \times_i [S_i]$$

Having available not all of z but only the signal s_i an agent can no longer make use of the function F_i to calculate the achievable transactions. Thus it is assumed that the kind of association that every individual establishes between the signal received, s_i, his own demand, z_i, and exchange, x_i, can be represented by means of a *perceived rationing function* H_i on the part of i:

$$\mathbb{R}^{IN} \times S_i \ni (z_i, s_i) \xrightarrow{\quad H_i \quad} x_i \in \mathbb{R}^{IN} \quad \text{for each } i = 1, \ldots, I$$

In equilibrium it will be a requirement, among other things, that exchanges are admissible from the individual point of view. Consequently, transactions expected by means of the function H_i and the signal s_i must not be too different from the transactions effectively achieved by means of the function F_i. Thus the following relationship between F_i, G_i and H_i is assumed:

$$F_i(z) = H_i(z_i, G_i(z)) \text{ for every } z \text{ and every } i$$

This simply means decomposing the rationing mechanism relative to the individual information structure, as in Fig. 6.1. That this decomposition is always possible is seen at once by putting $s_i = z_{-i} = (z_1, \ldots, z_{i-1}, z_{i+1}, \ldots, z_I)$ and $H_i(z_i, s_i) = H_i(z_i, z_{-i}) = F_i(z)$.

The following is an example of a non-trivial decomposition. Assume that for each $z \in \mathfrak{R}^{IN}$ and $n \in \{1, \ldots, N\}$ aggregate demand and supply on market n are given by

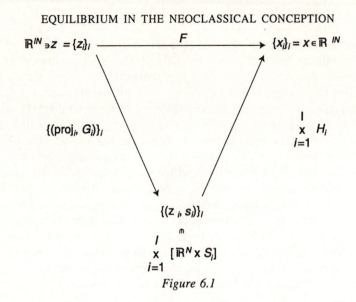

Figure 6.1

$$D_n(z) = \Sigma_i \max\{z_{in}, 0\} \text{ and } s_n(z) = -\Sigma_i \min\{z_{in}, 0\}$$

We then have *uniform proportional rationing* if

$$F_{in}(z) = \begin{cases} z_{in}\min\{S_n(z)/D_n(z), 1\}, \text{ if } z_{in} \geq 0 \\ z_{in}\min\{D_n(z)/S_n(z), 1\}, \text{ if } z_{in} \leq 0 \end{cases}$$

A decomposition of F_{in} is obtained by setting

$$s_{in} = G_{in}(z) = S_n(z)/D_n(z)$$

and

$$H_{in}(z_i, s_i) = \begin{cases} z_{in}\min\{s_{in}, 1\}, \text{ if } z_{in} \geq 0 \\ z_{in}\min\{1/s_{in}, 1\}, \text{ if } z_{in} \leq 0 \end{cases}$$

With the above assumptions the formalization of the decision-making problem of the ith agent is now immediate. Given (from the point of view of i) the prices vector p and the signal s_i, by choosing z_i the agent solves

$$\max u_i(H_i(z_i, s_i))$$

such that

$$H_i(z_i, s_i) \in B_i(p)$$

where $u_i(\cdot)$ is the utility function and $B_i(p)$ indicates the set of all admissible transactions for i, both from the physiological point of view and from that of his budget constraint. It is worth bearing in mind at this point that the agent bases his decision on a given signal s_i and that he or she does not know, or, at any rate, does not take into consideration, the link between his

126

or her action z_i and the signal s_i expressed by the function G_i. The solution to the problem above has been called by Benassy (1977) *generalized effective demand* $z_i(p,s_i)$. The demands of all agents give rise to the *generalized aggregate excess demand* $Z(p,s) = \Sigma_i \, z_i \, (p,s_i)$.

In this context $s^* \in S$ defines an equilibrium with rationing in quantities at fixed prices if

$$G_i(z_1(p, s_1^*), \ldots, z_I (p, s_I^*)) = s_i^* \quad \text{for each } i = 1, \ldots, I.$$

We note that, because of the assumed consistency of the rationing mechanism, transactions are logically feasible, i.e.

$$\Sigma_i F_i \, (z_1(p, s_1^*), \ldots, z_I \, (p, s_I^*)) = 0$$

Furthermore, and this is valid only in equilibrium, transactions are admissible for every agent because

$$F_i(z_1(p, s_1^*), \ldots, z_I(p, s_I^*)) = H_i(z_i(p, s_i^*), s_i^*) \in B_i(p)$$

In equilibrium all agents have rational expectations regarding the signals (and also the prices), which ensures that actual transactions x are the same as those that the agents expected when announcing their exchange proposals z.

RATIONING EQUILIBRIUM WITH EFFECTIVE DEMANDS ACCORDING TO THE 'DUAL DECISION HYPOTHESIS' (CLOWER–BENASSY)

Another concept of effective demand had already been introduced (which later proved to be, under a certain condition, a particular case of generalized effective demand) well before the model just described. Let us assume that signal s_i is a complete list of lower and upper constraints on the exchange possibilities in every market for the agent i:

$$s_{in} = G_{in}(z) = (\underline{G}_{in}(z), \bar{G}_{in}(z)) = (\underline{x}_{in}, \bar{x}_{in}) \; \forall \; i, n$$
$$H_{in}(z_i, s_i) = \min \, \{\max \, \{z_{in}, \underline{x}_{in}\}, \bar{x}_{in}\} \; \forall \; i, n \qquad (6.1)$$

Let us now consider the following problem for a given market n:

$$\max u_i \, (z_i) \text{ such that } [i] \; z_i \in B_i \, (p),$$
$$[ii] \; \underline{x}_{im} \leq z_{im} \leq \bar{x}_{im} \; \forall m = 1, \ldots, N, m \neq n$$

Let us denote the nth component of the corresponding solution $z_{in}^B(p, s_i)$. According to this plan, the agent, when he or she decides on his or her effective demand on market n, takes into account all existing constraints on all markets except those relative to market n, i.e. except those regarding the market on which he or she is to propose a transaction. This approach, following Clower (1965), is called the *dual decision hypothesis*; it obviously has the merit of enabling an agent to express a demand that can go well beyond the constraint effectively in force. Consequently, the desired discrepancy in the case of rationing between desired transaction and actual transaction is obtained. Benassy (1975) went a stage further by hypothesizing that the agent behaves as described on all markets simultaneously. This leads to his concept of effective demand $z_i^B(p, s_i)$

$$z_i^B (p, s_i) = (z_{i1}^B(p, s_i), \ldots, z_{iN}^B (p, s_i))$$

Since in effective demand according to Benassy the dual decision hypothesis is applied to every market, so also for the effective aggregate excess demand we have

$$\Sigma_i \, z_i^B (p, s_i^*) = Z^B(p, s^*) \neq 0$$

Even if the procedure according to which Benassy's effective demand has been defined is different from that of generalized effective demand, the following link holds true (see Grandmont 1977):

Lemma If u_i is strictly quasi-concave $z_i^B(p, s_i)$ is a solution to the problem

$$\max u_i \, (H_i(z_i, s_i)) \text{ such that } (H_i(z_i, s_i) \in B_i \, (p)$$

As a corollary $z_i^B(p, s_i)$ is a generalized effective demand if u_i is strictly quasi-concave.

Although what has just been set out gives Benassy's concept a certain justification, there are criticisms that point out its deficiencies. In the first place, effective demands are formed market by market without consideration of the overall consequences. This seems artificial and unconvincing from the point of view of the behaviour of the single individual. However, there is another even graver argument which is linked with the fact that the perceived rationing function H_i used by Benassy is *non-manipulable*. In order to understand this, let us observe that agent i expects the realization $x_{in} = H_{in} (z_i, s_i)$ to respect $\underline{x}_{in} \leq x_{in} \leq \bar{x}_{in}$. On the other hand, in the case of rationing (of demand, for example), $z_{in}^B > \bar{x}_{in}$. But this implies that every demand $z_{in}' \geq \bar{x}_{in}$ is equally optimal in that $H_{in} (z_i, s_i) = \bar{x}_{in} = H_{in} z_i^B, s_i)$. The choice of z_{in}^B as the effective demand in the set of all optimal demands $(\bar{x}_{in} \, \infty)$ is arbitrary. Consequently the celebrated excess of demand $D_n - S_n = Z_n \, (p, s)$ is also arbitrary and therefore anything but a reliable indicator of the intensity of rationing and even less so for the adjustment of prices.

The last point of the criticism just made against Benassy's concept of effective demand is not a criticism strictly related to this concept; it refers in fact to any concept of effective demand where the perceived rationing function is of the type expressed in (6.1). The fact that the quantitative signal consists of lower and upper constraints and that these constraints cannot be influenced by the agent is called non-manipulable rationing.

We can therefore summarize by saying that in circumstances of non-manipulable rationing it is impossible to obtain an indicator of the intensity of rationing which is not in some way artificial and unreliable. The conclusion is that the type of rationing to assume in the model under consideration must be manipulable.

There is a further argument in favour of manipulability. Let us consider the case in which the only signals communicated to economic agents are the aggregate demands and supplies on all markets, i.e.

$$s_{in} = (D_n(z), S_n(z)) \text{ for every } i \text{ and } n.$$

Let us moreover assume that the functions G_i and H_i are continuous and that on every market the 'short-sided rule' holds whereby at most one side of every market can be rationed. Furthermore, the sign of a transaction x_{in} cannot be different from that of the demand/supply z_{in}. In these circumstances the following result holds, which is a corollary of a theorem first formulated in Green (1980), subsequently corrected in Weinrich (1982) and generalized in Wu (1987) and Weinrich (1988).

Result Let $I \geq 4$. If $s_{in} = (D_n, S_n)$ for every i and n, then

$$H_{in}(z_i, s_i) = \begin{cases} z_{in}\min\{S_n/D_n, 1\}, & \text{if } z_{in} \geq 0 \\ z_{in}\min\{D_n/S_n, 1\}, & \text{if } z_{in} \leq 0 \end{cases}$$

In other words, if the rationing mechanism is such that the actual transaction depends only on the proposed transaction and on the aggregate values of demand and supply, then it must be the uniform proportional one.

A consequence of this result is that in the circumstances described the rationing mechanism must not be non-manipulable which favours the use of manipulable rationing schemes.

Unfortunately, manipulable rationing has a serious deficiency with regard to the model so far developed: it is not compatible with the existence of equilibrium (Benassy 1977). This can be easily understood by taking into account that, in the case of uniform proportional rationing, every agent exaggerates his or her own transaction offers to the exact extent that enables him or her to achieve the desired transaction. But doing so means that the factor of proportionality gradually becomes more and more unfavourable and the transaction offers go beyond every limit. Therefore equilibrium does not exist.

The conclusions, at this point, may appear discouraging. In fact, we either assume non-manipulable rationing and then it is not possible to define the adjustment of prices, or we hypothesize a manipulable rationing and then equilibrium does not exist. This is the dilemma that I think has led most scholars to abandon the theory of equilibrium with rationing at fixed prices. Actually, there is one way out. However, the bugs have not yet been ironed out sufficiently to make it easy going. I shall deal with this in the section that follows.

EQUILIBRIUM WITH STOCHASTIC RATIONING

Gale (1979) and Svensson (1980) had the idea of modelling the relationship between proposed transactions and actual transactions as a random function. This appears quite natural, since in a complex economy an agent often cannot forecast exactly the transaction that will emerge from his or her proposal. On the other hand, Gale's motivation for dealing with stochastic rationing seems to have been exactly what was set out in the previous section, i.e. that deterministic rationing cannot give rise to a satisfactory model of what happens in an economy with rigid prices and quantity constraints on the possibilities of exchange. As a possible solution, Gale proposed manipulable rationing and stochastic rationing. We shall see further on how this can do the job.

Formally there is only one element to be modified regarding the model constructed so far: the rationing framework must be assumed a random function instead of a deterministic one. To that end, we denote with $(\Omega, \mathfrak{F}, P)$ a probability space where every $\omega \in \Omega$ represents a specification of all the uncertain elements that can in some way influence the working of the rationing framework. Consequently the functions $\{F_i\}_i$ and $\{H_i\}_i$ become as shown in Fig. 6.2. Since $F_i(z, \omega) = H_i(z_i, G_i(z), \omega)$ $P - a.e.$, each agent i knows the distribution of the random function $F_i(z, \cdot)$ if his or her signal received s_i is that corresponding to z through G_i. This will be true in equilibrium and in that case will ensure the feasibility of the corresponding allocation.

The decision-making process of a single agent requires a minimal modification regarding the deterministic case. For a given p and s_i, it becomes

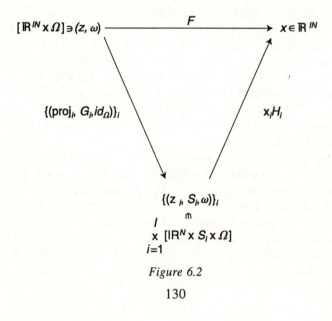

Figure 6.2

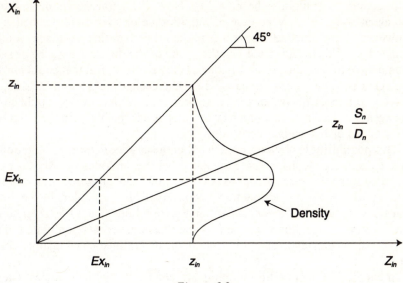

Figure 6.3

$$\max_{z_i} \int u_i \, (H_i(z_i, \, s_i, \, \omega)) \, P(d\omega)$$
$$s.t. \; H_i(z_i, \, s_i, \, \omega) \in B_i(p) \qquad P - a.e.$$

As before, an *equilibrium*, this time with *stochastic rationing*, is defined by an $s^* = \{s_i^*\}_i$ such that

$$G_i(z_1(p, \, s_1^*), \, . \, . \, ., \, z_I \, (p, \, s_I^*)) = s_i^* \quad \text{for each } i$$

The validity of the above-mentioned result of Green and others (1980) also transfers to the stochastic case.

Theorem Let $I \geq 4$ and $s_{in} = (D_n, S_n)$ for every i and n. Then

$$EH_{in}(z_i, \, s_i) = \begin{cases} z_{in}\min\{S_n/D_n, \, 1\}, \text{ if } z_{in} \geq 0 \\ z_{in}\min\{D_n/S_n, \, 1\}, \text{ if } z_{in} \leq 0 \end{cases}$$

Here $EH_{in}(z_i, \, s_i)$ indicates the expected value of the random function H_{in} $(z_i, \, s_i, \, \cdot)$.

In the deterministic case the manipulability was prohibitive for the existence of equilibrium. This is no longer true with stochastic rationing, as has been demonstrated in Weinrich (1984a) in the case of a general equilibrium model *à la* Arrow and Debreu and in Weinrich (1984b) in the case of a simpler macroeconomic model. It is easy to guess why this result holds true. In Fig. 6.3 demand z_{in} gives rise, in the case of stochastic rationing, to a distribution over the possible transactions with support $[0, \, z_{in}]$ while the expected transaction (in the probabilistic sense) is Ex_{in}. In the deterministic case the actual transaction, and therefore the one expected

131

with certainty, would also be $x_{in} = Ex_{in}$. Now, if the transaction desired by the agent were Ex_{in}, in the case of rationing he or she would demand z_{in}. However, in the stochastic case it is not at all certain that he or she would demand z_{in}. This is due to the fact that, if he or she demanded z_{in}, he or she would have to face the possibility of z_{in} being realized. But that could make the agent notably uneasy, since z_{in} is not the desired transaction; it is Ex_{in}. Having to honour his or her exchange proposals, to purchase z_{in} could cost the agent very dear, in fact much dearer than is acceptable from the point of view of his or her budget constraint.

This possibility is obviously excluded in the case of deterministic rationing. Thus in the stochastic case the agent behaves more cautiously than in the deterministic case as far as exaggerating the proposed transaction relative to the desired transaction is concerned. In particular, in the stochastic case, the agent's demand will not go to infinity even if S_n/D_n should tend to zero. It was, however, the fact that the demands were unlimited that prevented the existence of equilibrium in the deterministic and manipulable case.

In conclusion, stochastic rationing overcomes all the deficiencies listed above regarding deterministic rationing; more precisely, it possesses the following properties:

1 $\Sigma_i z_{in} (p, s^*) = D_n - S_n \neq 0$, i.e. in equilibrium with rationing there is an excess of demand/supply.
2 The effective demands are formed taking into consideration the consequences on all markets simultaneously.
3 $z_i(p, s_i)$ is uniquely determined (under standard assumptions as, for example, strict convexity of the preference relation).
4 The excess $\Sigma_i z_{in} (p, s_i) = D_n - S_n$ is uniquely determined.

A further step in the development of the model concerns the specification of the adjustment of prices. Given that the aggregate values D_n and S_n in the case of rationing are different one from the other, it is natural to assume that the new prices are determined depending on the old prices and the values $D = (D_1, \ldots, D_N)$ and $S = (S_1, \ldots, S_N)$, i.e.

$$p^{t+1} = f(p^t, D^t, S^t)$$

An exploratory study of the potentialities of this approach has been undertaken by Weinrich and Battinelli (1988) in the context of a simple macroeconomic model. Among the results of this investigation is the observation that some forms of wage indexation are desirable for the purposes of rendering the dynamic behaviour of the economy more stable; this type of stabilization, however, means living with a positive, although not necessarily high, rate of unemployment.

As was to be expected, as a consequence of the fact that there is rarely such a thing as a 'free lunch', so also in the case of stochastic rationing certain difficulties and problems emerge. These are linked not so much with conceptual aspects as with technical factors. In the first place, demonstrating the existence of equilibrium in a model with stochastic rationing is generally somewhat demanding. This is due to various facts.

1 The continuity of the perceived rationing function H_i does not transfer from the deterministic case to the stochastic one in such a way as to render fixed point theorems easily applicable. Weak continuity of the distribution $\mathscr{D} H_i (z_i, s_i)$ of $H_i (z_i, s_i, \cdot)$ is not sufficient and the continuity of the support of $\mathscr{D} H_i (z_i, s_i)$ relative to the topology of 'closed convergence' (Hildenbrand 1974: II, 15–19) is not generally valid.
2 The quasi-concavity of the utility function u_i does not transfer to the function of expected utility $\int u_i (H_i (\cdot, s_i, \omega)) P(d\omega)$.
3 The concept of equilibrium as defined above generally admits the trivial equilibrium $(z, s) = (0, 0)$. In order to exclude this possibility further assumptions are needed which are more delicate in the stochastic than in the deterministic case.

In the second place, agents' problems of maximizing do not, in general, enable the functions of effective demand to be calculated in an explicit form. Therefore all the analyses – for example, of comparative statics – must be carried out using implicit functions. This increases the analytical complexity in a way that is at times prohibitive. The application or not from a technical point of view of the stochastic approach seems to depend on the particular model being considered. Works that exemplify this aspect are Gerard-Varet *et al.* (1990), Honkapohja and Ito (1985), Weinrich (1984b) and Weinrich and Battinelli (1988).

REFERENCES

Publications that are asterisked deal with stochastic rationing.

Barro, R.J. and Grossman, H.I. (1971), 'A General Disequilibrium Model of Income and Employment, *American Economic Review* 61, pp. 82–93.
Barro, R.J. (1976), *Money, Employment and Inflation*, Cambridge, Cambridge University Press.
*Battinelli, A. (1988), 'Modelli di equilibrio economico generale con razionamento stocastico' in *Atti del Convengno su Incertezza ed Economia, Trieste 20–30 ottobre 1987*, ed. L. Crisma *et al.*, Trieste, Lint.
Benassy, J.P. (1975), 'Neo-Keynesian Disequilibrium Theory in a Monetary Economy', *Review of Economic Studies* 42, pp. 503–24.
Benassy, J.P. (1977), 'On Quantity Signals and the Foundations of Effective Demand Theory', *Scandinavian Journal of Economics* 79, pp. 147–68.
Benassy, J.P. (1982), *The Economics of Market Disequilibrium*, San Diego, Academic Press.
Böhm, V. (1978), 'Disequilibrium Dynamics in a Simple Macoeconomic Model', *Journal of Economic Theory* pp. 179–99.

Böhm, V. (1989), *Disequilibrium and Macroeconomics*, Oxford, Blackwell.

Böhm, V. and Levine, P. (1979), 'Temporary Equilibrium with Quantity Rationing', *Review of Economic Studies* pp. 361–77.

Clower, R.W. (1965), 'The Keynesian Counter-Revolution: Theoretical Appraisal', in *The Theory of Interest Rates*, ed. F.M. Hahn and F.P.R. Brechling, London, Macmillan.

Drèze, J.H. (1975), 'Existence of an Exchange Equilibrium under Price Rigidities', *International Economic Review* 16, pp. 301–20.

*Gale, D. (1979), 'Large Economies with Trading Uncertainty', *Review of Economic Studies* 46, pp. 319–38.

Gale, D. (1981), 'Large Economies with Trading Uncertainty: a Correction', *Review of Economic Studies* 48, pp. 363–4.

*Gérard-Varet, L.-A., Jordan, R. and Kirman, A.P. (1990), 'A Model of Temporary Equilibria with Stochastic Quantity Rationing', in *Economic Decision-making: Games, Econometrics and Optimisation*, ed. J.J. Gabszewicz, J.-F. Richard and L.A. Wolsey, Amsterdam, Elsevier.

Grandmont, J.M. (1977), 'Temporary General Equilibrium Theory', *Econometrica* 45, pp. 535–72.

Grandmont, J.M. (1982), 'Temporary General Equilibrium Theory', in *Handbook of Methematical Economics*, ed. K.J. Arrow and M.D. Intriligator, Amsterdam, North Holland.

*Green, J. (1980), 'On the Theory of Effective Demand', *Economic Journal* 99, pp. 341–53.

Hildenbrand, W. (1974), *Core and Equilibria of a Large Economy*, Princeton N.J., Princeton University Press.

*Honkapohja, S. and Ito, T. (1979), *Non-trivial Equilibrium in an Economy with Stochastic Rationing*, National Bureau of Economic Research Working Paper. 322, Washington, D.C., NBER.

*Honkapohja, S. and Ito, T. (1985), 'On Macroeconomic Equilibrium with Stochastic Rationing', *Scandinavian Journal of Economics* 87 (1), pp. 66–88.

*Ioannides, Y.M. (1978), 'Endogenous Trading Uncertainty and Macroeconomic Equilibrium', *Economic Journal*, supplement: Conference Papers, pp. 99–105.

*Ito, T. (1979), 'An Example of a Non-Walrasian Equilibrium with Stochastic Rationing at the Walrasian Equilibrium Prices', *Economics Letters* 2, pp. 13–19.

Malinvaud, E. (1980), *The Theory of Unemployment Reconsidered*, Oxford, Blackwell.

*Martin, C. (1985), *Simple Stochastic Rationing Schemes*, Birkbeck College Discussion Paper 182, University of London.

Svensson, L.E.O. (1980), 'Effective Demand and Stochastic Rationing', *Review of Economic Studies* 47, pp. 339–56.

*Svensson, L.E.O. (1981), 'Effective Demand in a Sequence of Markets', *Scandinavian Journal of Economics* pp. 1–21.

*Weinrich, G. (1982), 'On the Theory of Effective Demand', *Economic Journal* 92, pp. 174–5.

*Weinrich, G. (1984a), 'On the Theory of Effective Demand under Stochastic Rationing', *Journal of Economic Theory* 34, pp. 95–115.

*Weinrich, G. (1984b), 'L'effetto dei mutamenti del salario in uno stato di sottoccupazione keynesiana con razionamento stocastico', *Giornale degli Economisti e Annali di Economia* 7/8, pp. 531–46.

*Weinrich, G. (1988), 'On the Foundations of Stochastic Non-price Rationing and the Adjustment of Prices', *Rivista di matematica per le scienze economiche e sociali* 1/2, pp. 107–31.

*Weinrich, G. and Battinelli, A. (1988), 'Wage Indexation in a Simple Macro-economic Model with Stochastic Rationing', in *Non-linear Dynamics in Economics and Social Sciences*, ed. M. Galeotti, L. Geronazzo and F. Gori, Bologna, Pitagora.
*Wu, H.M. (1982), *Unemployment Equilibrium with Stochastic Rationing of Supplies*, IMS Technical Report 378, Stanford University, Stanford, Cal.
*Wu, H.M. (1987), 'On the Theory of Effective Demand under Stochastic Rationing', *Economic Journal* 97, pp. 487–92.

Part III

EQUILIBRIUM IN THE CLASSICAL CONCEPTION

7

ON SOME SUPPOSED OBSTACLES TO THE TENDENCY OF MARKET PRICES TOWARDS NATURAL PRICES*

Pierangelo Garegnani

1. I had thought of taking this occasion in order to tidy up some reflections which had been stimulated many years ago by my reading of a first draft of Ian Steedman's *Natural Prices, Differential Profit Rates and the Classical Competitive Process*, which was to be published some years later in the Manchester School 1984. However, the time to prepare the paper I intended has not been available, and here I am with some notes only a little more developed than they were then, and without the readings I had hoped to do in the meantime. Since I have managed to convince myself that the argument holds in its essential lines, I have come to submit it for discussion.

In his article Steedman (1984) argues that Smith, Ricardo and Marx 'associated a positive (negative) deviation of a commodity's market price from its natural price with a positive (negative) deviation of the corresponding industry's profit rate from the natural rate' (p. 123). He then asks:

> Could it not happen, . . . that an industry whose product's market price lies above its natural price, purchases as produced inputs commodities whose market prices lie 'even more above' their natural price, with the result that that industry has a profit rate below the natural rate? (ibid.)

This question, to which he devotes the first part of his paper, has of course an affirmative answer. Nothing prevents the compound commodity consisting of the means of production – among which we may for a moment include the real wages paid in advance at the given rate – from having a market price exceeding its natural price in a proportion larger than the output does, in which case the rate of profit will have to be below the natural rate.

Indeed, as far as can be seen from Steedman's own references, neither

* Except for minor changes, this text is the same published under the same title in *Political Economy, Studies in the Surplus Approach*, vol. 6 n. 1–12, pp. 329–59, 1990, I am indebted to Rosenberg Sellier for permission to reproduce that material.

Adam Smith nor Ricardo nor Marx stated that a market price higher than the natural price is *necessarily* associated with a rate of profit higher than the natural rate. This would have been wrong, even independently of the problem raised by the means of production, because opposite signs of the deviations of market price and profit rate could also result from wages and rents exceeding their natural levels sufficiently.[1] The classical authors appear rather to have confined themselves to the less restrictive statement that it is by *raising* the market price sufficiently high, relative to wages, rents, and the means of production, that the rate of profit of the industry whose output must be increased is elevated above that obtaining in other industries.[2] Indeed, as we shall see, the very notion of an excess of the market price over the natural price has an arbitrary element attached to it because it depends on the choice of the numeraire (para. 8 below).

2. However, let us leave aside history of thought and return to analysis. More important than the possibility of a high market price going together with a low rate of profit is the question which Steedman raises in the second part of his paper: namely, whether such a possibility might not prevent the ultimate tendency of the market price towards the natural price, by causing the output of the commodity to decrease, thus sending the market price even higher.[3] We shall here argue that this question can be answered negatively.

The reason for that result can perhaps be preliminarily surveyed in an intuitive way by noting that when *e.g.*, for a commodity A_1, a negative deviation of the market price accompanies a positive deviation of the profit rate, then, the same opposition of signs cannot be true for at least one of the direct or indirect means of production of A_1: that having the *minimum* ratio of market to natural price.[4] For that particular means of production the profit rate deviation will have to be negative like that of the relative market price, and the associated fall of output will tend to raise its market price, leading either directly or in a finite number of stages to a fall in the rate of profit of A_1, and thus to a reversal in the initial 'perverse' rise in output.

3. Our formal argument in this chapter will be founded on *three assumptions*. The first will be a fall in the output of the industry or industries showing the *minimum* rate of profit in the economy; the second will concern the conditions under which that fall in output will result in a rise of the profit rate of the industry in question. We shall claim that the generality of those first two assumptions is hardly disputable. The third assumption will instead be more restrictive, in that it will concern a *monotonic* rise of the minimum profit rate, rather than that *eventual* rise of the rate which it will be possible to demonstrate on the basis of the first two assumptions. It will then be possible to show that when the rise of the minimum profit rate reaches the natural rate, the natural position of the economy will have been achieved. The consequences of

abandoning the third assumption will then be discussed at the end of the chapter.

The layout of the chapter will be as follows. In the next section we shall introduce the postulate of given (normal) effectual demand, a basic premise of the classical treatment of market prices. There we shall also set out our definitions and assumptions about the kind of economy we shall be concerned with. In the following section (paras 9–18) we shall come to the rise of the minimum rate of profit in the economy and to the three assumptions mentioned above. The fourth section (para. 19) will instead be devoted to proving some propositions needed in order to draw the implications of that rise. In the fifth (paras 20–5) those propositions will be used to show how, when, in its rise, the minimum rate of profit reaches the natural rate r^*, convergence to the natural position of the economy will be achieved, whatever may have been the initial deviations of the market prices of the means of production from their natural levels. In the final section we shall conclude by discussing the generality of our conclusions, and the method of argument used in the chapter. We shall then claim that, though our primary aim has been to examine and reject the idea that divergences of market prices from natural prices for the means of production may prevent a tendency to the natural position, yet our argument may allow for some general affirmative conclusions.

PREMISES AND DEFINITIONS

4. In the course of our argument we shall follow in the footsteps of Adam Smith and the old classical economists and take as *given*, and therefore as *constant* during the process of adjustment, the normal effectual demand of each commodity – the quantity, that is, of the commodity which would be demanded when the prices and outputs of *all* commodities were at their normal levels.[5] It should be immediately noted that this classical postulate does not imply any assumption of stationarity of the economy. It only rests on the view that the forces of competition, which may bring market prices towards the natural prices, will be acting in a way which is broadly independent of what the normal outputs (effectual demands) happen to be, or of how they happen to evolve over time. It follows that market prices are best studied *separately* from the circumstances determining the normal quantities produced and the latter may be taken as given when studying the former.

This classical postulate of given effectual demands needs to be stressed because it seems to have been frequently overlooked in recent literature, at the expense of the generality of the results obtained.[6]

5. Though the subject is beyond the aim of the present chapter some observations may here be necessary with respect to the assumption, implied

in the above postulate, that the *aggregate* economic activity (on which the effectual demands of the individual commodities evidently depend) can be taken as given in analysing market prices. A first view which may be taken in that respect is that the deviations of the actual outputs from the respective effectual demands (and therefore their changes during the process of adjustment) will in general broadly compensate each other with respect to their effect on aggregate demand and its determinants. However, the classical postulate of given effectual demands does not appear to ultimately rest on any such eventual compensation of deviations. Here also what needs in effect be assumed is only the possibility of *separating* the two analyses. Thus, if we had reason to think that the effects on aggregate demand of the circumstances causing (or arising out of) certain kinds of deviation of actual from normal relative outputs were sufficiently important – then, it would seem, those effects could be considered in the separate analysis of the determinants of aggregate economic activity and hence of the individual effectual demands.

In this chapter, the level of aggregate demand is assumed constant in terms of the level of aggregate labour employment.

6. We may now proceed to the assumptions defining the economy we will be envisaging. We assume n commodities $A_1 \ldots A_n$, obtained, as in Steedman's paper, from single-product industries in a yearly production cycle, with wages advanced at the beginning of the year. Only one method of production will be available in each industry. All the n commodities will be 'basic products'[7] and, besides, labour will be assumed to enter all of them, directly or indirectly.

We shall also assume at first that the real wage is at its natural level and, in accordance with the premises of the classical economists, we shall take it to be given (separately determined). Our numeraire will be the composite wage commodity G, consisting of the g wage goods taken in the proportions in which they enter the natural wage rate. A quantity w^* of G will accordingly constitute the natural wage. We shall indicate the wage goods by

$$A_1, A_2, \ldots, A_g \; ; \text{ for } g \le n$$

and call

$$g_1, g_2, \ldots, g_g$$

the quantities in which these goods appear in the physical unit of the wage commodity G. The natural wage w^* is positive and less than the maximum wage W, for which the profit rate is zero. The usual equations

$$p_1 = (a_{01} w^* + a_{11}p_1 + \ldots + a_{n1}p_n)(1 + r^*)$$

$$\ldots$$

$$p_n = (a_{0n}w^* + a_{1n}p_1 + \ldots + a_{nn}p_n)(1 + r^*) \tag{7.1}$$

will then determine the natural profit rate r^* and the corresponding series of natural prices $p_1, \ldots p_n$, expressed in terms of the wage commodity:

$$1 = g_1 p_1 + g_2 p_2 + \ldots + g_g p_g \qquad (7.2)$$

The market rates of profits $r_1, r_2, \ldots, r_n$ obtainable in each industry in the given 'market position' – as we may call any position of the economy other then the 'normal position' – will, on the other hand, be given by the following equations, where by $m_1, m_2, \ldots, m_n$ we shall indicate the market prices of the n commodities:[8]

$$r_1 = \frac{m_1 - (a_{01}w^* + a_{11}m_1 + \ldots + a_{n1}m_n)}{a_{01}w^* + a_{11}m_1 + \ldots + a_{n1}m_n}$$

$$\ldots \qquad (7.3)$$

$$r_n = \frac{m_n - (a_{0n}w^* + a_{1n}m_1 + \ldots + a_{nm}m_n)}{a_{0n}w + a_{1n}m_1 + \ldots + a_{nn}m_n}$$

obtained from

$$m_1 = (1 + r_1)(a_{01}w^* + a_{11}m_1 + \ldots + a_{n1}m_n)$$

$$\ldots \qquad (7.4)$$

$$m_n = (1 + r_n)(a_{0n}w^* + a_{1n}m_1 + \ldots + a_{nn}m_n)$$

and

$$1 = g_1 m_1 + g_2 m_2 + \ldots + g_g m_g \qquad (7.5)$$

where, as indicated above, the market real wage has been assumed equal to the natural real wage w^*.

7. We may note that in equations (7.3) and (7.4) we have expressed both the inputs and the output of each industry at the same market prices, though the inputs are bought at the beginning, and the outputs are sold at the end, of the production cycle. To this it may be objected that, to the extent to which it can be foreseen by the entrepreneurs with sufficient exactness, the appreciation (depreciation) of the product relative to the means of production during the year[9] constitutes a non-accidental element which entrepreneurs would take into account when comparing the prospective rates of profits between different industries.

It does not, however, seem that a consideration of the price changes over the production cycle is necessary at the present stage of the argument. The requirement of the correct foresight necessary to make those price changes relevant will not generally be fulfilled. And economic theory, which cannot be expected to determine actual prices, but only prices corresponding to averages of actual prices, can hardly be expected to determine the actual changes in actual prices, as distinct from providing guidance to the *sign of* those changes. Appreciation or depreciation of the capital stock of each industry relative to its product seem accordingly to be best abstracted from in a first approximation – just as we abstract from, say, the non-uniqueness of the market price in any actual situation of the economy.[10] Corrections can always be made to the conclusions thus reached, should it be likely that the price changes be sufficiently large and correctly foreseen by the entrepreneurs.[11]

8. The numeraire equations (7.2) and (7.5) focus attention on the fact that the problem of the deviation of market from natural prices is a question of the deviation of *relative* market prices from *relative* natural prices. An implication of this relative nature of the deviation of market from natural prices should be noted. By definition, market and natural prices must coincide for the commodity which we use as our standard of value – and which, for the sake of clarity, we may for a moment suppose to be a single commodity, call it A_1 and not the composite commodity. This coincidence does not of course imply that output and effectual demand need coincide for A_1 any more than for any other commodity. For A_1, as for A_2, A_3, etc., an excess, say, of output over effectual demand will imply a *relative* market price which is below the relative natural price. Thus if, for example, all the other commodities happened to exchange among themselves according to their natural prices, the market prices of those commodities would all have to be uniformly higher than their natural prices, as an expression of the excess of output over effectual demand for A_1 (as well as of the corresponding shortage of the output of those commodities relative to the respective effectual demands).[12] This is evident when, as just assumed, the standard of value consists of a single commodity A_1, but the same element will be present when we refer to any composite commodity, like our commodity G above.

THE RISE OF THE MINIMUM PROFIT RATE

9. Let us then begin by considering a commodity A_h, in the production of which the rate of profit is the minimum among the market rates of profits $r_1, r_2, \ldots, r_n$ resulting from equations (7.3).[13] Competition will ensure that capital will flow out of the industry A_h, and its output O_h will decrease, possibly after a time lag.[14] We may accordingly write

$$\frac{dO_h}{dt} < 0, \quad \text{if } r_h \leq r_i \ (i = 1, \ldots, n) \tag{7.6}$$

with the strict inequality holding for at least one couple h, i.

This eventual decrease in the output of the industry (or industries) showing the minimum among the rates of profits in the economy, is the first of the two basic assumptions on which our argument will be based (para. 3 above).

The effect of that decrease in output in raising the market price of A_h,

144

relative to its means of production and wage costs – and therefore its effect in raising the rate of profit (see equations [7.3]) – cannot, however, be taken for granted. We shall see, in paras 16–17 below, that the input–output relations and the corresponding interactions between the market price of a commodity A_h and those of the means of production and wage goods used in its production will constitute no obstacle to the rise in r_h. The obstacles to such a rise which we must consider now are instead those which may conceivably affect the 'demand' in some sense for A_h because of the fall in O_h, and because of any adjustments simultaneously occurring in the outputs and prices of the *other industries*, about which nothing will be postulated in our argument. In fact, if those changes were to lower the 'demand' for A_h *more rapidly* than O_h is lowered, then clearly we could not expect a rise in r_h.

In order to deal with such changes in 'demand' we must first try to provide a sufficiently definite notion of that 'demand'. This we shall do by means of the concept of a 'market effectual demand', as distinct from that of the 'normal effectual demand' referred to so far.

10. By *market effectual demand* D_i^m for commodity A_i ($i = 1, 2, \ldots, n$) we shall mean the quantity of A_i which would be demanded for use[15] in the current 'market' position of the economy, but at a price m_i* of A_i which, unlike m_i, would yield the natural rate of profit $r*$ on the wages and the prices of the means of production estimated at their *market levels*. The price m_i* is therefore given by the equation

$$m_i* = (1 + r*)(a_{oi}w* + a_{1i}m_1 + \ldots a_{ii}m_i * + \ldots + a_{ni}m_n) \quad (7.7)$$

Except, that is, for the price m_i*, which we may for brevity call the *reference price* of A_i in the given market position of the economy, the market effectual demand for A_i will be referred to the actual prices and outputs of that position.[16]

The price m_i* is thus neither the market price m_i nor the natural price p_i. It is needed in order to define the market effectual demand, which in turn provides a common quantitative expression for the effects on the market of A_i of the adjustments in outputs and prices occurring in the whole economy. It will exceed, or fall short of the corresponding market price m_i according as r_i exceeds, or falls short of, $r*$. The price m_i* will on the other hand exceed, or fall short of, the natural price p_i because of the deviation of the market prices of the wage goods and means of production from the corresponding natural prices. The *market* effectual demand D_i^m will thus differ from the corresponding *normal* effectual demand D_i^n, not only because the price m_i* differs from the natural price p_i, but also, and above all, because of the deviations from the respective normal levels of all outputs, and of the prices of the commodities other than A_i. In fact D_i^m depends on the level of those market magnitudes to the extent to which A_i is required as an input for those commodities, or has a relation of complementarity or supplementarity in consumption with them, or, also, to the extent to which those magnitudes affect the distribution of the social income and the part of it spent on A_i.

11. The usefulness of this concept of market effectual demand lies in the fact that the current behaviour of market prices will depend on the 'proportion'[17] which the current output bears to it, rather than on the proportion it bears to the normal effectual demand. The consideration of the latter proportion as governing the current behaviour of market prices and rates of profit, such as we find it in Adam Smith and the other classical authors, appears in fact to have been implicitly founded on the idea that the effects on the demand for A_i of the deviations of the actual outputs and of the prices of the other commodities from their normal levels would tend to compensate each other. That compensation cannot however be assumed. The effects in question may in principle be appreciable enough to raise questions for the tendency of actual prices and outputs to their normal levels, and must accordingly be examined.

12. It would thus seem that the same reasons for which Adam Smith could postulate that when the quantity brought to market of the commodity A_i exceeded its *normal* effectual demand D_i^n, then m^i would fall short of p_i and *vice-versa* (Smith 1776, ch. VII, 49–52) now justify us in assuming that when O_i exceeds the *market* effectual demand D_i^m, then m_i falls short of $\dot{m}_i^*$ (and *vice-versa*).[18] Moreover, as Smith did for the corresponding magnitudes,[19] we may assume that as the proportion O_i/D_i^m rises, the ratio m_i/m_i^* falls (and vice-versa).[20] These conditions for which

$$\text{if } O_i \gtreqless D_i^m, \text{ then } m_t \lesseqgtr m_i^* \ (i = 1, 2, \ldots, n)$$

$$\text{and} \quad \frac{d(m_i/m_i^*)}{dt} \gtreqless 0 \quad \text{according as} \quad \frac{d(O_i/D_i^m)}{dt} \lesseqgtr 0 \qquad (7.8)$$

will constitute the second basic assumption of our argument (par. 3 above)[21] – an assumption the generality of which would not seem to fall short of the corresponding one in the classical economists.

13. Equation (7.7) and assumption (7.8) entail not only that $r_i \lesseqgtr r^*$ as $O_i \gtreqless D_i^m$ but also, and most importantly, that r_i rises as O_i/D_i^m falls. The problem we left at the end of para. 9, about the effect of the fall of the output O_h of commodity A_h on the minimum rate of profit r_h, then becomes the problem of the effect of the fall in O_h on the ratio O_h/D_h^m.

The difficulty is of course that, as O_h changes, D_h^m may also change, as a result, partly, of the change in O_h (for example, to the extent in which A_h is used as an input for itself) and, partly, of what may be happening in the rest of the economy, about which, as we said, nothing is assumed in our argument. We can, however, analyse the circumstances on which the market effectual demand D_h^m depends, and attempt to reach some general conclusions about the sign of the changes which $O_h/D_h{}^m$ will undergo because of the output and price changes mentioned above.

A main cause of the changes in $D_h{}^m$ is likely to be the change in the outputs of the commodities of which A_h is an input.[22] It is particularly because of these changes that we cannot exclude the possibility that, in some circustances, as O_h falls, the market effectual demand $D_h{}^m$ may fall even faster, leading to the result of a rise, and not a fall, in the ratio $O_h/D_h{}^m$; and therefore (by our second basic assumption above) to a further fall in the minimum rate r_h.[23]

However, it seems safe to assume that the market effectual demand for any basic commodity (as we have here assumed all the n commodities to be) has a positive minimum, below which it cannot fall for any length of time. Indeed, no commodity whatsoever could continue to be produced (to be produced, that is, while replacing its means of production) without giving rise directly or indirectly to a positive effectual demand for each of the basic commodities. Now, each of the n commodities in the economy will require different quantities of A_h per worker for its integrated production.[24] A *minimum market effectual demand* for A_h may accordingly be assumed to exist in the given economy, which can be no smaller than the amount of it which would be demanded if the net product of the economy (the size of which remains constant in terms of the total labour employed: above, para. 5) consisted only of the commodity requiring the minimum such amount of A_h. The market effectual demand for A_h could not indeed fall below that minimum for any length of time, unless the economy were on the way to extinction. The same minimum level of $D_h{}^m$ will evidently be there if the fall in that variable were to be the result of adjustments causing distributive changes or changes in prices and outputs for commodities which are complements or supplements of A_h.

It seems therefore possible to conclude that as O_h falls and approaches that minimum level of $D_h{}^m$, then, if not before, it will not be possible for $D_h{}^m$ to fall faster than O_h, and $O_h/D_h{}^m$ will have to *rise* together with r_h.[25]

14. Our conclusion as to the fall of $O_h/D_h{}^m$ when r_h is the minimum profit rate concerns an *eventual* fall of that ratio and rise in r_h. We shall presently simplify our argument by provisionally assuming that O_h/D_h falls (r_h rises), not only eventually, but whenever the condition that r_h is the minimum rate of profit is verified – thus in fact assuming a *monotonic* rise in the minimum profit rate in the economy (our third and last assumption: para. 3 above). In order to justify that assumption it is however necessary to consider first a complication which, were it not for the sake of a simpler exposition, we would have introduced before. In fact, our second basic assumption (7.8) should, strictly speaking, have been formulated in terms of the quantity supplied S_i of the commodity A_i, and not directly in terms of

its output O_i; the difference $(O_i - S_i)$ being given by the algebraic accumulation of *inventories* of A_i. Indeed, a sufficiently large running down of inventories could make the supply exceed the output sufficiently to render the condition $O_i{<}D_i^m$ compatible with $m_i{<}m_i^*$, and also to make a fall of O_i/D_i^m compatible with *a fall* of r_i.

However, it should be evident that any effect of the decumulation of inventories in making S_h/D_h^m rise, and the minimum rate r_h fall, in spite of the fall of O_h/D_h^m, could be only *temporary*. Any such running down of inventories could not proceed indefinitely, because the inventories would evidently be limited. Above all, by lowering the price of the commodity, any such liquidation of inventories would enhance the fall in the output O_h which, in the end, is bound to dominate the behaviour of the ratio S_h/D_h^m, and therefore the behaviour of r_h. The same applies in the opposite case, an accumulation of inventories of A_i, which would prevent a fall of r_i despite the rise of O_i/D_i^m. Such an accumulation could proceed only for a limited time (the costs of carrying such inventories would see to that) and it would enhance the rise of O_i/D_i^m and, therefore, the eventual rise of S_i/D_i^m.

Now, this temporary character of the effects of the building up or running down of inventories is in evident contrast with the fact that any tendency to the natural position of the economy cannot but be a long-period tendency, implying as it does changes in the size of plant and in the number of firms in the industry. And, with respect to any such long-period tendencies, build-ups or run-downs of inventories are likely to be mere episodes. This observation is strengthened by the consideration that a liquidation of inventories, which could make the minimum rate of profit r_h fall further, is rendered unlikely or, in any case, likely to be very short-lived, by the fact that it would occur for a commodity the value of which, relative to that of the mass of other commodities, could be expected to rise in the longer run. We shall, however, return to the question below (para. 29), when discussing the implications of abandoning the assumption about the monotonic rise of r_h to which we must now proceed, and by which we shall provisionally rule out the above possible influence of inventories (thus making it unnecessary to change the form in which we wrote condition (7.8)).

15. In fact the conclusions of para. 13 above on the *temporary* nature of any rise of O_h/D_h^m and those just reached in para. 14 about the similar nature of any liquidation of inventories, preventing the rise of m_h/m_h^* despite the fall of O_h/D_h^m, allow us now to simplify the exposition by adding the third assumption mentioned above. This third, provisional, assumption is that the rise in the minimum rate of profit will be verified whenever the rate of profit in question happens to be the minimum, so that the eventual rise of the minimum rate which we demonstrated at

para. 13 becomes, as we stated, a monotonic rise, though the commodity or commodities in the production of which that minimum rate can be obtained may be changing in the process.[26]

We may now see that this third provisional assumption entails a fall of O_i *fast enough* to overcome any effect of a fall of $D_h{}^m$ in raising the ratio $O_h/D_h{}^m$.[27] Moreover, it allows us to concentrate attention on long-run trends by excluding the possibility that a liquidation of inventories of the commodity may lower r_h despite the fall in $O_h/D_h{}^m$. As already mentioned, the consequence of dropping this third assumption will be discussed in para. 20 below.

16. What we must now consider is how the rise of r_h may in fact occur, without meeting any obstacles in the necessary relations between profit rates and prices which are established by the existing methods of production. The rise in the market rate of profit r_h will, as we said, require a rise of m_h, *relative* to the market prices of the means of production proper, *or to* wages, *or to both.*

1 A rise in the rate of profit r_h through a rise in the price m_h relative to the prices of the *means of production* of course requires that the production of A_h should use means of production other than A_h itself. That will always be the case because A_h is not the only commodity in the economy (no problem of deviations of market from natural prices would otherwise arise) and because, all commodities being basic (para. 5 above), at least one other commodity must appear among the means of production of A_h.[28]
2 A rise in r_h through a rise in m_h relative to wage costs is on the other hand always possible, except when A_h happens either to be the only wage good, or to be produced without any direct labour,[29] in which case the rise in r_h can occur only through route (1).

Which of the two routes, (1) or (2), the rise of r_h will mainly or exclusively take will depend partly on the technical conditions of production, and partly on what is happening to the prices of the other commodities about which, as already remarked, nothing is postulated here. (It may be interesting to note at this point how, because of our choice of the composite wage commodity as the numeraire, and of our assumption of a constant w, it is only when the rise in r_h involves a rise in m_h relative to wage costs that m_h will experience an *absolute* rise as the output of O_h falls. If the rise in r_h is exclusively due to a rise in m_h relative to its means of production, m_h will not rise, and may indeed fall as the profitability of its production rises).

17. Since, however, A_h enters directly or indirectly into the production of commodities which in turn enter directly into the production of A_h as means of production or as wage goods, the question may be posed as to whether the effect on the other industries of the rise in the relative market

price m_h of A_h may not pose some obstacle or constraint to that very relative rise in m_h and, therefore, some obstacle or constraint to the rise in r_h. The relative rise in m_h will in fact lower the rate of profit in the industries using A_h as a means of production, and therefore, were that profit rate to fall below the natural rate, it will set in motion forces tending to raise it again through rises in the relative market prices of the respective commodities. The question then arises of whether the impact of those secondary rises on the costs of A_h, may not conceivably annul the initial rise in m_h, relative to the means of production and wage goods, thus annulling the initial rise of r_h.

The answer to this question lies in the fact that the rate of profit r_h which is rising is the *minimum* in the economy and we are therefore sure that that rise cannot force any profit rate elsewere in the economy below itself. As soon as any rate of profit fell as far as r_h *because of the rise of the latter*, the process we are envisaging would raise it back jointly with r_h (cf. below, paras 20 ff). In fact the rise in r_h will not have to proceed beyond r^* where, as we shall presently see (para 19 below), all other rates will also have to be equal to r^*. Indeed, in principle, the rise in r_h could even occur while ensuring that no rate of profit ever falls below r^* elsewhere in the economy.[30]

We may thus conclude that the rise in r_h is entirely compatible with the possible secondary effects it may have on the market prices of its direct and indirect means of production. The convergence to natural prices could be prevented by a direct or indirect effect on the production expenses of A_h of its own relative price rise, if and only if some industries could 'resist' a fall in their profit rates at levels of those rates higher than the natural rate of profit r^*. The fact that such cannot be the case is at one with the assumption of free competition and the associated tendency towards a uniform rate of profit.[31]

18. As r_h continues to rise by finite increments, it will finally have to reach the level of one of the rates of profit obtaining in some other industry, say that for A_{h+1}. There are then two possibilities: either (1) r_{h+1} is already r^*, or (2) it is *less* than r^*. To see why $r_{h+1} > r^*$ is not possible, and in order to discuss possibilities (1) and (2) we shall, however, need first some propositions, to which we must now proceed.

THREE PROPOSITIONS ON MARKET AND NATURAL PRICES*

19. Of the three propositions to be demonstrated in this section, Proposition I and its strict complement, Proposition II, appear here only as a basis for Proposition III, which is the one central to our argument.

Proposition I *Whatever the deviations of market from natural prices, the production of a commodity A_m for which the ratio M_m of the market to the* *natural price is the minimum in the economy, will always yield a rate of profit which is below the natural rate.*

Let us indicate by $M_1, M_2 \ldots M_n$ the ratios of market to natural prices of the n commodities

$$M_1 = \frac{m_1}{p_1}, \qquad M_2 = \frac{m_2}{p_2}, \qquad \ldots, \qquad M_n = \frac{m_n}{p_n}$$

From the numeraire equations (7.2) and (7.5) above it follows that either $M_1 = M_2 = \ldots = M_g = 1$ or, if they differ, some of them will be larger and some smaller than unity. It may however be noted that the case $M_1 = M_2 = \ldots = M_g = 1$, does not entail $M_{g+1} = \ldots = M_n = 1$, and does not therefore coincide with the 'natural position' of the economy.

It follows that the minimum such ratio, let it be the ratio M_m for the commodity A_m, need not be less than unity. It is true that if the M's of the wage goods are not all equal, then, as we saw, the M of some wage goods will have to be smaller than unity, and therefore $M_m < 1$. We cannot, however, rule out the above possibility that the M's for the wage goods be all equal, and therefore equal to unity, with commodities other than the wage goods having different M's, none of which happens to be less than unity. In that case the minimum M would be unity. (The case would be the one we already noticed in the example of para. 8, of an excess in the output over the effectual demand for the numeraire commodity which will have to show in a general excess of the market prices of all the other commodities relative to their natural prices.)

In order to simplify the notation, let us now indicate by a the level of the minimum ratio M_m between market and natural prices, pertaining to the commodity A_m, so that we can write:

$$a \leq 1 \tag{7.9}$$

Let us also indicate by b the analogous ratio as it applies to the means of production of A_m, taken as a single composite commodity, i.e.

$$b = \frac{\sum\limits_{i=1}^{n} a_{im} m_i}{\sum\limits_{i=1}^{n} a_{im} p_i} = \frac{\sum\limits_{l=1}^{M} (a_{im} p_i) M_i}{\sum\limits_{l=1}^{M} (a_{im} p_i)}$$

We can of course be sure that b, which is the above average of the M's of the means of production of A_m, with the positive weights shown, will not be less than M_m. We cannot, however, immediately exclude the possibility $a = b$, i.e. that, for the chosen commodity, having the minimum ratio M_m between market price and natural price, the direct means of production of the commodity may all have the *same* minimum ratio M_m. In that case, the commodity – call it A_1, one, then, of the several sharing the same minimum

151

ratio M_m – would not yet be the commodity A_m we are looking for, which will instead show

$$a < b \qquad (7.10)$$

However, we shall then be bound to find A_m among those means of production of A_1, or (should also their own means of production all exhibit the minimum ration M_m), among the means of production of those means of production etc., within a number of steps which cannot exceed $(n-1)$. This is so because, by hypothesis, *some* commodity exists with an M larger than the minimum, and since all commodities are basic (para 6), such a commodity will enter (indirectly) into the production of A_1.

As for the maximum number of steps $(n-1)$ within which A_m must appear among the means of production of A_1 we know that, until all direct and indirect means of production have appeared through the several stages of the 'reduction to labour' (Sraffa 1960: 34 ff) of A_1, at least one *new* means of production other than A_1 must appear at each stage of that reduction: otherwise no new means of production could ever appear at any later stage of the same process. Thus the number of stages we may have before all means of production have appeared cannot exceed $(n-1)$.

We may now choose as physical unit of the commodity A_m thus traced that quantity of it which is of unit value when estimated at its natural price for the given r^*. Let v be the proportion of that value taken up by the (circulating) means of production, when estimated at their *natural prices*, so that bv will be the same proportion when estimated at *market price* of the means of production, and let u be the analogous proportion taken up by wages. We can then write the market rate of profit obtainable in producing A_m as:

$$r_m = \frac{a - (u + bv)}{u + bv} = \frac{a}{u + bv} - 1 \qquad (7.11a)$$

and the natural rate of profit as:

$$r^* = \frac{1 - (u + v)}{u + v} = \frac{1}{u + v} - 1 \qquad (7.11b)$$

(where, as we saw in para. 6 above, we assume wages to be at their natural level in dealing with the market prices of equation (7.11a)).

We must now show that under conditions (7.9) and (7.10), $r_m < r^*$, i.e. that

$$\frac{a}{u + bv} - 1 < \frac{1}{u + v} - 1$$

Since both the (7.11) expressions are positive (*or*, if $r_m < 0$, the positivity of r^* will make the demonstration of $r_m < r^*$ unnecessary) the above can be written as

$$\frac{a}{u + bv} < \frac{1}{u + v} \tag{7.12}$$

Since $(u + v)$ and $(u + bv)$ are both positive, inequality (7.12) simplifies into

$$u(1 - a) > v(a - b) \tag{7.12a}$$

which is always true, since $v(a - b) < 0$ by condition (7.10), whereas $u(1 - a) \geq 0$, by condition (7.9).

As we wanted to show, the production of a commodity A_m having the minimum M will always give a rate of profit below r^*.

Proposition II *The commodity, or one of the commodities, having M at its maximum level will necessarily have r>r*.*

This proposition can be demonstrated by a procedure strictly analogous to the one we followed for Proposition I.[32]

Proposition III *When none of the market rates of profit of the n industries lies below the natural rate, then all the rates of profits must be equal. They are therefore equal to the natural rate, and we are in the natural position of the economy with market prices equal to natural prices. The same holds true when none of the n rates of profits lies above the natural rate r*.*

In fact if, in the situation envisaged in Proposition III, the M's were not all the same, then by Proposition I above we would be able to single out a commodity A_m such that its production would yield a rate of profit $r_m < r^*$. Since by hypothesis no profit rate lies below r^*, we must conclude that the M's must all be the same. By the numeraire equations (7.1) and (7.2), they must then be all equal to unity. We are therefore in the natural position of the economy, with market prices equal to the natural prices, and with a uniform rate of profit r^*.

Strictly analogous reasoning will prove the proposition in the case in which none of the n rates of profit lies *above* the natural rate.

THE CONVERGENCE TO THE NATURAL POSITION

20. We can now return to the level $r_{(h+1)}$ which the rate of profit r_h has reached in its rise, and to the two cases $r_{(h+1)} = r^*$, and $r_{(h+1)} < r^*$, mentioned at the beginning of para. 18 above. Let us begin with the case $r_{(h+1)} = r^*$.

The market rate r_h was the minimum r in the economy, and, by the nature of the process envisaged above, it must have remained so. If $r_h = r_{(h+1)} = r^*$, then, by Proposition III, convergence to the natural position has been achieved.

21. We may proceed to the second case, where the level $r_{(h+1)}$ at which r_h meets the rate of profit of the industry of $A_{(h+1)}$ is below r^*. We can then envisage the continuation of the fall of O_h and rise of r_h, this time jointly

with a fall of O_{h+1}, and the rise of $r_{(h+1)}$, which is consequent upon that fall for the same reasons we saw in paras 9–18 for r_h. For the sake of simplicity, and without loss of generality, we may assume that the falls of O_h and O_{h+1} are such as to make the two rates of profit rise in step,[33] and we shall indicate by H the group of commodities (including A_h and $A_{(h+1)}$, so far) in the production of which the rate of profit is thus made to rise uniformly.

Everything that we said in paras 16–17 above, concerning the rise of r_h and its possibility, can now be repeated, with the slight reformulations made necessary by the fact that the rate of profit which is rising is the rate r_H common to the group of commodities H, and not that of the single commodity A_h. Thus, similarly to what we saw in para. 16, the possibility of a rise in r_H obtains because of one, or the other, or both of the following circumstances:

1 For at least one of the commodities H, one or more of its means of production must be commodities other than those of group H. This must be so because all commodities are basic and enter therefore, directly or indirectly, into the production of each of the commodities H (para. 3 above): evidently none of the commodities other than H could enter even indirectly into those of group H, if at least one of them did not enter *directly* into the production of at least one of commodities H (thus making it possible for all the commodities outside group H to enter *indirectly* into all those of the group: cf. the same point in the demonstration of Proposition I, para. 19 above). As a result a rise in the rate of profit r_H common to group H can always be achieved by raising the market prices of commodities H sufficiently, relative to those of the other commodities.

2 There must exist wage costs for the production of commodities H and, therefore, the possibility of raising the prices of commodities H relative to those wage costs. This will be so unless all wage goods are already included in group H, or no commodity of group H required any direct labour to be produced.

22. As in the case of the single commodity A_h, the further question then arises of whether the effect on the profits and prices of the remaining industries of the rise in the rate of profit obtained in the production of commodities H may not in fact ultimately undo that rise. The answer to this question is the same we gave in para. 17 above: no such obstacle can be met by the rise here required in r_H, which needs to proceed only up to r^* and is therefore compatible with any rise in the market price of the remaining commodities which may be necessary in order to keep the rate of profit obtainable in their production from falling below r_h or, indeed, below r^*.

23. It is now easy to see our way forward to the conclusion of the argument. As $r_h = r_{(h+1)}$ rise in step with each other, they will sooner or later

meet a third profit rate $r_{(h+2)}$ and there will again be two cases. Either we shall have $r_H = r_h = r_{(h+1)} = r_{(h+2)} = r^*$ and then, by Proposition III, the natural position would have been reached. Or, alternatively, $r_H < r^*$ and then, as commodity $A_{(h+2)}$ joins group H, all three can rise together in exactly the same way we saw above, until they meet a fourth rate of profit $r_{(h+3)} \leq r^*$, and so on until the rate of profit r_H common to the thus enlarging group of commodities H finally reaches r^* and hence, by Proposition III, all the remaining rates of profit. In a finite number of steps (that of the commodities joining the group H, which obviously cannot be larger than the number n of commodities) this process will lead to the normal position of the economy.

24. The fact that nothing is here being postulated about the behaviour of outputs and prices outside the industries H whose profit rate is being increased may, however, seem to raise a difficulty, with which we should deal before concluding our argument.

We have assumed a monotonic fall in the output of A_h and more generally of the commodities of group H, in parallel with a monotonic rise in the profit rate r_h obtainable from their production. We cannot, however, exclude the possibility that, in the initial situation, the market effectual demand for A_h – whose proportion to output, as we saw, plausibly governs the sign of the deviation of the market, from the natural, profit rate (para. 12 above) – be considerably below the normal effectual demand so that the output of A_h, while larger than the 'market' demand, thus explaining $r_h < r^*$ – will be below the 'normal' demand. In such a case the convergence towards the natural position will ultimately require some *rise* in the output of A_h (and thus be incompatible with a monotonic fall), and therefore also, presumably, that r_h at some stage rises above the minimum and possibly beyond r^* before falling back to it. In that special case we can see the *necessity* of a non-monotonic movement of the output and rate of profit for one of the commodities H, but of course the possibility of such non-monotonic movements is always there, as a profit rate may, so to speak, 'shoot' beyond r^* (*e.g.* as a result of a particularly rapid fall in the relative market price of its means of production) before getting back to it or to r^*.

However, the phenomenon we have then to envisage is entirely compatible with the process of convergence we have discussed. To see that this is so, it is sufficient to realize that in such cases r_h will have had to meet some other profit rate $r_{(h+1)} \leq r^*$ before it could 'shoot beyond' r^*. Its place in the progressive rise towards r^* will then have been taken by $r_{(h+1)}$. In fact our procedure only requires that none of the rates of profit of commodities H, which we accompany in their progressive rise, ever falls back below the uniform level of the group. Some rates of profits may be allowed to go ahead and even 'shoot' above r^*.

25. We may now finally drop the assumption that, during the process

155

envisaged above, the real wage is, and stays, at its natural level w^*, and suppose instead that we have a variable 'market' real wage w.

However, the tendency of w towards w^* is a different question from that with which we have been concerned here, and has to do with the forces which allow w to be treated as an independent variable in classical theory. This difference in the forces involved is what has induced us to separate the two questions by supposing that the wage is and remains at its natural level during the adjustment in prices and profit rates envisaged above.

What can be of concern to us here is therefore only whether the two tendencies, that of the real wage towards its natural level, and that of the profit rate and relative prices towards their own natural levels, may not interfere with each other. From what can be seen from the side of the latter tendency – without entering, that is, into the way in which the market real wage will gravitate towards its natural level – there do not seem to be grounds for any such interference.

One could in fact argue as follows. At any given level of the market real wage w', the tendency to the general rate of profit r' corresponding to that wage, and the connected tendency to the corresponding series of $(m\text{-}1)$ natural relative prices, will occur in the way discussed in this chapter. This should ensure that, as the general rate of profit r' itself changes by effect of the movement of the market wage w' towards the natural wage w^*, the former tendency will translate into a tendency towards the natural rate of profit r^*.[34]

SOME CONCLUSIONS

26. We may now try to pull together the threads of our argument and assess the meaning of our results. The argument in this chapter has been designed to examine the obstacles which the market prices of the means of production have been thought to raise against a tendency towards the normal position of the economy. The chapter has thus been focused on showing that a fall in the output of the industries yielding the minimum rate of profit is sufficient to bring the economy to its normal or natural position, irrespective of what the market prices of their means of production may initially have been or may have become in the course of the adjustment.

27. The results thus reached may, however, extend beyond the non-existence of those particular obstacles. This may be seen by taking now an overall view of the premises and assumptions used for those results.

Our argument has first of all been founded on the classical postulate of given 'normal' effectual demands. This postulate, which follows from the basic premises of the classical approach (para. 4 above), has in fact been frequently overlooked in recent literature purporting to deal with the classical tendency of actual or market prices towards prices of production.

This is a result of the difficulty many authors seem to have in coming to terms with the classical determination of outputs and its independence from the demand and supply forces of present-day mainstream theory. However, overlooking this classical postulate has imposed on that literature special assumptions about normal outputs like that of steady growth.[37] This has in turn favoured the choice of hypotheses about the behaviour of actual prices and outputs, the arbitrary character of which seems to have escaped attention, and to have led to unwarranted conclusions about an instability in the prices of production.

Cases in point have been some two-commodity models where the normal position of the economy has been taken to be that of uniform growth. Thus in Nikaido, 1985 (cf. also Lippi 1990 discussed in the Appendix to this paper) it has been assumed that, with real wages included among the means of production, the outputs of the given initial 'market position', whatever they might happen to be, will be totally absorbed by the production for the following period, except for a fixed consumption out of profits. The coefficients of production of the two commodities being given, that assumption will fully determine the outputs of the following period.

Then, if we assume that the production of commodity A_2 requires itself in a proportion to A_1 higher than the production of A_1 does, and, for the sake of simplicity, we further assume a zero consumption out of profits – then, an initial excess in the supply of A_2 relative to the quantity required for uniform growth would result in an even larger excess supply in the following period. For exactly the same reason the excess supply would be still larger the period after, and so on up to the point at which the proportion O_2/O_1 will exceed the maximum in which the two commodities can be absorbed (by assumption, that in which they are required for producing A_2). Hence Nikaido's conclusion that the 'natural position' is unstable.

It seems, however, to have escaped notice that such a conclusion would require the relative price of A_2 to be such as to provoke the above increase in the relative output of A_2, *i.e.* that it should lie *above* the natural level, and this should occur when the output of A_2 *exceeds* its 'market' effectual demand (which is here equal to the normal effectual demand, and bears therefore the proportion of uniform growth to the similar demand for A_1)[36] – contrary to what any competitive bidding would entail. It appears then that, when the effects of competitive bidding are correctly taken into consideration, that conclusion of instability can be neatly reversed. A relative price of A_2 below its natural level because of the initial excess supply will result in a progressive fall in the proportion in which A_2 and A_1 are produced towards the single proportion of the natural position of steady growth assumed there, and in that position any excess supply will disappear.[37]

The above conclusion about the stability of the position of steady growth of that model will be equally true when the two commodities are

157

'hetero-intensive'. Under either assumption about the coefficients of production, the excess in the supply of A_2, relative to the quantity to be used as
input for the production of the subsequent period, will of course result in
some accumulation of inventories to be liquidated later, just as the symme-
trical shortage of A_1 will have to be made good from inventories. Indeed, by
the very fact that a market position *is not* a normal position of the economy,
the kind of market clearing occurring in the former will generally involve
some building up or running down of inventories of the commodity.[38]

28. Let us proceed now to the assumptions we made in our analysis. If
we leave aside the assumptions of paras 4–8 regarding the kind of economy
with which we have been concerned, similar to those generally made in
dealing with our topic, our conclusions have been founded on the two basic
assumptions we mentioned in para. 4 above. The first has been the decrease
in the output of the industry (industries) yielding the minimum rate of profit
in the economy (para. 9). The second has been that a fall in the proportion
which the output of the commodity A_i bears to its 'market' effectual
demand, will raise its market price relative to the 'reference price' m_i^*,
yielding the natural rate of profit in the given 'market position' of the
economy, and *vice versa* (para. 12).

The generality of the first of these two basic assumptions would not
appear to be in doubt, since it is based on the tendency of investors to
maximize their returns.[39] The second assumption, on the other hand, is a
generalization of Adam Smith's postulate about the market price exceeding
the natural price when the output of the commodity falls short of the
normal effectual demand, and vice versa.[40] It seems therefore to be no
more disputable than Adam Smith's own postulate.

29. A third assumption of a more restrictive nature has, however, also been
used by us. The assumption is that, instead of *eventually* rising as demonstrated in paras 13–14 above, the minimum rate of profit will rise straight
away. As we noted (para. 15 above), that need not necessarily be true
because the ratio of the output of the commodity to its market effectual
demand may temporarily rise rather than fall. Also, the liquidation of inventories of some commodity of group H may temporarily depress the rate of
profit in the corresponding industry, even when O_h/D_h^m is falling. In these
cases the minimum rate of profit of the economy could temporarily fall.

The restrictions which this third assumption has imposed on our argument may be summed up by saying that it has excluded the possibility of
any but convergent oscillations in reaching the normal position of the
economy. Oscillations of constant or even widening amplitude in the profit
rate of some industries had not in fact been ruled out by our demonstration
of the *ultimate* rise of a profit rate which happens to be the minimum in the
economy. They have been instead assumed away by the monotonic rise in
the minimum rate of profit of the economy of our third assumption.

Before considering in the light of our previous analysis the sources and likelihood of any such constant or widening oscillations, we must, however, remind ourselves of a possible ambiguity concerning them, and make clear the nature of those oscillations which are the only ones we need to be concerned with. The oscillations around the normal position which can always be expected to occur in the actual economy will generally arise from the continuous occurrence of *exogenous* accidental circumstances. However, by their nature, those oscillations are excluded from an analysis of the tendency of the economy towards its normal position. If the latter tendency can be shown to exist – given an arbitrary initial deviation from that position, and in the absence of further disturbances – then there will be grounds for concluding that the continuously occurring exogenous disturbances will tend to compensate for each other over a sufficiently long-period of time, with the result that the market price will gravitate *around*, rather than *towards*, the natural price.

The only oscillations relevant to the analysis of the tendency to natural prices are therefore those of a different, endogenous kind, and that is the kind of those assumed away by our third assumption. However, it appears that the previous argument by which we could prove, in paras 13–14 above, the *eventual* rise of the minimum rate of profit, had in fact left little room for any but convergent oscillations.

Indeed there seem to be only two possible sources of those constant or divergent oscillations which have been assumed away by our third assumption. The first is the time lag between production decisions and realized outputs, for which O_h may temporarily rise even when A_h is a minimum-profit commodity (cf. condition (7.6) above, about an *eventual* fall of O_h): we have implicitly excluded the effect of that lag to the extent that the monotonic rise of r_h entails a corresponding fall of O_h/D_h^m and therefore, presumably, of O_h whenever A_h is a minimum-profit commodity. Now by assuming away those effects we have also assumed away the possibility of phenomena like the 'hog cycle'. The possibility is that for which in some industries a low rate of profit may cause decisions to decrease output which, when put into effect, will reveal themselves to have been excessive, thus causing a sharp rise in the profit rate above the natural level and then, conceivably, a rise in output well beyond its normal level and thus a widening cycle.

The second conceivable source of constant or widening oscillations of individual profit rates, ruled out by our third assumption, is inventory cycles of the commodity concerned. Although for the reasons we saw in para. 14 we cannot imagine a liquidation of inventories of the commodity to cause an indefinite continuous fall in the rate of profit yielded by its production, yet the rise in relative price (and profit rate and) following upon the end of that liquidation might provoke as a reaction a new liquidation of inventories, bringing the profit rate even below the minimum level previously reached, and so on and so forth.

However, with respect to this second source of oscillations, the reasons we saw at para. 14 above make it difficult to envisage the possibility of such widening inventory cycles. It would in fact seem that the effect of those cycles on the prospective rate of profits obtainable by producing the commodity would tend to be confined within narrow limits by the analogous, opposite effects on that rate due to the changes in output, and hence in supply, caused by those very cycles. Those cycles would also tend to be narrowly confined by the fact that, as the rate moves away from the normal level, the inventory change would run counter to plausible expectations about the longer-run behaviour of the relative price of the commodity.

On the other hand, with respect to the first possible source of divergent oscillations, the lag between production decisions and realized outputs relevant to the 'hog cycle' phenomenon will chiefly concern the short-period decisions regarding the outputs obtainable from existing plant (we are of course abandoning here our assumption about all capital being circulating capital). The long-period decisions concerning the size of plant will presumably have time to be revised as the effects on the relative price of the commodity of the short-period decisions gradually reveal themselves.

It seems, therefore, that when the demonstrated ultimate rise in the rate of profit (13–14 per cent) has narrowed the possibilities of instability in the prices of production down to the above cases of divergent oscillations, the conclusions about any such instability would have to be negative. Even leaving aside the considerations above those possibilities of non-convergent endogenous oscillations would have to rest on the possibility of indefinitely repeating, on the same, or an increasing, scale, the errors made possible either by the lags between output decisions and realized outputs, or by changes in inventories of the commodity.[41] Until convincing examples are brought to the fore to the contrary, it would seem legitimate to suppose that in such cases individuals could and would learn from their experience and that any such endogenous oscillations in the markets of individual commodities[42] would tend to decrease in amplitude.[43]

30. A feature of the argument put forward in this chapter may finally be commented on. Following the method of the classical economists, we have attempted to confine the assumptions on which our argument has rested to the *signs* of the changes in the relevant variables (a *fall* in the least profitable output O_h, a *rise* in r_h as O_h/D_h^m *falls*, etc.). The importance of this lies, in the first place, in that the simplicity of those assumptions allows direct comparison with, and hence confirmation (or lack of it) by, observation. No less important, these assumptions are by their nature quite general, since nothing is there postulated about the *size* of the rates of change over time of outputs and prices.[44] They render possible, therefore, equally general con-

clusions. This generality and possibility of conclusive comparisons with observation are on the other hand essential for a problem as central as the tendency to the positions of the economy determined by the theory, on which tendency the validation of classical theory, as of any conceivable alternative theory, does ultimately depend.

The fact that – once some essential premises of classical theory, like that of given effectual demand, are correctly understood and taken into account – results appear to be obtainable by means of such simpler and more general assumptions, confined to the signs of the changes, seems, on the other hand, to confirm the basic correctness of the classical method.

NOTES

1 I. Steedman describes Adam Smith as stating that when 'the market price is *e.g.* below the natural price, then the wage *and/or* the profit rate *and/or* the rent paid in the industry must fall below their natural rates' (1984: 124, our emphasis). Steedman admits there that Smith leaves open the *possibility* of *e.g.* a market price below the natural price, while the profit rate is above the natural level (rent and/or wage rates bearing the brunt of both the lower price and the higher profits). He argues however that Smith's analysis ignored the means of production and therefore the question he is specifically addressing (Steedman 1984: 125). In this connection it should, however, be remembered that Smith thought that the value of the means of production could be reduced to wages, profit and rents (Smith 1910: ch.VI, 44–5). Therefore when he refers to wages, profit and rents, he could be interpreted as referring to those accruing in the *indirect*, as well as in the direct, production of the commodity in question, and thus, in fact, to the value of the means of production.

2 See *e.g.* 'It is only in consequence of variations [in market prices] that capital is apportioned precisely . . . to the production of the different commodities. *With the rise or fall of prices, profits are elevated above, or depressed below their general level*' (Ricardo 1951: 88, our emphasis).

3 Cf. *e.g.* 'If a "low" market price in a particular industry can be associated with a "high" profit rate . . . then it is clear that one cannot immediately assume that the "low" market price will tend to gravitate towards the corresponding natural price' (Steedman 1984: 134; see similar passages at pp. 23–4, 127).

4 See Proposition I, para. 19 below. Assuming, as Steedman assumes in the relevant part of (1984), that all commodities are *basic*, each commodity, including that with the minimum ratio of market to natural price must enter directly or indirectly the production of A_1.

5 Cf. Smith (1776. I, 73). Our definition of the effectual demand of a commodity modifies that of Adam Smith by specifying that demand also in relation to the natural prices of the other commodities and to the normal outputs of all commodities. The reason for qualifying the effectual demands in the text as 'normal', will be seen in paras 10–11 below.

6 Cf. *e.g.* the argument in Nikaido (1985), which we shall consider in para. 27 below.

7 Sraffa (1960), p. 8.

8 Since the economy is not in its normal position, frictions of several kinds render free competition compatible with different *actual* prices being paid for the same commodity in different transactions occurring at the same instant of

time. We shall, however, assume, as is generally done, that these different prices can be adequately represented at any given instant of time by a single 'market' price.

9 In the case of 'continuous production' the same problem arises in the form of a change in the value of the output relative to the aggregate of intermediate products (capital) required to achieve simultaneity of the input and output flows, during the period for which those flows are reckoned. (For the notion of continuous production cf. Garegnani 1990: 25–6)

10 See note 8 above.

11 *E.g.* we may note how forecasts that the relative market price of a commodity in the production of which a low rate of profit can be obtained will rise over time, and *vice versa*, would decrease somewhat the divergence between the market profit rates.

12 See the assumption of constant aggregate demand made in para. 5 above.

13 In case more than one industry happened to have that same minimum level, what we shall say should be referred to that group of industries, in the form which we shall see in paras 20-5 below.

14 Cf. para. 29 below for the implications of the lag between production decisions and realized outputs. Cf. also the Appendix to this paper, for a discussion of what would have to be understood by changes in the output O_i, when we abandon the assumption that all capital is circulating capital, and accordingly introduce the distinction between outputs changing merely because of a change in the degree of utilization of production capacity and outputs which change together with a corresponding change in the level of capacity.

15 We exclude, that is, from market effectual demand any quantity demanded for changes in inventories.

16 The present concept is close to that of 'actual' effectual demand put forward in Ciccone (1990: 4–5). Though intended to take into account the effects of accidental circumstances on demand, that concept is, however, still defined for a price of the commodity equal to the natural price.

17 For the characteristic classical concept of 'proportion' between demand and supply cf. Garegnani (1987: 565).

18 It may be noted that even when A_i happens to be the numeraire, and therefore $m_i \equiv 1$, m_i^* will not generally be unity. Also in that case, therefore, m_i/m_i^* can change as O_i/D_i^m changes.

19 Smith writes: 'The market price will rise more or less above the natural price according as . . . the greatness of the deficiency [of the quantity brought to market] . . . happens to animate more or less the eagerness of competition' and a similar passage can be found to explain how 'the market price will sink more or less below the natural price' (Smith 1910: 50).

20 See the Appendix below on the conflict sometimes claimed between the classical assumption of a *rise* in the market price in situations in which supply exceeds the effectual demand and the assumption in modern theory of a *fall* in price in the presence of excess supply.

21 This second basic assumption should be interpreted as referring to quantities *supplied* inclusive, that is, of any (algebraic) de-cumulation of inventories of the commodity, rather then to outputs only. The presentation chosen here has been preferred for reasons of exposition and is justified by the assumption about inventories which we shall discuss in para. 14 below and which will be used for our third general assumption of para. 15.

22 Only changes in the outputs for which the commodity A_h is a *direct* input need be considered, since the case in which A_h is an *indirect* input for a third

commodity will be taken care of by the changes in the output of the commodity A_j, which, while entering the production of that third commodity, requires A_h as a *direct* input.

23 *E.g.* if A_h is used directly for the production of itself, an element of D_h^m will be proportional to the O_h of the subsequent year, and will therefore fall faster then O_h, if O_h falls at an increasing speed. It is then possible that O_h/D_h^m will rise as O_h falls.

24 For this notion of integrated production cf. Sraffa's concept of a sub-system producing a net physical quantity of the specified commodity (Sraffa 1960: 90).

25 For O_h/D_h^m to fall sufficiently there will be no need for O_h to fall below the minimum level indicated in the text. By assumption, O_h/D_h^m is initially higher than unity, and it must remain so, so long as the minimum rate r_h remains below the natural level r^*. When, on the other hand, O_h/D_h^m has become unity, thus indicating that the minimum rate r_h has become equal to r^*, the natural position of the economy will have been achieved (as we shall see in para. 19 below) and market effectual demand will coincide with normal effectual demand.

26 A less restrictive assumption would in fact seem sufficient for our argument in this chapter: it is that, should the minimum rate of profit of the economy ever (temporarily) fall, each minimum level then reached would lie above the previous one. Since in either form the assumption would have been dropped in the last section of the chapter, the form given in the text has been preferred because it allows of a simpler exposition. In either formulation the assumption is of course taken to be verified under that condition of absence of new disturbances which constitutes the necessary premise of the analysis of the tendency of market prices to natural or normal prices (cf. para. 29 below).

27 It may seem that this third assumption is in conflict with what we said in note 23 about the way in which increasing speed in the fall of O_h may cause a rise in the ratio O_h/D_h^m, when A_h is a means of production of itself. However, the present assumption concerns the absolute speed of the fall in O_h, and not its variation over time.

28 For a demonstration of this proposition see para. 19 below.

29 Our assumption (para. 6 above) is that labour is required directly or *indirectly* in the production of every commodity. All products being here assumed to be basic, that assumption could be satisfied even if only one of the commodities required direct labour. We cannot therefore exclude the case of A_h having no wage costs (the ageing of wine is the example traditionally envisaged of a production process requiring no direct labour).

30 Cf. note 32 below.

31 Under competitive conditions no 'resistance' to a fall in the rate of profit can be effected in any industry except by means of a fall in the output and of the consequent (eventual) rise of the market price of the product relative to the means of production and/or wage goods. This is unlikely to happen and in any case cannot last at a rate of profit above the natural rate r^*.

32 If now we return to the commodity A_m of Proposition I, in the production of which the rate of profit must be below the natural rate r^*, we may note that the production of at least one of the other commodities would have to yield a profit rate higher than r^*. Indeed, we cannot exclude that this will be the case with *all* commodities other than A_m. Thus, as mentioned in para. 17 of the text, we cannot exclude that, when one market rate is below r^*, all the others are above that same natural rate.

33 No difference to our conclusions would in fact be made if the two rates did not

rise uniformly. The only element on which our present argument rests is that the minimum rate, whether r_h or r_{h+1}, or the two together, should monotonically rise (cf. paras 13 above and 27 below). The assumption of a uniform rise of the two allows an easier exposition of the answer to the problems which that joint rise presents us with.

34 The effect of the change in real wages in changing the 'market' effectual demand for commodity A_h (or for the commodities of group H) should not, on the other hand, affect the conclusions we reached in para. 13 above about the fall in A_h ultimately entailing a fall in the ratio O_h/D_h^m. Though it cannot be excluded that the adjustments in the real wage might temporarily cause falls in the market effectual demand D_h^m for A_h which are faster than those of the output O_h, such a faster fall obviously could not last as the market wage got progressively closer to the natural rate.

35 As I have had occasion to point out elsewhere (Garegnani 1990: 52), the assumption of steady growth seems to have been often adopted in the belief that it would allow an analysis of the average rate of growth of the economy. This overlooks the fact that no reason exists why any such average growth of the real economy should or ever could entail a proportional increase in all sectors and employed resources.

36 We have here assumed no consumption out of profits and therefore the demand for consumption good A_2 comes exclusively from wages. The general assumptions of Nikaido's model entail, on the other hand, a level of labour employment which, though growing from period to period, is given in any given period. The market effectual demand for A_2 will therefore be equal to aggregate real wages and thus to the *normal* effectual demand, whatever the market position of the economy (and therefore the reference price m_2^*) may be. The same will then be true for A_1.

37 Nikaido's argument may perhaps emerge more clearly by using a *curve qq* where the abscissa x measures the proportion O_2/O_1 between the outputs of the two commodities A_2 and A_1 of the model, and the ordinate y, the proportion in which the two commodities are *demanded as inputs* when the output proportions are those on the abscissa. Figure 7.1 depicts the case in which the production of A_2 is 'self-intensive' and therefore y rises from the minimum a_{21}/a_{11} for $x = 0$, and tends to its maximum a_{22}/a_{12} as $x \to \infty$. Fig. 7.2 depicts the opposite case of hetero-intensity. Suppose now in Fig. 7.1, that the relative outputs of the initial situation happen to be x', with a relative *market* effectual demand which, for the reasons seen in note 36 above, will correspond to the proportion x^* of uniform growth and therefore of the *normal* effectual demands. There will be a positive excess demand for A_2, indicated by the horizontal difference $(x^* - x')$, (or by the vertical difference between $y^* = x^*$ and the ordinate y' of the bisectrix through the origin.) The proportion x'' in which the two commodities should be produced the following year in order to absorb the current outputs available in proportion x' can then be found as the abscissa x'' of the intersection q'' between the q curve and the horizontal line drawn from the point of ordinate $y' = x'$ on the bisectrix. As can be seen from Fig. 7.1, the proportion x''' would then indicate the next output proportion required to absorb the two commodities thus produced in the proportion x'', with no proportion of outputs being then any longer capable to absorb the two commodities thus produced in the proportion x'''. Similarly in the case of an initial proportion x_1 of the outputs, with an excess supply of A_2 expressed by the difference $x_1 - x^*$ (also shown vertically by $y_1 - y^*$), the sequence of outputs x_1, x_2, would show a similar instability. However, the leftward instability

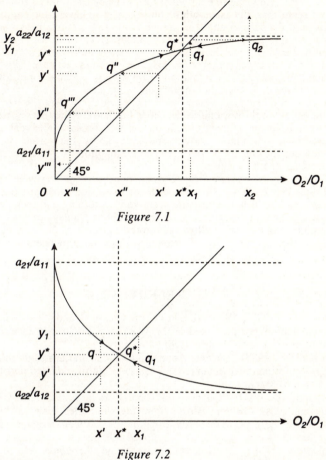

Figure 7.1

Figure 7.2

disappears as soon as we observe that, to be ever realized, the sequence x', x'', x''' would require $m_2/m_1 < p_2/p_1$, which cannot be the case with the excess demand expressed by $(x^* - x')$ – just as the rightward instability would require $m_2/m_1 > p_2/p_1$ which is not possible with an excess supply $(x_1 - x^*)$. Such excess demands or supplies will instead be accompanied by relative market prices ensuring the tendency to the relative effectual demand x^*. And the same tendency will be there in the hetero-intensive case of Fig. 7.2.

38 This building up or running down of inventories would probably be generally considered as 'unintended'. It does not, however, seem to be easy to distinguish such 'unintended' inventory changes, clearly connected with reservation prices and, therefore, with expectations about future prices, from 'intended' inventory changes.

39 The implications of the possibility of a temporary rise of output in the least profitable industry because of the lag between production decisions and realized outputs (para. 9 above) will be considered presently.

40 Cf. para. 12 above.

41 A word may be added about the continuity which for simplicity of exposition

we have here sometime assumed for the changes in prices and outputs. It does not seem that this assumption can in any way have affected our conclusions. Even in the case of an economy with only two commodities – where discontinuity might seem essential to oscillations, since when the two market rates of profit became equal in the course of their continuous change no further endogenous changes might seem possible – even in that case, as we saw, production lags, rather than discontinuity, are what is essential for oscillations. In fact continuity in the variation of the relative prices would not prevent 'overshooting', to the extent to which the changes in output when the two rates of profit are equal would respond to decisions taken when they were unequal.

42 Oscillations in aggregate demand are of course a different question from oscillations in market prices and accordingly the former have here been excluded by means of the classical assumption of given 'normal' effectual demands (para. 4 above).

43 Thus taking as an example the 'cobweb' of a divergent 'hog cycle' (*e.g.* Samuelson 1980: 381–2), it would seem difficult to imagine that producers – far from learning about their errors in excessively increasing and then decreasing their outputs, and that speculators, far from taking advantage of any such persisting, visible errors – would allow them to be repeated on an ever increasing scale.

44 Except of course for the *finiteness* of those rates of change, which has been assumed throughout the chapter.

REFERENCES

Ciccone, R. (1990), 'Short-run Prices in Classical and Neoclassical Analysis', unpublished paper presented at the Workshop on Convergence to Long-period Positions, Siena, 5–7 April, 1990.

Garegnani, P. (1987), 'Surplus Approach to Value and Distribution' in J. Eatwell, M. Milgate and P. Newman (eds), *The New Palgrave: a Dictionary of Economics* 4, London, Macmillan.

Garegnani, P. (1990), 'Quantity of Capital' in J. Eatwell, M. Milgate and P. Newman (eds), *Capital Theory*, New Palgrave Series, London, Macmillan.

Lippi, M. (1990), 'Comment on Boggio' in *Political Economy, Studies in the Surplus Approach*, Vol. 6, n. 1–2; pp. 59–68.

Marshall, A. (1898), 'Distribution and Exchange', *Economic Journal* 8, pp. 37–59.

Marshall, A. (1920) *Principles of Economics* 8th ed, London, Macmillan, 1949.

Nikaido, H. (1985), 'Dynamics of Growth and Capital Mobility in Marx's Scheme of Reproduction', *Zeitschrift für Nationalökonomie, Journal of Economics*.

Ricardo, D. (1821), *The Works and Correspondence of David Ricardo*, ed. by P. Sraffa with the collaboration of M.H. Dobb, vol. I, Cambridge, Cambridge University Press.

Samuelson (1980) *Economics*, New York, McGraw Hill, pp. 381–2.

Smith, A. (1776), *The Wealth of Nations*, London, Dent, Everyman edition, 1910.

Sraffa, P. (1960), *Production of Commodities by Means of Commodities: Prelude to a Critique of Economic Theory*, Cambridge, Cambridge University Press.

Steedman, I. (1984), 'Natural Prices, Differential Profit Rates and the Classical Competitive Process', *Manchester School* 52, pp. 123–40.

ACKNOWLEDGEMENTS

In putting together the earlier notes I have drawn benefit from comments by M. Caminati, G. Duménil, H. Kurz, D. Lévy, F. Petri, B. Schefold and, in particular, from discussions with R. Ciccone. Work on this chapter has been facilitated by research grants from the Consiglio Nazionale delle Ricerche and from the Ministero dell'Università e della Ricerca Scientifica e Tecnologica.

APPENDIX

A contrast seems to have sometimes been seen, between the assumption of the classical economists of a *fall* of the market price when effectual demand exceeds supply, and the modern assumption of a *rise* in price whenever there is 'excess demand'. Thus in Lippi 1990 the modern assumption is taken to entail a rise of the market price until output reaches effectual demand where, the price being then necessarily *above* its natural level, output would have to increase further, engendering cycles, which, in Lippi's view, would prevent convergence to the natural price.

However, at a closer examination, no such contrast between the classical and the modern assumptions appears to exist since the two refer in fact to *different stages* of the process of adjustment which generally follow one another, and are equally admitted in either theoretical approach. And once that is made clear, it also becomes clear that Lippi's instability results are due not, as he seems to think, to 'feedbacks' between outputs and prices ignored by the classical economist but, rather, to Lippi's own mathematical model which ignores the distinction between such two stages.

Indeed the first reaction to an unforeseen change, say a rise, in effectual demand will be a rise in price up to a level where a *temporary equality* between quantity demanded and supplied is achieved and where the rise in price will accordingly stop. We shall presently consider the temporary nature of the demand and supply there involved, but what needs to be stressed straightaway, for clarity's sake is that their *equality* will be generally reached *before*, often long before, the more permanent equality characterizing the new long-period position: indeed a lasting increase of demand for, say, coal, cannot be expected to cause a continued *increase* in its price – as distinct from a continued price *higher than normal* – for all the years before new coal mines are opened up.

On the side of supply, this first stage of the adjustment will generally include, so far as increase in output are concerned, only those increases which might be possible in the time *before* the above temporary demand and supply equality is achieved – output increases which may even be zero. What that supply will instead generally include will be purely temporary adjustments like the running down of sellers' inventories[1].

---

[1] Thus, for the opposite case of a glut, Smith explains that 'when the quantity brought to market exceeds the effectual demand . . . the market price will sink more or less below the natural price, according . . . *as it is more or less important to [the sellers] to get immediately rid of the commodity. The same excess in the importation of perishable, will occasion a much greater competition than in that of durable commodities, in the importation of oranges, for example, than in that of old iron' (1776, I, p. 50 our italics).

Temporary factors will be even more important on the demand side. Quite apart from any substitution which might conceivably be possible even in such a very short time run, and any likely effect of the price rise in reducing the purchasing power of buyers, we would generally expect delayed purchases, liquidation of buyers' inventories – and even queuing and other forms of rationing – which, when confined, as they would here be, to the very short-run, would appear to be compatible with *long run* free competition.

This first stage of the adjustment is that which Marshall represented as a 'temporary equilibrium' (1920, 369–70), and which the classical authors *took for granted* by referring to a market price higher than the normal price, when the quantity 'brought to market' fell short of effectual demand. It is indeed a stage which quite naturally draws more attention in modern theory, since it is the *only* stage possible under the hypothesis of 'pure exchange' common in its standard expositions[2]. However also in modern theory that stage of the adjustment recedes to its proper role of a first preliminary stage when production is introduced.

A second stage has in fact to begin as soon as the first is completed. It consists of the gradual fall in the price of the commodity because of the increase in output made possible by the higher price and the longer time run which can now be considered. In this second stage the price ensuring the 'temporary' equality of demand and supply moves downwards toward its normal level, as the initial shortage of the commodity is gradually removed while output is increased towards what the classical economists called the 'effectual demand', and modern theorists describe instead as the long-period equilibrium output.

To show the form in which this second stage of the adjustment – the one which drew the almost exclusive attention of the classical economists – is equally present in modern theory, we have recalled in Fig. 7.3 below its

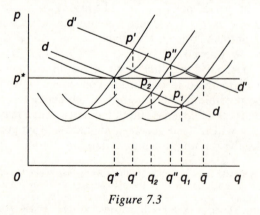

Figure 7.3

---

[2] It generally is the only stage of adjustment possible also in the market for 'factors of production' envisaged in modern theory.

standard description in terms of a sequence of the short-period equilibria of that theory. As the demand has unexpectedly risen from dd to $d'd'$, the price initially rises from its long period equilibrium level of $p*$ to the short-period equilibirum level p' (involving here *some* rise in output) along the short-period supply curve resulting from the summation of the short period marginal cost curves of existing firms (similar summations of variable and total short-period average costs, are also shown). However as firms increase in number and (initially) in size because of the higher profitability, the short-period supply curve shifts gradually to the right and the short-period equilibrium price progressively falls to p'' ... etc. down to $p*$, while the output rises to q'' etc. to finally reach $q*$. (The opposite process of a fall in price from $p*$ to p_1, followed by a rise to p_2 ... etc., up to $p*$, is also depicted for the case of an unexpected lasting fall in demand from $d'd'$ to dd).

No *necessity* can evidently emerge, either here or in classical theory, of the cycles around the normal price envisaged by Lippi. The reason of these different results is simple. It is that Lippi's mathematical model has put together the output increases of the *second* stage of adjustment and the price increases of the first, ignoring the temporary equality between demand and supply that separates the two stages. This has been done by *assuming* that prices continue to rise until output reaches effectual demand. Indeed in his equation [4] p. 6, Lippi supposes that the (relative) price p_t of the commodity will *continue to rise*, so long as (relative) output Q_t is below the quantity required to produce the output Q_{t+1} of the following period, the two becoming equal only when both will equal the effectual demand $Q*^3$. No trace then in Lippi's equations of the temporary demand-and-supply equality which closes the first stage of the adjustment and the associated temporary phenomena.

Lippi however coments as follows on a Ricardo passage (Ricardo, 1951, 119) describing the usual Smithian gravitation of the market price back to the natural price after a rise of effectual demand and price:

> Ricardo's statement does not appear to contain any immediately apparent mistake. Nonetheless, it must be pointed out that: (i) while Q_t rises between some point to the [left of the level of effectual demand] the simultaneous rise of P_t is not mentioned; (ii) while P_t falls, between some point to the right of [the level of effectual demand] the simultaneous rise of Q_t is not mentioned. Thus, one has the impression that Ricardos's firm belief in convergence relies on his inability to keep under control the feedback determination of quantities and prices, or perhaps on taking the two directions of causation one at a time. Firstly

---

[3] For what interests us here it would make no difference if, in Lippi's equation [4], $Q*$ appeared directly, replacing the quantity demanded in order to produce Q_{t+1} and thus cutting through the 'feedbacks' of outputs on demand.

high price causes quantity ratio to rise, but price ratio rises as well[4]. Subsequently, price falls and equilibrium is reached; by contrast, quantity ratio rises *at the same time*, and equilibrium, if reached, can only occur as the limit of an oscillatory process. (1990, 64).

However Ricardo (and Marshall) realised so well the 'feedbacks' price-quantity that they explained the falling price of their second stage, by the increasing output of that stage. Hence comes the fact noted by Lippi that while the 'quantity rises between some point to the [left of the point of effectual demand] the simultaneous rise of [the price] is not mentioned' by Ricardo: that rise is not mentioned because there is a *fall* and not a *rise* of the price, and there is a fall just because of the 'feedback' of the increasing output. That 'feedback' is indeed the same which Lippi places to the *right*, and not the *left*, of the level of effectual demand (which is what under (ii) Lippi then reproaches Ricardo for not doing).

The difference between the two arguments is thus due to the *different feedbacks* assumed, and not to 'Ricardo's inability to keep under control the feedback determination etc.'. It seems then that 'Ricardo's firm belief in convergence' is a result of his keeping a *correct* control of 'the feedback determination etc.' in its normal form and that it is Lippi's opposite belief which instead contemplates a very special case – that for which, in our previous example, a rise of the effectual demand for *coal* would cause a *continued rise of coal prices* over all the years before the new mines are in production. When therefore in the conclusion of his article Lippi writes

'once . . . we understand that the working of the system is more complicated than in the naive classical representation . . . we should no longer be committed to the idea that market prices must converge' (*ibid.* p. 65),

it seems natural to observe that a naivety may also lie, at times, in a modern excessive trust on mathematical treatments requiring assumptions which are too simple to adequately represent the complications of the economic system.

---

[4] Thus the 'feedbacks' which Lippi accuses Ricardo of ignoring would seem to consist of the interactions between prices and quantities, and not the feedback of outputs on the demand of the commodity because of its use in production – a feedback present in Lippi's model. However, as implied in n.3 above, consideration of that feedback would not alter our conclusions: the fact that coal is used to produce coal does not entail that the price of coal will have to continue to rise until new mines come to be exploited.

Part IV

EQUILIBRIUM IN THE KEYNESIAN CONCEPTION: THEORETICAL ANALYSIS AND HINTS FOR ECONOMIC POLICY

8

THE CONCEPT OF EQUILIBRIUM AND THE REALITY OF UNEMPLOYMENT

Bruno Jossa

E12
E24

DEFINING PROBLEMS

The main reason why the theory of general economic equilibrium for many economists is, at most, a point of departure and certainly not the point of arrival for every theory that wishes to explain the reality of the world in which we live is that it is not able to explain the persistence of unemployment (cf. Hahn 1986: 1). Persistent unemployment, we need to say, is a phenomenon that belongs to the very nature of capitalist economy, as evidenced in the 1930s, 1950s and 1960s in many different countries throughout the world, but it has never appeared so incurable as in the last decade, the 1980s. And, as the more aware economists view it, if unemployment is so persistent, for so long and in such a noticeable way, it cannot reasonably be seen as a phenomenon of disequilibrium without depriving the theory of equilibrium of any interpretative value.

Every explanation of unemployment that wishes to be Keynesian, in particular, must, in my opinion, reconcile unemployment with equilibrium, because Keynes was not a theoretician of circular causation or unstable equilibria, and every explanation of unemployment that hypothesizes rigidities of various kinds (without basing them on rational behaviour) challenges the letter and the spirit of the *General Theory*. As has been correctly observed, Keynes was prepared to assume that the system of prices functioned perfectly, that both prices and wages would move with flexibility to smooth out any disequilibrium between supply and demand, and it is therefore truly strange that Keynes's theory is often accused of hypothesizing the rigidity of prices and/or wages (cf. Kregel 1975: 11–12; and cf. also, for example, Hahn and Solow 1986: 2–3 and Patinkin 1984: 101).

Keynes explicitly said that he theorized equilibrium positions (cf. Keynes 1936: 25, 247–9, 252–3) and in fact for many years the prevalent interpretation of the *General Theory* was that it had explained *equilibria with* unemployment.[1] Today, however, the concept of equilibrium has so many specifications that the first problem is to clarify how it is to be used.[2]

According to a widely held opinion, if there are unemployed workers prepared to work for current wages, then by definition there is a disequilibrium (cf., for example, Greenfield 1986: 267–8). 'In the equilibrium view – Solow has written – a worker who is not employed must have chosen not to work' (cf. Solow 1979: 345). Some economists, in other words, sustain that unemployment is always, and by definition, voluntary because in economic activity everything that happens without force being exerted is voluntary. Every unemployed person, they say, could be selling small handicraft objects on pavements, or cleaning windscreens at traffic lights, or selling tissues in the street and, if he or she does not do so, it means that, in the present conditions of the labour market, he or she prefers not to work.

Strange as it may seem, today there are still many difficulties concealed behind such apparently banal phrases.[3] To say that every unemployed person is, by definition, someone who has chosen to be so is an obvious error, because even if we want to suppose that variations in prices always balance demand and supply, it may well happen that someone stays unemployed because *others* (employers, a union of which he or she is not a member, Parliament, etc.) can keep wages rigid and thereby prevent prices from adjusting.

The evidence of the facts also suggests that unemployment is partly involuntary. The idea that the unemployed are such only because they are looking for the best job that is available is in fact in obvious contrast with reality even in the United States, where the rule is that many accept the first job that is offered to them and those who are looking for work, as Blinder (1987: 131) has pointed out, do not spend more than an average of four hours a week looking for it. (This obviously suggests that job-searching unemployment, which is the type of voluntary unemployment to which the most attention is paid today, is not so important.) Those who leave a job do so, for the most part, because they are fired, not because they voluntarily quit.

As already emerges from what has been said so far, the divergence of opinions on the existence or not of involuntary unemployment is also due to the fact that neither the concept of involuntary unemployment nor the concept of full employment is clear or easy to define.

Blinder wrote: 'it may be that involuntary unemployment is like pornography; it is hard to define, but you know it when you see it' (1988: 3). As for the concept of full employment, a widely used definition is that which identifies full employment with 'that natural rate of unemployment' which it defines as a situation in which there is a lack of involuntary unemployed people. However, this seems to overlook the fact that only if we suppose that the unemployed have all voluntarily left their jobs can we say that there is full employment when those who are looking for work are equal in number to the jobs available. Thus more than one author considers the unemployment that corresponds to the natural rate of unemployment as involuntary (cf., for example, Prachowny 1985: 45, 49–50).

UNEMPLOYMENT AND EQUILIBRIUM IN THE 'NEOCLASSICAL SYNTHESIS'

We have mentioned the necessity for theory to reconcile unemployment with equilibrium and, we can add, the prestige and consensus the Keynesian theory enjoyed for many years are doubtlessly due to the fact that it appeared to reconcile the reality of unemployment with a theory of equilibrium.

It is believed that Keynesian theory has the defect of not explaining what determines the downward rigidity of wages. But Keynes attempted to explain this rigidity beginning from the idea that workers, individually and as a group, are more interested in relative wages than in absolute ones. He wrote in the *General Theory*: 'any individual or group of individuals, who consent to a reduction of money-wages relatively to others, will suffer a *relative* reduction of real wages, which is a sufficient justification for them to resist it' (1936: 14). But Keynes himself appraised his explanation of the rigidity of money wages as 'theoretically not fundamental' (1936: 8) and in summing up his theory he expressly said that he considered the money wage as an exogenous given (1936: 246–7)[4] and this explains how, for many years, 'very little attention has been paid to the sources of such inflexibility in Keynes's own analysis' (Trevithick 1976: 327) and how, as a consequence, the conclusion was reached that 'the *critical* assumption in Keynes's theory is that wages are *rigid downwards*' (Leijhonhufvud 1969: 49).

When, in more recent times, Keynes's explanation of the rigidity of money wages was reproposed by Trevithick (1976) and Tobin (1972), it was judged as not completely satisfactory because, as Hahn has argued, if it is to have interpretative capacities, there has to be a discontinuity in the utility function corresponding to the traditional relative wage (1986: 68). Furthermore, Keynes's explanation which brings relative wages into play is not altogether compatible with the model of 'the neoclassical synthesis', where labour is assumed as perfectly homogeneous, and for this reason it has not served to prop up the tottering edifice of Hicks and Modigliani's interpretation of the Keynesian theory.[5]

There is, however, a simple argument that can be useful in giving a microeconomic foundation to the downward rigidity of wages which has been strangely neglected in traditional interpretations of the Keynesian theory. In the model of the 'neoclassical synthesis', as we have just noted, the labour force is supposed homogeneous; and, if money wages are negotiated by the union (and are then respected), the supply of labour is monopolized. This model of the neoclassical synthesis with a monopolistic

175

union, according to Tobin, is not a correct interpretation of Keynes, because he 'did not appeal to trade union monopolies' and was, instead, 'anxious, perhaps over-anxious, to meet his putative classical opponents on their home field, the competitive economy' (Tobin 1972: 3); and the model in question, we repeat, cannot explain the rigidity of wages in the manner of Keynes because, according to the argument of the *General Theory* (as we have just said), 'rigidities in the path of money wage rates can be explained by workers' preoccupation with *relative* wages and the absence of a centralized economic mechanism for altering all money wages together' (Tobin 1972: 5). But the model of the neoclassical synthesis with a monopolistic union is certainly faithful to the Keynesian tradition of thought and lends itself in our view better than any other to explaining unemployment as a phenomenon of equilibrium.

Let us assume, then, that unions know economic theory perfectly or that they have rational expectations regarding levels of employment. In the model of the neoclassical synthesis with 'inside money' (therefore without real balance effect) and unitary elasticity of expectations, a reduction in money wages provokes an equiproportional variation both in current prices and in future prices and leaves the level of employment unchanged.[6] Thus a union with rational expectations does not have any interest in this case in allowing a reduction in wages, even if it has the fate of 'outsiders' at heart and tries to maximize the level of employment. In this case, then, the downward rigidity of money wages can be explained as rational behaviour, micro and macro-founded, on the part of the unions.

The same thing can be said of a model with 'outside money' and without a precise hypothesis of the elasticity of expectations. In a model of that kind the decrease in money wages sets forces in motion that act in different directions, which can favour or hinder a higher level of employment. The decrease in wages and prices will probably give rise to higher levels of consumption through real balance effects; but investments can increase or decrease, as has been argued a thousand times, and thus nothing guarantees that the level of employment will increase. (For recent discussion of the matter, cf. Wells 1984; McCombie 1985–6; Hahn and Solow 1986.) Thus, in this case too, a union that behaves rationally and has the fate of the unemployed at heart has no reason to negotiate a lower wage level.[7]

The explicit consideration of the union is, then, all that is needed in the model of the neoclassical synthesis to abandon the *hypothesis* that money wages are rigid and to explain that rigidity with rational behaviour. But then, if equilibrium is a situation of rest, the unemployment theorized by this interpretation of Keynesian theory is equilibrium and involuntary unemployment (cf. Costabile and Jossa 1990).[8]

THE NATURAL RATE OF UNEMPLOYMENT

The conviction that unemployment must be reconciled with equilibrium has, as is well known, led the monetarists to define a natural rate of unemployment.[9] For monetarists, if unemployment is the situation in which work is sought, and if a certain frictional unemployment always exists, because at any given moment there is always someone who is looking for work, full employment can only be defined as a situation in which available jobs, for which entrepreneurs need labour, are equal to the number of unemployed, who offer labour. But then, it is better to change the terminology regarding the old definition of full employment and, taking into account that a certain rate of unemployment cannot be eliminated, speak of a 'natural rate of unemployment' as the rate of unemployment in correspondence with which the jobs available are equal to unemployed workers and hence the demand for labour is equal to the supply (so that the wage rate tends to remain constant).

At times the natural rate of unemployment is defined as the level that would exist, in equilibrium, *in a perfectly competitive economy* (cf. Jenkinson 1987: 21). Friedman, however, has clarified that for him it is the unemployment rate that

> would be ground out by the Walrasian system of general equilibrium equations, provided there is imbedded in them the actual structural characteristics of the labor and commodity markets, *including market imperfections*, the stochastic variability in demands and supplies, the cost of gathering information about job vacancies and labour availability, the costs of mobility and so on
>
> (Friedman 1968: 8)

and there is actually no reason to define the natural rate of unemployment as the level of unemployment of equilibrium of a perfectly competitive economy. As is clear, Friedman's definition of the natural rate of unemployment does not coincide with the definition we have given above, which is often attributed to him and which is the most widely accepted definition of the natural rate of unemployment. The point has been explained, beyond the possibility of ambiguity, by Friedman himself, who, after having given the definition stated above, added in a note: 'It is perhaps worth noting that this "natural" rate did not correspond to equality between the number unemployed and the number of job vacancies' (1968: 8 n.).

It must be said, therefore, that Friedman's definition is not the one usually given by monetarist economists when they speak of a NRU (Natural Rate of Unemployment), i.e. the rate of unemployment at which the demand for and supply of labour are equal, but it is the one that is given by Keynesian economists, when they, with Modigliani and Papademus, talk about a NAIRU (Non-accelerating Inflation Rate of Unemployment), i.e.

the rate of unemployment in which inflation does not accelerate or decelerate (cf. Modigliani and Papademus 1975: 141–2).[10] But the NRU and the NAIRU are oceans apart because they are two very different definitions,[11] and, in our view, consideration of the difference between the two concepts enables us to greatly further the discussion.[12]

Friedman's opinion, however, is not the only one that can be mentioned to criticize those who at present maintain that macroeconomic equilibrium implies equality of supply and demand, because the events of the 1980s removed all foundation from the idea that the demand for and supply of work continuously tend to be equal. To bring theory into agreement with reality, already in 1976 Sargent had observed that the natural rate of unemployment undergoes strong and lasting oscillations from period to period, to the extent that the increase in unemployment historically registered may very well be due to structural changes that have caused a clear increase in unemployment of equilibrium (Sargent 1976: 213–23). This 'structuralist' vision takes into consideration, among the causes that can make the natural rate of unemployment increase, every type of obstacle on the side of supply, including high wages demanded by unions and government intervention, and can end up being tautological, because every lasting increase in the unemployment rate can be regarded, in the final analysis, as proof that the natural rate of unemployment has increased. Taking the example of Germany, a study conducted in 1984 spoke of an increase in the natural rate of unemployment from a level of 1.3 per cent at the end of the 1960s to a level of 6.2 per cent in the period 1981–3 (Various authors 1984) and subsequent studies have calculated an increase in the natural rate from less than 1 per cent for the period 1970–4 to 8 per cent for 1984–5 (Coe 1985; Franz 1987). For Great Britain the data tell us that unemployment was (on average) at 4 per cent between 1970 and 1975 whereas it was 10–11 per cent between 1981 and 1988. Likewise, for France unemployment was (on average) at 3 per cent between 1970 and 1975 whereas it was at 9–10 per cent between 1981 and 1988. For the countries of the European Community on the whole, since 1982 the rate of unemployment has been on average five times the average value of the period 1960–73.

Without lingering on these and other available data, which are in themselves sufficiently eloquent, we shall limit ourselves to saying that such considerable increases in the rate of unemployment can be considered as compatible with the labour market in equilibrium only if it is believed that the equilibrium unemployment rate is the NAIRU, and not the NRU, or if, to say the same thing in another way, the NRU is *identified* with the NAIRU according to Friedman's definition.[13] The existence of a NAIRU, we repeat, does not at all exclude that the supply of labour can systematically, and greatly, exceed the labour demand.

However, if we admit that the supply of labour can (systematically and greatly) exceed the demand for labour even when the labour market is in

equilibrium, unemployment in equilibrium will be, at least partially, involuntary.

What has been said above is confirmed by an argument formulated by
Hahn, in which search unemployment necessarily gives rise to involuntary
unemployment (1987: 2).

THE ANOMALY OF THE LABOUR MARKET AND EQUILIBRIA WITH UNEMPLOYMENT

'The greatest blow to the textbook Keynesianism of the 1950s and 1960s –
it has been written – was the advent of the idea of the natural rate of
unemployment' (Jackman *et al*. 1986: 111). This widespread view is based
on the idea that, if there is a single level of income in correspondence with
which inflation neither accelerates nor decelerates, there is no room for the
Keynesian policies of control of global demand.[14] But if the demand for
labour systematically exceeds the supply of labour at an unemployment
rate which does not accelerate or decelerate the inflation, the macroeconomic models based on the NAIRU (or on the NRU defined as the NAIRU)
are macroeconomic theories that are based on a very Keynesian concept of
equilibrium, equilibrium as the position of rest, but with involuntary
unemployment.[15]

Solow has written a brief but effective essay to criticize an important
tradition in economic thought, 'perhaps the dominant tradition right now,
especially in macroeconomics', according to which 'in nearly all respects,
the labour market is just like other markets', and must be analysed using
always and only the conventional apparatus of the curves of supply and
demand (Solow 1990: 3). According to Solow, in order to understand the
working of the labour market, it is necessary to take into account that in
this market opinions on correctness and loyalty are important, to both
employers and workers; and the explanation of the persistence of involuntary unemployment and the absence of underbidding is to be found in the
fact that behaviours that only follow the logic of supply and demand would
be considered unfair (and are thus avoided). In Solow's view, then, the
interpretation according to which the equilibrium unemployment rate is
that in which the equilibrium unemployment rate is that in which the
demand for and supply of labour are equal 'is only an interpretation, the
most popular one, but not the only one possible' (1990: 64).[16]

The idea that judgements on loyal and correct behaviour are important in
the labour market is also at the basis of the model for determining wages
proposed by G. Akerlof (Akerlof and Yellen 1990) known as the 'fair
wage' model of the class of models in the theory of efficiency wages.
More generally, regarding this theory, we are interested here in mentioning
the demonstration according to which an excess of supply over the demand
for labour does not usually give rise to underbidding.[17] This, as is known,

is only one of the main theses of the theory in question, but for our purposes it is the most interesting, as it can be detached from the other lines of reasoning on the links between wages and efficiency and used to complement to other theories.[18]

According to the theory of efficiency wages, then, the productivity of labour depends greatly on the level of wages because the incentive to work well depends heavily on job satisfaction, since lower wages induce workers to produce less or less well (the 'incentive effect') (Akerlof 1982, 1984; Bulow and Summers 1986). A decrease in wages impels many workers to look for a new job and thus increases the rotation of workers within firms, giving rise to higher costs, both in recruitment and in training (the 'rotation effect') (Stiglitz 1974; Hall 1975; Salop 1979; Stiglitz 1985). Furthermore, workers vary in their efficiency, but firms have difficulty in evaluating workers' capacities before hiring them and it is probable that a reduction in wages makes the best workers leave: this induces firms to keep wages high in order to procure the most efficient workers (the 'selection effect') (Weiss 1980; Malcolmson 1981; Nalebuff and Stiglitz 1985).

The incentive effect, if taken in a limited sense, has a clear meaning. But it can be taken in a broader sense in order to understand the increase in efficiency due to the increased stimulus to work that occurs with higher wages, since the opportunity cost of losing one's job is higher when wages are higher. In this broader sense, the incentive effect works only if there is unemployment, i.e. only if the worker fears being fired (if he or she is not very efficient) and fears not finding another job if he or she is fired (Calvo 1979; Calvo and Wellisz 1979; Shapiro and Stiglitz 1984; Bowles 1985).

For any of these reasons it is possible that profits will be reduced when wages are reduced, especially when a firm takes the initiative on its own of lowering wages, and this may very well explain why there is no under-bidding. But if, usually, there is no underbidding, the labour market can be in equilibrium and will often be in equilibrium even when the supply of labour is greater than the demand. This goes to confirm Solow's view that the interpretation in which the equilibrium unemployment rate is the one that brings supply and demand for labour into equilibrium is only one of many, and not the most convincing.[19]

THE VITALITY OF THE KEYNESIAN TRADITION

The above has attempted to emphasize there is a long tradition of thought, that starts with Keynes and is still alive and well today, which holds that the labour market is often in equilibrium even when supply is greater than demand. This tradition of thought also embraces those who, following the monetarist critique of the Phillips curve, maintain that there is a NAIRU, a single unemployment rate which does not nurture inflationary tendencies, but they specify that the NAIRU is different from the NRU. The theory of efficiency wages and every other theory that explains downward rigidity of wages with rational behaviour are a central part of this tradition.[20] According to this Keynesian version of capitalist reality, equilibrium is a position 'of rest', a situation the system tends not to move away from, even if there is involuntary unemployment.[21]

The demonstration that wages are rigid downward that has been supplied by the theory of efficiency wages, for those who believe it to be convincing and realistic, scores heavily in favour of Keynesian theory. It has already given rise to interesting developments in the tradition of Keynesian thought and will give rise, presumably, to further developments.[22] The enormous importance of the demonstration that there is no underbidding lies in the fact that it gives the system a 'degree of freedom' because it is as if it cancelled the equation that expresses the labour supply curve. To say that there is no underbidding is to say that in the labour market it is as if there were only the demand curve and thus the only condition to worry about if we are to have equilibrium is equality between wages and the marginal productivity of labour, i.e. the 'first postulate' of the 'classical' theory.[23]

In order to evaluate fully the relevance of a demonstration that in effect cancels the labour supply curve, it must be borne in mind that, in the words of Keynes, while the first postulate of the 'classical' theory 'gives us the demand schedule for employment, the second gives us the supply schedule' (1936: 6); because it is clear that, in explaining involuntary unemployment by the fact that 'the second postulate does not hold good' (1936: 10), Keynes explicity said that involuntary unemployment is an equilibrium position precisely because the labour supply curve does not exist.

The idea that the labour supply curve does not exist in the Keynesian model is to be found in Tuchscherer and Kregel (Tuchscherer 1979: 97–9, 1984: 528–30; Kregel 1980: n. 7); but Tuchscherer, then, strangely assumes that the money wage is exogenously given (1984: 530–1), which detracts from the value of his argument.

In recent years, as we know, Blanchard and Summers (1987) have put forward the theory of hysteresis which, in a radical version, sustain the thesis that the labour supply curve coincides with the labour demand curve and, in consequence, singles out 'fragile' equilibria. In this version Blanchard and Summers's theory fully places itself in the tradition we are discussing, because it says that labour supply has no importance in determining employment levels. In a more general version, the theory of hysteresis sustains that the equilibrium wage is fixed by the unions and comes to establish itself at the point of intersection between the labour demand curve and the 'wage setting curve', the curve which gives us the wage chosen by unions in relation to different levels of unemployment (Blanchard and Summers 1987, 1988; Johnson and Layard 1986; Alogoskoufis and Manning 1988). But in this version too the theory in question places itself in the

181

same tradition, because it singles out the fact that in the labour market equilibrium is compatible with a systematic excess of those seeking work over available jobs.

Already in 1980 Tobin had observed that the unemployment rate gravitates towards the average rate experienced in the past because of the several mechanisms – such as improvements in unemployment allowances, the loss of training experienced by the unemployed, the existence of the so-called 'black economy', and the slowing down of the process of capital formation that occurs when entrepreneurs reduce their estimates of the production capacity required (cf. Tobin 1980: 61).

These are precisely the basic ideas of the theory of hysteresis, and Tobin's quote can thus be used here to conclude that the Keynesian tradition in which equilibrium is compatible with involuntary unemployment is still alive today and a fertile source of new ideas. This confirms the ideas of those who believe that the criticism 'from inside' which can be levelled against neoclassical theory today (after Keynes and Sraffa) is stronger than ever. (For an overview of this matter, cf. Lunghini 1988.)

NOTES

1 Recently, the interpretation of the Keynesian theory as the theory of equilibrium has been re-proposed, for example, by Harcourt and O'Shaughnessy (1985: 20); Hahn (1987); Costabile and Jossa (1990).

2 On the concept of equilibrium, with particular reference to the *General Theory*, cf. Caravale's recent excellent essay (1992).

3 Hahn quite rightly begins his article on involuntary unemployment with a section on its definitions (Hahn 1987: 14).

4 As Tuchscherer has observed, few affirmations in the *General Theory* are more explicit than the affirmation that money wages are taken as an exogenous given of which no explanation is supplied (cf. Tuchscherer 1984: 530; cf. also, for example, Leijhonhufvud 1969: 49; Brothwell 1988).

5 For those who find Keynes's explanation of the downward rigidity of money convincing, involuntary unemployment is clearly compatible with equilibrium if equilibrium is conceived of as a position 'at rest' (as Keynes clearly did; cf., for example, Hansen 1970: 4; Asimakopulos 1989: 16).

6 A central idea of Keynes's theory, which Hicks called 'the wage theorem', is that 'when there is a general (proportional) rise in money wages the *normal* effect is that all prices rise in the same proportion, provided that the money is increased in the same proportion (when the rate of interest will be unchanged)' (cf. Hicks 1974: 59–60).

7 As has been rightly observed, the "wage theorem" assigns 'a dynamic role to exogenous wage change that is in some ways strikingly similar to the growth of the money supply in the quantity theory' (Crossley 1988: 93).

8 The matter under discussion has been quite rightly defined as 'involuntary unemployment in the spirit of Keynes's (cf. d'Aspremont *et al.* 1989, 1990: 896). Keynes, in fact, as we know, held the view that unemployment is involuntary when there is no available way for labour as a whole to reach full employment by renegotiating the money wage with entrepreneurs.

9 The concept of a natural rate of unemployment was first introduced in Phelps (1967: 254 ff.) and Friedman (1968: 8).

10 Another definition of the natural rate of unemployment much used today is that it is the only rate of unemployment that enables the effective level of prices to equal the expected level (cf., for all, Parkin and Bade 1988: ch. 20).

11 The concepts of a NRU and a NAIRU are very different if the NRU is defined as the rate of unemployment in which the demand for and supply of labour are equal; but the NRU, we repeat, can be identified with the NAIRU. As Modigliani and Papademus have written, all the principal opinions on the relationship between inflation and unemployment imply the existence of a NRU (cf. Modigliani and Papademus 1975: 145) and the existence of a NRU is implicit both in the school of a 'vertical' Phillips curve and in that of a 'non-vertical' Phillips curve (p. 142).

12 Among those who stress the clear-cut distinction between the NRU and the NAIRU, cf., in particular, Cornwall (1983: 66–9, 1989: 99–100).

13 Among those who identify the NRU with the NAIRU cf., for example, Blanchard and Fischer (1989: 543–4) and Taylor (1988: 131).

14 An interesting discussion of a certain orthodoxy which claims to be Keynesian, although it (almost) deprives the policies of control over the global demand of any role, can be found in Bruno (1988).

15 As we said at the beginning, those who define the NRU as the rate of unemployment in which demand for and the supply of labour are equal mostly hold the view that in equilibrium unemployment is voluntary.

16 Already in the past considerations of this kind have led Solow to deduce that the labour market is multifaceted, because heterogeneous forces operate in it and thus many pieces of theory or combinations of different theories are needed to give a realistic, or sufficiently complete, representation of that market (cf. Solow 1980).

17 For ample exposition of other theories of the working of the labour market that are compatible with the absence of underbidding cf. Lindbeck (1991).

18 For reviews of the theory of efficiency wages cf. Yellen (1984); Stiglitz (1986: 182–92); Katz (1986); Carmichael (1990).

19 An objection against the argument that wages are downwardly rigid is that it can be convincing only for the 'primary' or 'formal' sector and not for the 'secondary' or 'informal' sector where wages always tend to equalize supply and demand (cf. Artis 1988: 10).

20 Lindbeck's and Snower's theory of insiders is another of the recent strands of research that can be placed within this tradition (cf. Lindbeck and Snower 1985, 1988a).

21 In a Hayekian conception, on the contrary, every excess of supply over demand, or vice versa, is the consequence of a lack of coordination between economic agents and cannot occur if there is perfect information. Disequilibrium, by its very nature, is the result of imperfect information (cf. O'Driscoll 1977: 16; Garrison and Kirzner 1987: 120).

22 The main reviews of the theory of efficiency wages have given a positive evaluation of this, with the exception of the more recent one by Carmichael (1990).

23 The interpretation of Keynesian theory that places the absence of underbidding at the centre of the argument is in clear contrast with that of those who, following Davidson and Weintraub, maintain that 'Keynes's main point is that, in a monetary production economy, the classical labour market mechanism

does not work since its 'demand curve,' the marginal product of labour curve, is not a demand curve at all' (Brothwell 1988: 62 n. 11).

REFERENCES

Acocella, N., Rey, G., and Tiberi, M., (eds) (1990), *Saggi di politica economica in onore di Federico Caffé*, I, Milan, Angeli.

Akerloff, G. (1982), 'Labor Contracts as Partial Gift Exchange', *Quarterly Journal of Economics* 95, 4.

Akerloff, G. (1984), 'Gift Exchange and Efficiency Wage Theory: Four Views', *American Economic Review* 74, 2.

Akerloff, G., and Yellen, J. (1990), 'The Fair Wage–Effort Hypothesis and Unemployment', *Quarterly Journal of Economics* 105, May.

Alogoskoufis, G.S., and Manning, A. (1988), 'On the Persistence of Unemployment', *Economic Policy* 7.

Artis, M. (1988), 'Are Market Forces Adequate to Maintain Full Employment? If not can Demand Management Policies be Relied upon to Fill the Gap?, in Eltis and Sinclair (1988).

Asimakopulos, A. (1989), 'The Nature and Role of Equilibrium in Keynes's General Theory', *Australian Economic Papers* 28, 57.

d'Aspremont, C., Dos Santos Ferreira, R., and Gérard-Varet, L.A. (1989), 'Unemployment in an Extended Cournot Oligopoly Model', *Oxford Economic Papers* XLI, 3.

d'Aspremont, C., Dos Santos Ferreira, R., and Gérard-Varet, L.A. (1990), 'On Monopolistic Competition and Involuntary Unemployment', *Quarterly Journal of Economics* CV, 4.

Bean, C. (1992), *European Unemployment: a Survey*, Centre for Economic Performance, Discussion Paper 71, Brussels, CEP.

Beckerman, W. (ed.) (1988), *Wage Rigidity and Employment*, London, Duckworth.

Blanchard, O.J. (ed.) (1986), *Restoring Europe's Prosperity*, Cambridge, Mass., MIT Press.

Blanchard, O.J., and Summers, L.H. (1987), 'Hysteresis in Unemployment', *European Economic Review* 31, 2.

Blanchard, O.J., and Summers, L.H. (1988), 'Beyond the Natural Rate Hypothesis', *American Economic Review* 78, 2.

Blanchard, O.J., and Fischer, S. (1989), *Lectures on Macroeconomics*, Cambridge, Mass., MIT Press.

Blinder, A.S. (1987), 'Keynes, Lucas and Scientific Progress', *American Economic Review* 77, 2.

Blinder, A.S. (1988), 'The Challenge of High Unemployment', *American Economic Review* 78, 2.

Bowles, S. (1985), 'The Production Process in a Competitive Economy: Walrasian, neo-Hobbesian, and Marxian Models', *American Economic Review* 75, 1.

Brothwell, J. (1988), 'The "General Theory" after Fifty Years; Why Are we not All Keynesians Now?', in Hillard (1988).

Bruno, S. (1988), 'The Secret Story of the Rediscovery of Classical Unemployment and of its Consequences on Economic Advisers', *Studi economici* XLIII, 36.

Bulow, J.I., and Summers, L.H. (1986), 'A Theory of Dual Labor Markets with Applications to Industrial Policy, Discrimination, and Keynesian Unemployment', *Journal of Labor Economics* 4, 3.

Butkiewicz, J.L., Koford, K.J. and Miller, J.B., (eds) (1986), *Keynes's Economic Legacy*, Praeger, New York.

Calvo, G.A. (1979), 'Quasi-Walrasian Theory of Unemployment', *American Economic Review* 69, 2.

Calvo, G.A., and Wellisz, S. (1979), 'Hierarchy, Ability and Income Distribution', *Journal of Political Economy* 87, 5.

Caravale, G. (1992), 'Keynes and the Concept of Equilibrium', in *The Notion of Equilibrium in the Keynesian Theory*, (ed.) M. Sebastiani, London, Macmillan.

Carmichael, H.L. (1990), 'Efficiency Wage Models of Unemployment: One View', *Economic Inquiry* 28, 2.

Coe, D.T. (1985), *Nominal Wages, the NAIRU, and Wage Flexibility*, OECD Economic Studies 5.

Cornwall, J. (1983), *The Conditions for Economic Recovery: A Post-Keynesian Analysis*, Oxford, Martin Robertson.

Cornwall, J. (1989), 'Inflation as a Cause of Economic Stagnation: a Dual Model', in Kregel (1989).

Costabile, L., and Jossa, B. (1990), 'La disoccupazione involontaria come posizione di equilibrio', in Acocella *et al.* (1990).

Cross, R. (ed.) (1988), *Unemployment, Hysteresis and the Natural Rate Hypothesis*, Oxford, Blackwell.

Crossley, R. (1988), *Inflation, Unemployment and the Keynesian Wage Theorem*, in Hillard (1988).

De Long, J.B., and Summers, L.H. (1988), *How Does Macroeconomic Policy Affect Output?* Brookings Papers on Economic Activity 2. Washington, D.C., Brookings Institution.

Eltis, W. and Sinclair, P. (1988), *Keynes and Economic Policy: the Relevance of the General Theory after Fifty Years*, London, Macmillan.

Fischer, S. (ed.) (1986), *Macroeconomics Annual*, Cambridge, Mass., National Bureau of Economic Research.

Franz, W. (1987), 'Hysteresis, Persistence and the NAIRU: an Empirical Analysis for the Federal Republic of Germany', in Layard and Calmfors (1987).

Friedman, M. (1968), 'The Role of Monetary Policy', *American Economic Review* 58, 1.

Garrison, R.W., and Kirzner, I.M. (1987), *Friedrich August von Hayek*, reprinted in *The New Palgrave, The Invisible Hand*, London, Macmillan, 1989.

Greenfield, R.L. (1986), 'Walras' Law in Macroeconomic Disequilibrium', *Australian Economic Papers* 25, 47.

Hahn, F.H. (1986), *Three Lectures on Monetary Theory*, (ed.) F. Marzano and G. Chirichiello, Milan, Angeli.

Hahn, F.H. (1987), 'On Involuntary Unemployment', *Economic Journal* 97, supplement.

Hahn, F.H. and Solow, R.M. (1986), 'Is Wage Flexibility a Good Thing?', in Beckerman (1988).

Hall, R. (1975), *The Rigidities of Wages and the Persistence of Unemployment*, Brookings Papers on Economic Activity 2, Washington, D.C., Brookings Institution.

Hansen, B. (1970), *A Survey of General Equilibrium Systems*, New York, McGraw-Hill.

Harcourt, G.C., (ed.) (1985), *Keynes and his Contemporaries*, London, Macmillan.

Harcourt, G.C., and O'Shaughnessy (1985), 'Keynes' Unemployment Equilibrium: Some Insights from Joan Robinson, Piero Sraffa and Richard Kahn', in Harcourt (1985).

Hicks, J.R. (1974), *The Crisis in Keynesian Economics*, Oxford, Blackwell.

Hillard, J. (ed.) (1988), *J.M. Keynes in Retrospect: the Legacy of the Keynesian Revolution*, Aldershot, Edward Elgar.

Jackman, R.A., Layard, P.R.G., and Pissarides, C. (1986), 'Policies for Reducing the Natural Rate of Unemployment', in Butkiewicz *et al.* (1986).

Jenkinson, J. (1987), 'The Natural Rate of Unemployment: Does it Exist?', *Oxford Review of Economic Policy*, autumn.

Johnson, G., and Layard, P.R.G. (1986), 'The Natural Rate of Unemployment: Explanation and Policy', in *Handbook of Labour Economics*, Amsterdam, North-Holland.

Katz, L. (1986), 'Efficiency Wage Theories: a Partial Evaluation', in Fischer (1986).

Keynes, J.M. (1936), *The General Theory of Employment, Interest and Money*, London, Macmillan.

Kregel, J. (1975), *The Reconstruction of Political Economy: an Introduction to post-Keynesian Economics*, London, Macmillan.

Kregel, J. (1980), ' I fondamenti marshalliani del principio della domanda effettiva', *Giornale degli economisti* 39, 3–4.

Kregel, J., (ed.) (1989), *Inflation and Income Distribution in Capitalist Crisis: Essays in Memory of Sidney Weintraub*, London, Macmillan.

Layard, R., and Calmfors, L. (ed.) (1987), *The Fight against Unemployment*, Cambridge, Mass., MIT Press.

Leijonhufvud, A. (1969), 'Keynes and the Classics: First Lecture', in Leijonhufvud (1981).

Leijonhufvud, A. (1981), *Information and Coordination: Essay in Macroeconomic Theory*, London, Oxford University Press.

Lindbeck, A. (1991), 'Microfoundations of Unemployment Theory', *Labour* 3.

Lindbeck, A., and Snower, D.J. (1985), 'Explanations of Unemployment', *Oxford Economic Policy* 1, 2.

Lindbeck, A., and Snower, D.J. (1988a), 'Cooperation, Harassment and Involuntary Unemployment: an Insider–Outsider Approach', *American Economic Review* 78.

Lindbeck, A., and Snower, D.J. (1988b), *The Insider–Outsider Theory of Employment and Unemployment*, Cambridge, Mass., Blackwell.

Lunghini, G. (1988), 'Equilibrio', in *Dizionario di economia politica* 14, Turin, Boringhieri.

Malcolmson, M. (1981), 'Unemployment and the Efficiency Wage Hypothesis', *Economic Journal* 91.

McCombie, J.S.L. (1985–6), 'Why Cutting Real Wages will not Necessarily Reduce Unemployment: Keynes and the Postulate of the Classical Economics', *Journal of Post-Keynesian Economics* VIII, 2.

Modigliani, F., and Papademus, L. (1975), *Targets for Monetary Policy in the Coming Year*, Brookings Papers on Economic Activity 1, Washington, D.C., Brookings Institution.

Nalebuff, B.M., and Stiglitz, J.E. (1985), 'Quality and Prices', in Econometric Research Program, Memorandum 297, Princeton University.

O'Driscoll, G.P. (1977), *Economics as a Coordination Problem*, Kansas City, Sheed Andrews and McMeel.

Parkin, M., and Bade, R. (1988), *Modern Macroeconomics*, New York, Philip Allan.

Patinkin, D. (1984), 'Keynes and Economics Today', *American Economic Review* 74, 2.

Phelps, E.S. (1967), 'Phillips Curves, Expectations of Inflation and Optimal Unemployment over Time', *Economica* 34, 35.

Prachowny, M.F.J. (1985), *Money in the Macroeconomy*, Cambridge, Cambridge University Press.

Salop, S.C. (1979), 'A Model of the Natural Rate of Unemployment', *American Economic Review* 69, 1.

Sargent, T.J. (1976), 'A Classical Macroeconomic Model for the United States', *Journal of Political Economy* 84, 2.

Shapiro, C., and Stiglitz, J.E. (1984), 'Equilibrium Unemployment as a Worker Discipline Devise', *American Economic Review* 74, 3.

Solow, R.M. (1979), 'Alternative Approaches to Macroeconomic Theory: a Partial View', *Canadian Journal of Economics* XII, 3.

Solow, R.M. (1980), 'On Theories of Unemployment', *American Economic Review* 70, 1.

Solow, R.M. (1990), *The Labor Market as a Social Institution*, Cambridge, Mass., Blackwell.

Stiglitz, J.E. (1974), 'Alternative Theories of Wage Determination and Unemployment in LDCs: the Labour Turnover Model', *Quarterly Journal of Economics* 89, 2.

Stiglitz, J.E. (1985) 'Equilibrium Wage Distribution' *Economic Journal* 95.

Stiglitz, J.E. (1986), 'Theories of Wage Rigidity', in Butkiewicz *et al.* (1986).

Taylor, J. (1988), 'Inflation and Fiscal Expansion', in Eltis and Sinclair (1988).

Tobin, J. (1972), 'Inflation and Unemployment', *American Economic Review* 62, 1.

Tobin, J. (1980), *Stabilization Policy Ten Years After*, Brookings Papers on Economic Activity 1, Washington, D.C., Brookings Institution.

Trevithick, J.A. (1976), 'Money Wage Inflexibility and the Keynesian Labor Supply Function', *Economic Journal* 86.

Tuchscherer, T. (1979), 'Keynes' Model and the Keynesians: a Synthesis', *Journal of Post-Keynesian Economics* 2, 1.

Tuchsherer, T. (1984), 'Metzler on Keynes's Labor Market Theory: a Review of the *General Theory's* Second Chapter', *Journal of Post-Keynesian Economics* IV, 4.

Various authors (1984), *Europe: the Case for Unsustainable Growth*, CEPS Paper 8–9, Brussels, reprinted in Blanchard (1986).

Weiss, A. (1980), 'Job Queues and Layoffs in Labor Markets with Flexible Wages', *Journal of Political Economy* 92, 3.

Weitzman, M. (1987), 'Steady State Unemployment under Profit Sharing', *Economic Journal* 97.

Wells, P. (1984), 'Modigliani on Flexible Wages and Prices', *Journal of Post-Keynesian Economics* II, 1.

Yellen, J. (1984), 'Efficiency Wage Models of Unemployment', *American Economic Review* 74, 2.

9

LONG-PERIOD POSITIONS AND KEYNESIAN SHORT-PERIOD EQUILIBRIUM

Paola Potestio

In this chapter I present a number of considerations of two concepts of equilibrium: the concept of equilibrium of classical tradition and of the modern theory inspired by that tradition and the concept of equilibrium that emerges from the main body of the *General Theory*. The comparison I wish to draw between these two concepts of equilibrium seems worthy of consideration because a widely held idea within the critiques of traditional theory is that an alternative analytical approach to the neoclassical approach can be constructed by uniting *essential* elements of classical and Keynesian analyses. The comparison between the two concepts of equilibrium aims to verify the consistency of this idea. More precisely, the comparison is directed to determine whether this idea finds its roots in a direct inspiration from the *General Theory*, so that the alternative theoretical project developed within these critiques emerges through an actual continuity of analysis from the main body of that book, or whether it is grounded in a sort of 'free' or generic inspiration from the *General Theory*, so that that project is similarly linked with it generically and indirectly. Moreover it is worth underlining that only one aspect of this idea will be discussed in this chapter: I shall not consider the claim to represent an alternative approach to neoclassical theory, only the possibility of uniting crucial elements of classical analysis and Keynesian analysis.

In the first section the characteristics of long-period positions of the classical type are briefly examined, while in the second the characteristics of Keynesian short-period equilibrium are discussed. The basic elements of the two analytical schemes under consideration immediately reveal a radical difference. The comparison in the third section between the two schemes and the two respective concepts of equilibrium stresses this difference and the alternative character of the two schemes from an analytical viewpoint. Brief conclusions close the chapter.

LONG-PERIOD POSITIONS

In outlining long-period positions I shall dwell only on some essential elements. Here we are obviously not interested in the diffrences and the debates within the theoretical approach that refers to classical economists up to Marx. Hence I intend not to analyse exactly what the long-period position is or what it expresses, but rather to single out some elements which, on the one hand, express basic characteristics of the entire neo-Ricardian approach and, on the other, are essential for the comparison between the two concepts of equilibrium that are discussed here.

The analytical structure underlying the definition of long-period positions and its direct derivation from the classical approach are illustrated by numerous contributions by P. Garegnani (in particular 1981 and 1990). It is an analytical structure 'characterized by "separate" logical stages', and is therefore 'deeply different from the "simultaneous" determination of distribution, outputs and prices we find in "neoclassical" theories' (Garegnani 1990: 113).

The approach to the analysis of distribution and relative prices in the classical tradition is characterized by the consideration that real wages can be determined separately from the social product and that the social product, in turn, can be determined separately from wages, quotas of social product different from wages and relative prices. As a result social product and real wages can be considered as given in the analysis of the determination of relative prices and quotas of product different from wages. This same structure underlies the long-period positions of modern theory and the eventual substitution of the profit rate with the wage rate as the exogenous distributive variable leaves the structure intact. Given the exogenous distributive variable, the long-period position is identified by a uniform real wage and relative prices that guarantee the uniformity of the profit rate in the system's production processes.

These elements, as can easily be seen, leave a series of questions open: for example, the role and the importance of a hypothesis of constant returns to scale; whether production prices can be associated with situations of market clearing, and so forth. The authors who in one way or another refer to long-period positions differ on the individual, specific questions. Nevertheless, this debate must necessarily remain outside the analysis of this chapter. Staying on a more general level, it is still worthwhile insisting on the implications or the characteristics of the basic elements of the long-period positions.

The determination of the long-period position presupposes and reflects a clear-cut distinction between 'systematic', 'permanent' or 'persistent' forces that operate in the system and the variegated range of transitory and accidental phenomena that emerge in the single, specific circumstances. Only the persistent forces constitute the object of the analysis of value and distribution, and the long-period position, with the aforementioned characteristics (uniformity of the rate of profit and of the real wage), is but the expression of such forces (see, for example, Eatwell 1983: 94–5 or Bharadwaj 1983: 18). It is worth while specifying two things: first, the values of the variables that characterize a specific long-period position will not generally be the magnitudes uniformly observed in the real world. Nevertheless, precisely because the long-period position is the expression of persistent tendencies in the system, it represents a centre of gravitation for those variables. The second specification is that this kind of approach to the problem of value and distribution, founded on a concept of long-period equilibrium as an expression of dominant and persistent tendencies in the economy, is not at all exclusive of classical analysis. There is a whole tradition in the neoclassical strand (think of Marshall or Wicksell) that utilizes a concept of long-period equilibrium. While the *content* of the theory is quite different, from the point of view of the method no important distinction can be drawn between the classical school and the modern theory that refers to it and an extensive tradition of the neoclassical school.

A crucial element in the comparison between long-period positions and the Keynesian short-period equilibrium is the different role uncertainty plays in them (uncertainty regarding the future value of the variables on which it is assumed the behaviour of subjects depends). It is therefore useful to complete this brief examination of long-period positions with some consideration of the relationship between uncertainty and positions of this type.

In quite general terms, and therefore without particular reference to the concept of equilibrium of the classical school, uncertainty cannot play an important role in the long-period equilibrium for the simple reason that in such an equilibrium expectations are all fulfilled; or, more precisely, in order to account for different theoretical content, the expectations of agents whose behaviour is considered by the theory are all fulfilled. Turning to long-period positions, it should first be pointed out that it is immediately evident from the examination conducted that uncertainty, or another analogous subjective factor, has no bearing on the determination of the long-period position.

That said, however, the fact that in the long-period equilibrium, and hence also in long-period positions, the expectations of agents are all fulfilled is a drastic simplification. The long-period position is not a set of *actual*, *observed* values of variables but the centre of gravitation of the economic system. The simplification is nevertheless legitimate and useful, since, as uncertainty has no bearing on the determination of the long-period position and as that position – which is upheld and affirmed by the theory – is a centre of gravitation, whether those expectations are fulfilled or not does not produce any substantial difference in the consequences and it is therefore quite irrelevant to the representation of the working of the economic system proposed by the theory.[1] In particular, it is important to stress that the theory implies that the fact that expectations are not fulfilled leaves the long-period position intact as a centre of gravitation of the system.

In conclusion, if the economy works for 'long-periods', for long-period positions, and it is in some sense a sequence of such positions, uncertainty cannot have a determining role in it. As Eatwell and Milgate write:

> The influence of uncertainty is just one of those multitude of influences which cause day-to-day circumstances of the economy to deviate from the long-run normal position. Uncertainty and expectations may thus be confined to the category of 'temporary' or non-systematic effects, as distinct from the persistent and systematic forces which act to determine the long-run position
>
> (1983: 12)

THE KEYNESIAN SHORT-PERIOD EQUILIBRIUM

The approach and the viewpoint of Keynes are radically different from those of the classical tradition. My reference point for Keynesian analysis is the model of the main body of the *General Theory*, that is, substantially, chapters 1–15. The reference to chapters 1–15 only is motivated by the fact that the remaining chapters either do not add anything substantial to the model outlined in chapters 1–15, or they express (chapter 17) an alternative analytical approach to that underlying the model of those chapters.[2] As with long-period positions, this examination of Keynesian analysis underscores only the elements that represents basic characteristics and which at the same time are essential in the comparison with the concept of equilibrium of the long-run positions.

The element that characterizes Keynes's analysis and which is at the basis of his radical departure from the classical approach, understood in Keyne's sense, i.e. the approach of both classical economists until Marx and the neoclassical tradition, is the recognition that uncertainty characterizes the actions of subjects *in an essential way*. If the analysis has to incorporate a positive consideration of uncertainty, the only concept of equilibrium that can be used (obviously if one holds, as Keynes did, that the positive consideration of uncertainty does not preclude the use of the equilibrium method) is the short-period equilibrium. In very general terms, the latter differs from the long-period equilibrium in that not all the expectations of subjects whose behaviour is considered by the theory are fulfilled.

In the *General Theory* the method of long-period equilibria is abandoned and the analysis develops around a concept of short-period equilibrium which reflects a positive consideration of uncertainty. Here it is important

191

to point out only one element of the content of this concept of equilibrium in the main body of the *General Theory*, which characterizes in a crucial way the short-period method used by Keynes. Some expectations, those whose fulfilment is irrelevant to the concept of equilibrium utilized in chapters 1–15, are assumed as given or arbitrary. As we know, these are the expectations that underlie investment decisions, the so called long-term expectations.

This hypothesis is crucial in the model of chapters 1–15. However, the hypothesis in itself, i.e. the mere fact of considering as given or arbitrary a certain kind of expectations, is not at all the main aspect. Keynes himself, after setting out the model in chapters 1–15, drops this hypothesis – in particular, in the model in chapter 17 and in the description of the shifting equilibrium in the first section of chapter 21. The main aspect is what such a hypothesis means and what it implies. And it is precisely in this respect that the given or arbitrary long-term expectations crucially characterize the equilibrium in chapters 1–15. The meaning of this hypothesis lies in the recognition of a subjective element of reaction to uncertainty in the formation of at least a certain type of expectations. The implications of this hypothesis – the recognition of a subjective element of reaction to uncertainty in the formation of expectations – makes the long-period perspective redundant, and renders the short-period and long-period methods *generally* incompatible.

If the short-period approach opens the way to a positive consideration of uncertainty, the recognition of an intrinsically subjective element of reaction to uncertainty in decisions bars the way to any general possibility of connection between short-period and long-period equilibrium. In other words, there is no basis for considering the short-period equilibrium *in any general sense* as a step towards a long-run one. This crucial implication of Keynes's approach in the main body of the *General Theory* does not seem to be sufficiently taken into account in the literature, or at any rate not always sufficiently taken into account.

While the role of uncertainty in Keynesian analysis is very often emphasized, and appreciated in various ways, the radical departure of Keynesian analysis from all previous tradition that this role implies is certainly not a generally accepted or acquired result. And yet Keynes himself, leaving aside the widespread lack of precision in the *General Theory* and even his reference to alternative analytical frameworks, is very clear on the rupture that the essential elements of his model (naturally that of chapters 1–15) imply for both the method and the content of previous theory. It therefore seems worth while, in conclusion, to refer to the words Keynes himself used on this rupture with previous tradition in the fundamental article of 1937 in the *Quarterly Journal of Economics*.

It is generally recognized that the Ricardian analysis was concerned with what we now call long-period equilibrium. Marshall's contribution mainly consisted in grafting on to this the marginal principle and the principle of substitution, together with some discussion of the passage from one position of long-period equilibrium to another. But he assumed, as Ricardo did, that the amounts of the factors of production in use were given and that the problem was to determine the way in which they would be used and their relative rewards.

(Keynes 1973b: 112)

Keynes contrasts this approach with one founded on the recognition that decisions are taken in conditions of uncertainty. Emphasizing the role of uncertainty and what he means by it in an economy that produces and accumulates wealth, he writes:

The whole subject of the accumulation of wealth is to produce results, or potential results, at a comparatively distant, and sometimes at an *indefinitely* distant date. Thus the fact that our knowledge of the future is fluctuating, vague and uncertain, renders wealth a peculiarly unsuitable subject for the methods of the classical economic theory.

(Keynes 1973b: 113)

Or again, further on, in quite general terms, without referring to a specific type of decision, Keynes states, 'I accuse the classical economic theory of being itself one of these pretty, polite techniques which try to deal with the present by abstracting from the fact that we know very little about the future' (1973b: 115).

A COMPARISON BETWEEN THE LONG-PERIOD POSITIONS AND THE CONCEPT OF EQUILIBRIUM IN CHAPTERS 1–15 OF THE *GENERAL THEORY*

From the brief outline of the basic elements of long-period positions and the concept of equilibrium in the main body of the *General Theory* in the previous sections, I should like first to make two observations. As is evident, the long-period positions and the Keynesian equilibrium, quite apart from any question of reciprocal compatibility, have different theoretical contents. The theoretical problem underlying the long-period positions is the determination of distribution and relative prices, while the theoretical problem that Keynes aims to deal with in the *General Theory* is the determination of the aggregate product and the level of employment.

But there is a second difference. The long-period positions emerge from an analytical scheme which is substantially well defined. As we have noted, on the single specific questions there is no uniformity in the views of the authors who in some way look to the classical approach; this can be observed within any theoretical strand. Nevertheless, the basic neo-Ricardian analytical scheme is sufficiently complete and clear. A similar affirmation cannot be made regarding the model of chapters 1–15 of the *General Theory*. In other words, there is no well-defined and complete analytical scheme in the work. The *General Theory* is above all a book of ideas, of extremely general indications. On this ground, that is, from the point of view of general indications about the theoretical approach, it is, in my opinion, a very clear book, but the development of these indications into a precise model is something on which the *General Theory* is not equally clear. The enormous number of models elaborated in a Keynesian spirit, interpreted and felt in very different ways, are the most evident and irrefutable demonstration of this.

Now, these two elements of diversity in the concepts of equilibrium under discussion – the long-period positions and Keynesian equilibrium – although obviously important, do not *per se* prevent a possible integration of the theoretical approaches from which they emerge. Thus the diversity of the theoretical themes dealt with, or the different degree of analytical completeness, is not relevant to the comparison. On the contrary, since the themes dealt with in any case come from critical approaches in respect of neoclassical theory, the diversity of these themes is an element which has prompted many critics of the neoclassical theory to seek ways of integrating them.

We can thus come, at this point, to the main question: do the basic elements of Keynesian analysis and long-period positions express theoretical approaches that are in some way and at some level compatible? The answer, in reality, is already contained in the outline of the basic elements of the two theories in the previous section.

The short-period context in which Keynes develops his analysis in the *General Theory* obviously does not in itself constitute the reason for the incompatibility of the two approaches. The incompatibility lies in the specific use Keynes makes of the method of short-period equilibrium, that is to say, in the contents with which he characterizes this method. These contents, and I am referring to the crucial role of uncertainty in the behaviour of subjects, make Keynes's short-period method incompatible with the method, however, developed, of long-period equilibria. Keynes, as the article of 1937 in the *Quarterly Journal* clearly shows, is fully aware of his theory's opposition, *on this ground*, to the 'classical' approach. If we recognize that uncertainty bears in an essential way upon the behaviour of the agents and, further, that this behaviour is the result of a subjective reaction to uncertainty, then we move irrevocably away from the approach of *all* classical economists. Actually, that is what Keynes does in the *General Theory*. Consequently, seen in these terms, Keynes's analysis, although only by means of extremely general suggestions, represents an alternative not only to neoclassical theory, or to a great deal of it, but also to the long-period positions of classical derivation.

One last question before proposing some conclusions. On what basis does the attempt to integrate Keynesian analysis with analysis inspired by the classical approach develop? Or, on what could the possibility of reconciliation and compatibility between the two strands be founded? Obviously, on a reading of Keynes different from that offered here. Without entering into debates about interpretation, which it is not the aim of this chapter, I would like to touch upon just one point. Quite aside from the interpretative differences between those who claim compatibility between the reappraisal of the classical strand and Keynesian analysis, differences which are not insignificant, there is an idea common to all of them. The idea is that the basic innovation and the nucleus of Keynesian analysis can be fixed in the principle of effective demand, intended as saving decisions adapting to investment decisions by means of variations in the level of national income. Where this nucleus has been cleansed by the neoclassical influence on Keynes's definition of an investment function inversely related to the rate of interest, the nucleus of Keynesian theory could easily be integrated with the classical strand.

Certainly the principle of effective demand, as defined above, is fundamental in Keynes. Nevertheless, the weakness of the proposed reading lies in the fact that it neglects Keynes's original contribution in the treatment of the investment function, overestimating the neoclassical influence on his treatment. Consequently, this reading neglects the fact that the principle of effective demand in the *General Theory also* depends on Keynes's original contribution in the analysis of investment decisions. When that contribution is adequately recognized (the incidence of uncertainty is particularly considered by Keynes in relation to investment decisions), we would be forced to admit that the principle of effective demand, as Keynes developed it, is placed in an analytical light which is radically different from that, as we have repeatedly said, of all 'classical' economists.

CONCLUSIONS

In conclusion, I would like to stress the limits of the comparison that has been drawn. I have sustained the incompatibility on the analytical plane between the long-period positions and the short-period equilibrium in chapters 1–15 of the *General Theory*. In the first place, in this comparison, I have intentionally proposed no assessment of the two respective theoretical frameworks, the object being simply to show their general incompatibility in analytical terms. Second, another question, which is a distinct theme of research, has not been considered: if long-period positions and Keynesian short-period equilibrium express theoretical approaches which are *generally* alternative and incompatible, we cannot exclude (or, at least, it would be an interesting theme of research) the possibility of establishing some kind of *specific* connection between the theoretical approaches of Keynes and the neo-Ricardians. Actually, the possibility of defining a *particular* context and *particular* paths of revision of expectations that permit the progresive overcoming of the subjective aspects of reaction to uncertainty in the formation of expectations has never been explored. Correspondingly, the possibility of integration, which generally does not exist analytically, could be evaluated on a 'historical' plane. That is, it cannot be excluded that the two approaches constitute a theoretical reference point in the analysis and interpretation of different phases in the life and the development of market economies.

Lastly, reviewing the analysis above, it can be concluded that the attempt to integrate Keynesian elements with elements of the classical tradition is, so to speak, freely inspired by the *General Theory*. Naturally this conclusion does not imply any type of appraisal of such an attempt and the theoretical project it could give rise to, but only the comment that a project of this type cannot hope to hold a deep and substantive continuity with the analysis of the *General Theory*.

NOTES

1 It is evident that here I am only pointing out the implication of the neo-Ricardian theory. Perhaps it is worth adding that, whether this theory is correct or not, or whether sufficient demonstration of its propositions is available, is a very different question.
2 The existence within the *General Theory* of two alternative and incompatible analytical approaches and concepts of equilibrium is shown and fully discussed in Potestio (1986, 1989).

REFERENCES

Bharadwaj, K. (1983), 'On Effective Demand: Certain Recent Critiques', in Kregel (1983).
Bharadwaj, K., and Schefold, B., eds (1990), *Essays on Piero Sraffa*, Unwin Hyman, London.
Eatwell, J. (1983), 'Theories of Value, Output and Employment', in Eatwell and Milgate (1983).
Eatwell, J., and Milgate, M. eds (1983), *Keynes's Economics and the Theory of Value and Distribution*, Duckworth, London.
Eatwell, J., and Milgate, M. (1983), Introduction to Eatwell and Milgate (1983).
Garegnani, P. (1978), 'Notes on Consumption, Investment and Effective Demand' I, *Cambridge Journal of Economics* 2, pp. 335–53.
Garegnani, P. (1979), 'Notes on Consumption, Investment and Effective Demand' II', *Cambridge Journal of Economics* 3, pp. 181–7.
Garegnani, P. (1983), 'Two Routes of Effective Demand', in Kregel (1983).
Garegnani, P. (1990), 'Sraffa: Classical versus Marginalist Analysis', in Bharadwaj and Schefold (1990).
Keynes, J.M. (1973a), *The Collected Writings of John Maynard Keynes* VII, *The General Theory of Employment, Interest and Money*, Macmillan, London.
Keynes, J.M. (1973b), *The Collected Writings of John Maynard Keynes* XIV, *The General Theory and after* II, Defence and Development, Macmillan, London.

Kregel, J.A., ed. (1983), *Distribution, Effective demand and International Economic Relations*, Macmillan, London.

Potestio, P. (1986), 'Equilibrium and Employment in *The General Theory*, *Giornale degli economisti e annali di economia* XLV, pp. 365–88.

Potestio, P. (1989), 'Alternative Aspects of Monetary Theory in the *General Theory*: Significance and Implications', *Recherches Economiques de Louvain* 3.

10

THE NOTION OF OPTIMUM DISEQUILIBRIUM

Luca Meldolesi

Perhaps it is worth briefly considering two propositions that have arisen from our debate. After a hundred years (or is it two hundred?) of analysis of equilibrium, Enrico Zaghini said, it cannot be denied that it must have some practical relevance. Whereas Siro Lombardini stated that with the analysis of equilibrium only some aspects are observed while others are not. Taken together, these ideas have brought to mind some reasons that may suggest working in another direction, on a complementary side, somewhat secluded compared with the Champs Élysées of the economy of equilibrium.

In the first place, we have to focus on a certain spirit of self-contradiction that lurks in the soul of every economic theoretician. There is a sense of fascination with equilibrium (static and dynamic), which – he or she may perceive – conceals a trap; that is to say, it hides a series of characteristics of the economy that are relevant to economic policy. Instead of just observing the tendency of market forces towards equilibrium in order to determine it (however, defined), the opposite should also be done in order to study the effects of that same tendency on the operation of the economy.

This suggests a methodological question. Our field of study, even in its university curriculum, is based on a separation between analysis and policy. A vast spectrum of approaches – from the ultra-liberal to the ultra-radical – accepts the idea that analysis must live in its own light, while economic policy must shine, in a certain sense, with reflected light. Instead of this traditional point of view, perhaps Keynes's suggestion that the elements of analysis and policy are intimately linked should be taken seriously.

In my opinion, whoever shares these concerns is more or less knowingly in search of a more open approach than the severe rigidity of his or her theoretical upbringing. He or she begins to struggle between belonging to the ivory tower of economics and the need to open the way to concrete problems and the cognitive and normative contributions that other social disciplines can offer. On this delicate and intermediate path of debate an equilibrium can be encountered which is very different from those evoked

198

so far. I am referring to the controversy over balanced versus unbalanced growth that animated development economics in the 1950s and 1960s and which was taken up once again at a Buenos Aires conference on 'The work of Hirschman and a new development strategy for Latin America' (November 1989, now in Teitel 1992).

Here, in the place of the traditional notion of an optimum equilibrium point or path (which is considered to be of limited heuristic value), one comes up against the concept, at first glance paradoxical, of optimum disequilibrium (Hirschman and Lindblom 1962). The idea is simple and incisive. Disequilibrium is defined as optimal compared with disequilibria, which are too feeble or too strong in terms of the effects they have on the working of the economy; that is, on the working of markets induced by variations in demand (and price), on the consequent effects of appeal and enrolment for the development of capacities and resources that are hidden, dispersed or badly utilized, and hence on production and income growth rates. Incidentally, I should like to point out that this problem continues to be crucial to the economic policy of Italy, which suffers from insufficient utilization of available capacities and resources. Furthermore, I should like to point out that it concerns most of humanity: development in the Third World, like that of the second (which is now transforming itself into a market economy). And, as Herbert Simon, Richard Cyert, James March, Nathan Rosenberg and Harvey Liebenstein have shown, the problem still exists in the more advanced countries. Is it possible that economic theory can just shrug it off?

It is first a question of recognizing the so-called slack paradigm, that is to say, the familiar experience whereby resources and capacities are not given and are not scarce. Rather, they can be increased through doses of successive disequilibrium which attract them. This doubtless upsets the theoretician's way of thinking but should not be a reason for him or her to give up. Since disequilibrium tends towards equilibrium, he or she could think, it is always possible to logically transfer, in terms of equilibrium, any configuration of disequilibrium. But by doing so, it could be objected, the focus of discussion is lost from view, that is, how disequilibrium attracts and sets capacity and resources and capacities into action. Furthermore, the equilibrium (however, it is defined) towards which, in the absence of other events, the economy would head is not that which corresponds *prima facie* to the observed phenomenology of disequilibrium, because the latter brings new resources into being and thus modifies the quantitative data on which the eventual equilibrium depends. Lastly, it is a well known fact that economists assume the behaviour of automatic reaction, whereas in reality, for entrepreneurs and economic decision-makers, things are quite different.

Personally, I am open to such reasoning and I would like to contribute to unravelling the tangle. The optimum degree of disequilibrium, it is clear, cannot be identified *a priori*, once and for all. It is a problem that must be

199

solved in reality through iterative processes that, in different situations, lead to the most efficient rate of disequilibrium in terms of development. It is, in fact, a question of economic decision-makers cultivating a 'nose' or an 'art' in this regard.

Should not this pragmatic research be bolstered (or even suggested) by theory? A step in that direction is to take up the comparison between equilibrium and disequilibrium behaviour in a model with two interdependent sectors (cf. in Hirschman and Lindblom 1962). With regard to the balanced growth rate based on given factors of production, unbalanced growth initially manifests a certain comparative inefficiency, but it also sends out signals to economic agents and politicians and, by means of their reactions to increase the output of the delayed sector, it induces the mobilization of additional resources. Thus, if the intersectoral disequilibria are self-correcting, the pressure mechanisms that they set in motion enable investment, hours of work, productivity and decision-making capacities to be squeezed out of initially dormant resources and a higher growth path to be reached. In this way, the energy that holds the different economic nuclei together can be utilized for the construction of other nuclei.

Now, while an *a priori* of optimal doses of disequilibrium to be imposed on real economic policy would make no sense, a logical clarification concerning the alternatives in question would be useful if associated with pragmatic work to identify and create appropriate disequilibria and to elicit resources. In the first place, different possible disequilibrium paths exist in every situation, and the economic decision-maker must learn to compare them and evaluate them. Furthermore, as mentioned above, the degree of disequilibrium can be inappropriate: it can be too weak or it can be too strong (and so produce bottlenecks, inflation, etc). Lastly, the nature of disequilibrium can be antagonistic, i.e. it can mean a step backwards for the relatively disadvantaged sector.

As far as I can see, there are no insurmountable difficulties in setting out along this road once the elements of departure have been specified – the resources to be employed and those which can be mobilized, their reaction times to the demand, the sectors, territories and possible disequilibria, entrepreneurial behaviour, degrees and forms of disequilibrium, etc. (In fact this reasoning has revealed in time, in Albert Hirschman's work, a surprising capacity to develop new results, even analogically, in other economic, economic-political and socio-political fields, by means of the principle of optimum oscillation.)

What appears difficult (but not impossible), however, is the full attainment of the mental attitude that this option requires, to the point of redefining the very role of the equilibrium. This latter is not only an accident or a plan, as Marx and Keynes believed (and as Giorgio Lunghini has reminded us in his contribution to this book). It is also a ghost that hovers over our capacity to understand the real process. Its usefulness lies essentially, *a contrario*, in the notion of disequilibrium that it enables us to explicate. Thus, having freed ourselves (with a certain sense of relief) from the sway of its fascination, we can at last gratefully deal with equilibrium as it is, namely a pure spirit.

REFERENCES

Hirschman, A.O. (1958), *The Strategy of Economic Development*, Yale University Press, New Haven.

Hirschman, A.O. (1971), 'Political Economics and Possibilism', in *A Bias for Hope*, Yale University Press, New Haven.

Hirschman, A.O. (1986), *Rival Views of Market Society and other Recent Essays*, Viking, New York.

Hirschman, A.O., and Lindblom, C.E. (1962), 'Economic Development, Research and Development Policy-Making: Some Converging Views', *Behavioural Science* 7, pp. 211–22.

Meldolesi, L. (1991), 'Dietro le quinte d'una strategia', *Studi Economici* 45(177, 3,) pp. 23–75; Spanish translation in *El Trimestre Ecónomico* 59, 1 (1992), pp. 65–106.

Teitel, S., ed. (1992), *Towards a new Development Strategy for Latin America*, Washington, D.C., Interamerican Development Bank.

AUTHOR INDEX